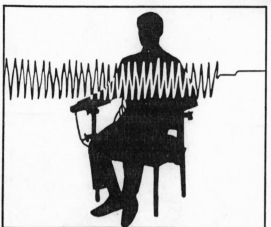

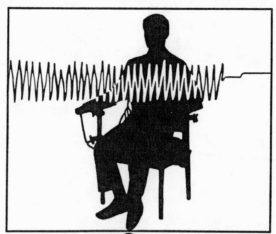

THE SILENT WITNESS

A Polygraphist's Casebook

Chris Gugas

PRENTICE-HALL, INC.
Englewood Cliffs, N. J.

The Silent Witness: A Polygraphist's Casebook
by Chris Gugas
Copyright © 1979 by Chris Gugas

Printed in the United States of America

Prentice-Hall International, Inc., London
Prentice-Hall of Australia, Pty. Ltd., Sydney
Prentice-Hall of Canada, Ltd., Toronto
Prentice-Hall of India Private Ltd., New Delhi
Prentice-Hall of Japan, Inc., Tokyo
Prentice-Hall of Southeast Asia Pte. Ltd., Singapore
Whitehall Books Limited, Wellington, New Zealand

10 9 8 7 6 5 4 3 2 1

Library of Congress Cataloging in Publication Data

Gugas, Chris.
    The silent witness.
    1. Lie detectors and detection. 2. Criminal
investigation—United States—Case studies.
I. Title.
HV8078.G84   364.12'8   79-180
ISBN 0-13-810069-1

Dedication

I am dedicating this book to the two most important women in my life. To my mother, Vera, whose Greek heritage and wisdom instilled in me the need for honesty, morality, and kindness. To my wife, Anne, whose patience far exceeds that of Job. She has been my friend, companion, and sweetheart for more than thirty-five years. I have been blessed with two adorable women, without whom I could never have accomplished anything worthwhile.

Acknowledgments

My thanks to my wife, Anne, whose constant encouragement and helpful suggestions really forced me to complete this project; to my sons, Major Chris Gugas, Jr., USAF, Steven Edward Gugas (also a polygraphist), and my daughter, Carol Anne Giovan, for their comments and guidance; to my sisters, Helen Galas, Marina Swoboda, Angeline Sleder, Georgia Abdouch, and their husbands, for their faith in my work and their encouragement of this book; and to my typist, Marti Cone, for her skill and criticism.

My grateful appreciation to the staff of the University of Beverly Hills, which reviewed the book and found it was worthy of a Master of Arts degree from that institution; to Joseph Hansen for his helpful comments and his assistance in preparing this book; and to my editor, Oscar Collier, whose assistance in the final phase of this book brought it to completion.

Preface

The following cases are all true. I have changed most names, dates, places, and details to protect the subjects I have polygraphed, and those innocent persons who involuntarily became involved in these situations. Truth, indeed, is stranger than any fiction generated by the most creative writer. My work has taken me to almost every state in the nation and to many parts of the world. I feel that I have the most interesting, exciting, and rewarding of jobs. I enjoy helping people in trouble and I hope to continue my efforts for a few more years.

The "truthseekers" who daily examine thousands of persons accused of the most dastardly crimes imaginable are the real heroes of this book. Dedicated polygraphists such as John E. Reid, C. D. Lee, C. B. Hanscom, Robert J. Ferguson, Jr., Richard O. Arther, Warren Holmes, Cleve Backster, and Leonard H. Harrelson have helped make our criminal justice system work just a little bit better.

Thousands of persons have had their innocence confirmed—and their lives salvaged—by the polygraph technique and through the dedication of the more than 1200 polygraphists of the American Polygraph Association.

The immense strain suffered by most polygraphers takes a severe toll in their health. There are no more than two or three hundred examiners in this country who have worked steadily as polygraphists for more than twenty years, and the average work span of many is no more than ten years because of the stress inherent in this profession.

It is not easy to render opinions daily on the guilt or innocence of any human being. We are bound to be caught up in the emotionally charged atmosphere surrounding our subjects. We have cried, stewed, and worried right along with them.

The following chapters will give the reader an idea of what goes on in all polygraph examination. I have tried to include my personal feelings in each case so the reader will understand the importance of seeking the most competent examiner available.

I am aware that at times the language may disturb some readers, but please try to understand that the narratives are those spoken by the subject while under tremendous emotional strain. Persons react in various ways when under pressure and anxiety, and the examiner's task is much easier when rapport has been established between both parties and subjects speak freely without any inhibitions.

I sincerely hope this book will enlighten people about the merits of the polygraph technique when used by skilled and dedicated polygraphists who are constantly seeking the truth—the whole truth!

—*Chris Gugas*

Contents

1

The Truthseekers

This is a casebook. It's made up of true stories taken from files I've kept during the thirty and more years I've been a polygraph examiner—a "lie-detector expert," as they say on the six o'clock news. Some time ago, I made my twenty-thousandth examination and stopped counting. But I never forgot. How could I? Face to face, and absolutely alone, I've probed the secrets of murderers, spies, bribe-takers in office, political assassins, arsonists, defrauders of insurance companies, rapists, international financiers, movie stars, teenagers stuck in foreign jails for dope smuggling, saboteurs, million-dollar-a-year preachers—people of every sort, in every sort of trouble you can name, some of it terrifying, some of it laughable, some of it a little of both. There's no way I could forget.

This is a casebook, not a textbook. But it differs from other casebooks in a very special and important way, because it is about the solving of crimes not by man alone but by a man working in tandem with a remarkable and little-understood instrument, the polygraph, that complex, delicate, and totally impartial device that almost always enabled me to clear the innocent and make certain of the guilty. So it's essential right here at the start to tell something about the polygraph, what it is and what it is not, what it can and cannot do, how it operates, how an examiner goes about his job, and who can and can't, will and will not, make use of the results—and why.

In 1923, a man named Frye, on trial for murder, asked to bring to his defense the results of an early lie-detector test. He was refused. And more than half a century later, except in cases where both sides agree to its use, or where a judge calls for it, polygraph evidence is still banned from the courtroom. Appeals judges have been known to rule that even mention of a polygraph test during a hearing—whether by the accused, saying that he has taken one, or by the prosecution, asking why he has refused to take one—is reason enough to declare a mistrial. This is ironic, since the polygraph was devised to aid justice, a root problem of which has been, so long as man has walked the earth, doubt as to who is lying and who is telling the truth.

The first polygraph was built by Dr. John A. Larson in 1921. It measured blood pressure, pulse, and breathing rates. In 1926, Leonarde Keeler introduced a fourth measurement, of skin resistance to electricity. And twenty years later, a system for registering muscular contractions that might upset blood pressure readings was added by John E. Reid. When we lie, our blood pressure goes up, our heart beats faster, we breathe more quickly (and our breathing slows once the lie has been told), and changes take place in our skin moisture. A polygraph charts these reactions with pens on a moving strip of graph paper, in much the same way your heart action is recorded when your doctor gives you an EKG as part of a physical checkup. The result is jagged lines that don't convey a lot to you. But, in the case of the EKG, your doctor can read in them whether or not your heart is behaving. In the case of the polygraph, an examiner can tell from those mechanical scribbles whether or not you've spoken the truth.

The process gone through to reach that point is far from simple,

2

but in its barest outlines, here is how it works. It starts with an interview that takes much more time than the actual tests. Each test—and there may be as many as three or four—lasts only a few minutes. In the interview before testing, the examiner will try to put you at your ease, get to know a little about what sort of person you are, explain the polygraph and what it does, and listen to your side of the story. If you've been accused of a crime, he'll already have read the arrest report, the statements of witnesses, your own statement to the police.

Let's say you're a bookkeeper charged with falsifying accounts. The examiner will try to learn your attitude toward this kind of misconduct in general, and your feelings about this incident in particular. Then, between the two of you—you and the examiner are alone in a plain room, air-conditioned, soundproof—you will decide on the questions that will make up the first test. There will be only ten or twelve. They will be brief. The words in them will be basic and easy to understand. For example, "steal" will be used, not "embezzle." There will be as few words as possible in each question, and every question will be answerable with a simple yes or no.

After each answer you give, there will be a pause of fifteen to twenty seconds. Some of the questions will have nothing to do with the reason you're taking the test. Some will touch on your attitudes toward stealing. Only three or four will go to the heart of the matter. And these will be blunt. After all, what is wanted is a strong, unmistakable reaction. After the test is done, the examiner will talk over the results with you, try to learn the reason for your responses as recorded on the chart, and the two of you may start again with a revised set of questions. People overreact, underreact, have guilt complexes, are frightened, are angry. The examiner has to take these and a lot of other variables into account, such as health, intelligence, emotional stability, reaction to shock. The process is never cut-and-dried.

Human beings are involved, so errors can be made. A polygraph chart can be misread. But so can an electrocardiogram. An electroencephalographer can make a wrong judgment from the lines his instrument scratches to show brain activity. An X-ray photograph can mean this to one radiologist, that to another. The microscopic scratches on a bullet can suggest to one ballistics expert that it was fired from a suspect's gun, to another that it was not. The scrutiny of questioned documents can cause clashes between specialists. Graphoanalysts can disagree about a handwriting sample. Psychiatrists can offer conflicting judgments about a suspect's mental state. Yet the testimony of physicians, lab technicians, psychiatrists, and experts in scores of other disciplines is accepted in thousands of courtrooms, as a matter of course, every year. Why is it, then, that extra barriers are set in the way of the polygraph examiner?

Perhaps because of a dubious early history. If judges and appeals courts in the 1920s rejected the polygraph as untested and unproven, police, sheriffs and other law-enforcement agents welcomed the idea of a "machine" that could tell them whether or not suspects and witnesses were lying. They rushed out and bought the so-called lie-detectors by the gross and put them to work—too often with little or no idea of how to use them. Even the earliest models were intricate and highly reactive, and demanded skill and patience of their operators. Clumsiness and haste could only have produced faulty results.

Yet newspapers and magazines kept feeding the public melodramatic stories about the infallibility of this latest scientific marvel. The picture they gave readers was of a diabolical machine that would ring bells and flash lights when the unhappy man or woman forcibly hitched to it by painful wires told a falsehood. The twenties and thirties were not our brightest and best period in law enforcement. If criminals are overprotected today, they were underprotected then, and public ignorance and fear of the infamous lie detector encouraged some unscrupulous officers of the law to use it as a threat to coerce and intimidate witnesses and suspects. Which didn't help the polygraph's reputation. Neither did the fact that anyone with enough money in his wallet could go out, buy a polygraph, and set himself up in business as an expert.

Yet at the same time, serious attention was being given the instrument. Leonarde Keeler improved it, worked out guidelines for its effective use in police work, and started training examiners. Laboratory experiments on polygraph testing began early, and over a span of decades, reports in such publications as the *Journal of Applied Psychology* and the *Journal of Criminal Law* showed results averaging 86.6 percent accuracy. In real-life situations, in which the outcome of testing can have serious results, where sharper physiological reactions show up in those tested and examiners are apt to be more experienced, accuracy rates were even higher.

World War II accounted for quantum leaps in technology. Wide use of the polygraph by the armed services not only produced a whole new breed of carefully trained examiners, but in a few short years it took testing and analysis techniques a long way toward standardization. In 1953, when two outstanding examiners, John Reid and Fred Inbau, tested 4,280 criminal suspects, their accuracy rate was 95 percent. And in 1971, Reid, working with F. S. Horvath, in a striking demonstration of the new exactness and uniformity of polygraph data showed examiners the charts of forty tests in which they had not been involved. Trained but inexperienced examiners scored 79 percent accuracy, experienced examiners 91.4 percent!

Yet the courtroom doors that slammed on polygraph evidence in 1923 remain shut still, with few exceptions. The root argument against admitting such evidence is that it results in self-incrimination. No one, says the Fifth Amendment to our Constitution, "shall be compelled in any criminal case to be a witness against himself." And what about the drunk driving suspect made to walk a chalk line, to close his eyes and touch his nose with a fingertip? Has he become a witness against himself? If not, then how can anyone be said to have done so in taking a polygraph test?

No, speech is not the issue. A polygraph test can be given without either examiner or subject uttering a word—as you'll see from one of the cases in this book. And on the subject of words, lawyers opposed to the polygraph like to say, "You can't cross-examine a machine." This is true. It's true of most of the equipment in today's big-city crime laboratories. But medical examiners and others able to use such equipment are cross-examined every day in courtrooms all over the country.

As recently as 1958, three California Supreme Court justices ruled that the polygraph examination "is offensive to the traditions of the law." But what is traditional about the electron microscope, semen-typing, voiceprints, and the hundred other scientific advances law enforcement uses today, and which trial lawyers and judges accept? Less than a hundred years ago, fingerprinting was

5

still a novelty! The word of witnesses, physical evidence, circumstantial evidence—these are traditional. It's safe to say they reach back beyond written history. Yet what judge or attorney of today would ban every other means but these of determining guilt or innocence, because they are "offensive to the traditions of our law"?

In their Stone Age attitude toward the polygraph, the courts stand almost alone. Every major police force in the United States uses the polygraph, not as a substitute for investigating crimes, but to help sort out lies from truth. Much time and many tax dollars are saved. And countless citizens every year have polygraph tests to thank for clearing them of mistaken suspicions of wrongdoing. Attorneys, public and private, regularly call on polygraph examiners to determine the truth or falsehood of stories told them by clients, witnesses, suspects.

Business and industry use the polygraph examination widely in screening job applicants and as a means of curbing employee thefts, a multibillion-dollar-a-year headache. Our Army, Navy, Air Force, and Marines all use polygraph testing. I myself set up the lie-detection program for the Criminal Investigation Department of the Marine Corps when I was a Marine major in 1953. The Armed Services operate a joint school for the training of polygraph examiners at Fort McClellan, Alabama. Private polygraph schools throughout the country offer intensive examiner-training courses. So do a growing number of universities.

The American Polygraph Association requires that its members—they number some twelve hundred—must be college graduates, have successfully completed a minimum of three hundred hours of classroom training at an accredited polygraph school, and have served an internship, during which they must have given two hundred or more polygraph examinations. As the Reid-Horvath experiment showed, the expertise of these young men and women is high, and field experience, day-to-day, real-life encounters with people in trouble, steadily raises it. Seminars for Polygraph Association members are held every year to keep examiners informed of the latest advances in instrumentation, testing, and diagnostic techniques.

Twenty-one states, mostly in the South and Southwest, demand that polygraph examiners be licensed. I hope that soon all fifty states will pass such laws, the stiffer the better, because the polygraph is only an instrument for measuring and recording physiological reactions. It can't tell truth from lies. It can draw a graph, that's all. The meaning of the graph has to be judged and expressed by a human being, the examiner. It is on his accuracy and integrity that the usefulness of polygraph evidence depends. Only when uniform standards for polygraph examiners are written into law throughout the fifty states can such evidence hope to be admitted into court along with that provided today by other scientific instruments.

In their book, *Truth and Deception,* John Reid and Fred Inbau suggest that for an examiner to qualify as an expert witness at a trial, he should not only meet the standards of the American Polygraph Association but have had at least five years' professional experience. I agree. A polygraph examiner needs more than the technical training that enables him to read the tracings of his instrument's sensitive pens. He must himself be sensitive—a keen observer, a shrewd questioner, a close listener. He must be a psychologist in the most down-to-earth sense of that word. He must know people. More—he must know people under stress. And that kind of knowledge, that kind of awareness, can be gained only through experience.

Unfortunately, licensing of polygraph examiners is still the exception, not the rule. And while the number of well-trained and highly disciplined examiners grows, there are still far too many around whose only qualification is that they have their hands on a polygraph instrument. This is true inside police departments and other official agencies, and outside them—which is bad not only for you and me as ordinary citizens, but for the future of the polygraph and, hence, the future of our overworked and sometimes floundering system of justice. The day of standardized requirements for polygraph examiners cannot come too soon.

Meanwhile, a personal word to you. Naturally, I hope you never get into trouble with the law, but if it happens—and you'd be amazed at how easily it can happen—and you want a polygraph examination to help you prove your innocence, make sure your lawyer finds you a qualified, experienced examiner. If you're not sure of his credentials, and if his results are inconclusive (a certain percentage always are), or if his charts indicate to him you were lying when you weren't (which can result from flaws in test questioning), then do as you would do if a doctor told you that you had cancer. Get another opinion.

But, you are probably asking, if most courts, most of the time, won't accept his testimony, then what good can a polygraph examiner's test results do you? I've said this is a casebook. Suppose we get down to cases.

2

The Mistaken Witness

Let's say your name is Jerry Smith. You're thirty-two years old, married, with three kids. You just recently moved from the East Coast to California. You're a barber, and you hope someday to have your own shop, but for the time being you're working for another man, cutting hair. Your wife is a dentist's receptionist. Together, you bring home about $800 a month. The move to California was expensive. You've got only about $1,500 in the bank.

It's a clear, crisp, sunny winter day when you finish with a customer at noon, shed your white barber's smock, shrug into your leather jacket, and step out the door on your way to lunch up the street. You've just collected your Big Mac and large Coke from the cheerful black girl at the counter, and you're looking for a place to sit down, when you notice a police patrol car swing into the parking lot. You figure the officers inside it are coming for lunch. They aren't. They're coming for you.

Why? There's a supermarket at the corner. Like a dozen others in the area, it was recently robbed. At gunpoint. By a man in his thirties, medium height, medium build, dark jeans, leather jacket—a man who looks like you. He looks so much like you that the market manager, passing in his car, seeing you leave the barbershop, is sure you are the holdup man. While the crowd in McDonald's watches, one officer reads you your rights and another snaps handcuffs on your wrists. You're folded into the rear seat of the black-and-white and driven to the market where, in a cold, cavernous storeroom filled with crates of oranges and cartons of canned soup, half a dozen more market employees—box boys, the women who punch the cash registers, a butcher in a bloody apron—nod grimly to each other and to the police. Yes, you are the one.

You're shoved into the black-and-white again and driven downtown. The contents of your pockets are sealed in a brown envelope. You're fingerprinted, photographed, locked up. Later you stand in a blinding glare of spotlights with half a dozen other men, lined up against a green wall. You've seen your share of television cop shows. You know what's happening. It's an identification lineup. Out there in the darkness, people are pointing fingers. At you? This is a nightmare. It can't be happening to you. But it is.

You were allowed one telephone call: Your wife shows up with a lawyer. But he didn't come cheap. You're strangers newly arrived in the state, the city. He needed a retainer, $1,500—which is all there was. Your bail is set but you can't make it. The barber you work for won't help you out. You're a stranger to him too. And he's made it clear to your wife that you're a stranger he doesn't want working for him again. Your wife is afraid to tell the dentist what's happened. He might lend the money; on the other hand, he might fire her. And there's the rent to pay, there are the kids to feed. You don't have any other friends out here. So you stay in the county jail.

Your lawyer telephones me and outlines the case.

"They don't have any evidence," I point out. "No gun, no money from the supermarket."

"They've got ten eyeball witnesses," the lawyer says. "Six at

10

the market and four more at the lineup. He's got to be guilty as hell, but he claims he's innocent. I don't know what to think."

I drive downtown and talk to you through wire mesh. Why do you want to sit in jail? You could have saved the attorney's fee—you're entitled to a public defender. You shake your head. You're not about to accept charity. Anyway, what do you need with a defender? You didn't do it. You've never been inside that market. You don't prowl around at night with a gun. You stay home with your wife and kids watching television. Or your wife and you do the shopping or the two of you do the wash at the neighborhood coin laundry. She works an eight-hour-a-day job too. It's only fair that you share the other chores. I arrange for an interrogation room, set up my equipment, and polygraph you.

"Jerry Smith didn't rob that supermarket," I tell your lawyer on the phone. "He doesn't know anything about it. Get the police to run their own polygraph on him. I promise you, they'll get the same result."

But the police refuse. So does the district attorney. They're satisfied with their crowd of witnesses. No jury is going to find against the sworn testimony of ten respectable citizens. They don't need their own polygraph test to send you to prison. And without their consent, under California law, my test results can't be admitted as evidence at your trial. I'm not discouraged. I'm angry. When I had you seated in the examining chair, the corrugated tube fastened around your chest to register your breathing, the blood-pressure cuff on your arm, the electrodes on your hand, and when I asked you if you robbed that store and you said, calmly and stubbornly, "No!" you were telling the truth. The polygraph chart said so. My common sense said so. I have no doubts. I phone an investigator friend.

When I tell him about you and how your case stacks up, he offers to work without a fee—which is nice, but he can't come up with anything. There's no proof, other than your wife's word, that you weren't at that supermarket on the night of the robbery, waving a gun, grabbing money out of the cash drawers. But I'm not ready to quit and neither is he. He's going to check out the police reports again. Maybe there's something we all overlooked.

Two days later we meet for lunch. I'm at the table with a drink when he comes toward me through the well-lighted room, swinging

11

something in his hand. He tosses it into the padded leather booth beside me and sits down. I pick the thing up, frowning. It's a shiny white plastic safety helmet, the kind motorcyclists wear. I turn it over in my hands. It is cold and sleek. The waiter comes and the investigator asks for Scotch on the rocks. Then he reaches over and takes the helmet from me and puts it on.

"What do you see?" he says.

"You could be anybody," I say.

"You've got it," he says. "The dude that robbed the supermarket was wearing one of these. All the witnesses say so. It's in every description. The leather jacket, the black trousers, the motorcycle helmet."

"They couldn't see his face," I say. "Not really. The tip of the nose, the mouth, the chin."

"Exactly." His drink arrives. The waiter raises an eyebrow. The investigator grins, takes off the helmet, and lays it on the seat again. The waiter goes off laughing. The investigator says, "And Jerry Smith never owned a motorcycle helmet in his life." He lifts his glass. "Here's to Jerry Smith."

I touch his glass with mine, drink, and rush to the phone to try to get the news to you as quickly as possible. Your lawyer isn't in, but I leave word for him to phone me at my office. The investigator and I are happy and we have a good lunch. Back at the office, I take the lawyer's call and tell him about the helmet. He will get to the police on the case and to the district attorney right away. He does, but it turns out he needn't have bothered. We needn't have bothered.

This morning, only a few blocks from the barbershop where you used to work, the owner of a small market had got out of his car in the still-empty parking lot, pulled keys from his pocket, and unlocked the market's rear door. As he opened it to go inside, a man appeared from nowhere. He held a gun. He wore a leather jacket and dark trousers—and a big motorcycle helmet. He started to shove the market owner through the door when a police car drove down the alley. The man in the helmet plunged on into the dark store. But there was no way out. The front doors were barred and padlocked. The police officers caught him among the frozen foods. He dropped the gun. They took him in. At the station he admitted to all the supermarket burglaries in the neighborhood—including the one you are in jail for.

The case against you is dropped. Keys rattle. Your cell door slides open. They hand you back the contents of your pockets from the sealed brown envelope. Your wife is there to kiss and hold you tight. But you don't want to draw another breath of the disinfectant stink of that jail. You want out into the open air again. You want to know what it is to feel free once more. Only you never will.

You're a decent man. You've never intentionally done anything to hurt anyone. That's you, and that won't change. But for the rest of your life, you're going to be braced for the next time some citizen as decent as yourself makes an honest mistake about you that will cost you your job, your savings, and grim weeks in jail. Weeks or perhaps your whole life. You were lucky this time. Lucky that your lawyer, against long odds, believed your story because a polygraph test showed you were telling the truth. And lucky that the real supermarket bandit turned up before you had to sit in a courtroom and watch a jury's sure and certain reaction to the testimony of ten eyewitnesses positive you were guilty. Because the polygraph test that proved the opposite wouldn't even have been whispered about in that courtroom.

You barely made it and you know it. Your knees still weaken when you think about it. Your lawyer finds you a temporary job. Doggedly you save every dime you can. And when there's enough, you load your wife and kids into the car and head back East where you came from. If you never see California again, it will be too soon for you. Just one thing: What happened to you can happen any-where, any time. I know. I've been connected in one way or another with law enforcement all my adult life. And I can tell you that arrests like yours are, if not the rule, certainly far from exceptional. They happen all over this country, all over the world, in big cities and small towns alike, every single day.

13

3

The False Witness

All right. You're not Jerry Smith. You're not a young stranger trying to get started in a city far from home. You're older. You're established. You're senior vice-president of a thriving building and loan firm. You earn over $50,000 a year. You own a pleasant home in a suburb of wide green lawns, curved streets, overarching trees. You're past president of the Junior Chamber of Commerce, an elder of the Episcopal Church, a member of a gracious and exclusive country club where you golf on Wednesday afternoons, scoring in the low eighties. You have a son at Harvard, and a daughter at Smith. Your wife is intelligent, charming, and beautiful. We'll call you John Thomas. And nothing like what happened to Jerry Smith could ever happen to you.

Then one day your secretary's pleasantly modulated voice speaks through the intercom on your desk. And two men in off-the-

14

rack suits come through the polished oak double doors of your handsome office. They cross the lush carpet. Police badges glint from leather folders. You're easy in your mind. You give them a smile and invite them to sit down. What can you do for them? They don't return your smile. They don't sit down. They have a warrant for your arrest. And what you can do for them is accompany them to police headquarters. Now, please.

"Are you serious?" You look from one blank, close-shaven face to the other. "Is this some sort of joke?"

"No, sir," one of them says. "No joke."

"Well, then, it's a mistake. You've got the wrong John Thomas."

"Not if you own the car parked downstairs, Mr. Thomas. And you do own it, don't you? It's registered to you."

You're bewildered. "What's my car got to do with it? I haven't been in any accidents."

"No, sir. But nine months ago, at the corner of Eighth and Elm, you picked up a girl who was hitchhiking. She's filed a complaint against you."

"What?" You're on your feet. "What sort of complaint?"

"She says you drove her out of town to a wooded area and raped her. Repeatedly."

You sit down again. Your legs won't hold you. "But—but that's not true. Wait a minute. Nine months ago? If it was true, why did she wait until now?"

The second detective is standing staring at a painting on your wall. He doesn't turn to you. He says tonelessly, "Because she just had a baby. She claims it's yours."

"But that's ridiculous," you shout. "It's impossible."

"Yes, sir," the detective says, turning back from his appraisal of the picture. "Well, we can straighten it all out down at headquarters."

"Headquarters, hell! I'm not going anywhere. I haven't done anything. You have no right to—"

But they have more than a right. They have a warrant and a job to do. And it was a mistake for you to lose your temper. You end up riding downtown with your wrists in handcuffs cramped behind your back. Just like Jerry Smith. Just like Jerry Smith, the contents

15

of your pockets are dropped into a brown envelope and sealed. Just like Jerry Smith, you are fingerprinted and photographed. Shiny steel bars clang shut on you just as they did on Jerry Smith. The difference is that you have money for bail, so it's not weeks but only hours until you get your possessions back and can walk out of the police building with your lawyer. You feel soiled. You want to get home and into the shower.

But there's another difference between you and Jerry Smith. He was a nameless stranger. You're well known. Only two years ago you were honored as Man of the Year. You've been chairman of the United Fund in your city. Your name and your wife's appear on sponsors lists for the local art museum, concert, and recital series. You were a leader in setting up a ball park for the Little League. You've insisted that your firm's building loans go only to contractors who will respect the environment. You're a newsmaker.

And that's the real difference between Jerry Smith and you. You push out the glass doors into the welcome fresh air, and bulky men with TV cameras strapped to their shoulders surge toward you. You're surrounded by reporters. Shiny microphones are thrust into your face. You know some of these people. You've talked to them amiably on interview shows. They're different now. They come at you like screaming birds in the Hitchcock film. You want to crouch down with your arms over your head. You can't. You can only stare. Your lawyer takes a bruising grip on your arm. It's a warning to say nothing. He smiles. He speaks. You're too stunned to pick up more than fragments.

"Sorry. No comment at this time. No truth in the charges, no. Don't know why the warrant was issued. A mistake. Mr. Thomas is not involved, not in any way." Then he speaks close to your ear. "Come on. There's my car. Break for it together. One, two, three. Now."

And you make your break. It catches them by surprise. The cameras and sound equipment make them clumsy. But before you can get away, a young woman in denims stitched with glass bead flowers catches the handle of your door. The microphone comes at you like a missile. Her question is shrill and taunting:

"But you do know Karen Benson, don't you, Mr. Thomas?"

16

"I never heard of her," you say, and slam the door.

But you do know the girl. You've had a shower. You're sitting, shocked and drained, beside the pool. Your wife and the lawyer are with you. In your hand is a stiff whiskey over ice. It isn't helping. You've remembered, and you're sick with anger. And with disgust at yourself. You look wryly at these two people—one of whom you love, the other an old friend whom you trust.

"Part of what she says is true," you say. "I'd worked late on that town-house deal in Simmons Orchards." You smile and shake your head. "They're completely built now. Occupied. I'd telephoned you to say I couldn't make some dinner we were supposed to go to. You said you'd go alone. I left the office about sunset. Drove home the same route I always take. And there she was. Fragile little thing, standing at the corner with her thumb out for a ride. What an idiot I was. She reminded me of Barbara." You mean your daughter, and you silently thank God she's a thousand miles from here today, she won't know what's happening to her father. "She wasn't the least bit like Barbara. We hadn't gone four blocks when she was asking me for money. I pulled to the curb, leaned across and opened the door on her side. I said this was as far as I could take her. She got out but she was angry. I'd be sorry, she said." You laugh grimly. "Well, she was right about that."

There's film at eleven. You get up and switch to another channel. There you are again in front of the police building, looking shocked and scruffy and guilty as hell. You snap the tuning knob but you're on Channel 3 as well. You groan and turn off the set. It means gritting your teeth, but you go into the office next morning. And it's not the same. How could you expect it would be? The change isn't obvious. But there's a disturbing quietness around you, and you catch odd looks from associates. Faces are stiff that used to smile with easy friendliness.

It's the same at the country club. The surgeon that always made up part of your foursome drops out. Then the insurance broker. Your lawyer and you play alone. In the club bar silence falls when you walk in. For a long second there's only the clink of ice in glasses, the thread of music from the ceiling speakers. Then conversation starts again, backs turn shutting you out. You give up the

17

club. After Sunday service, you phone the rector. You think it would be more comfortable for everyone if you didn't seat people and pass the offering plate for a while.

He tells you you're being oversensitive, that no one believes you've done anything wrong. But you know better, and you stay away from church. Meetings come up, of civic committees on which you serve. If your showing up doesn't surprise you, it surprises others. Eyes won't look at you when you speak. When the meeting breaks up, there don't seem to be any hands to shake. You'd like to think you imagine it, but you're pretty sure you hear one committeewoman ask another in a hissing whisper, "What's he doing here? The nerve of the man!"

The nerve of the man begins to crack. You can't eat. You can't sleep. In your teens, you had migraine headaches. Suddenly they're back, and no medication relieves the blinding pain. But pain isn't the worst. The worst is fear. You can't prove that what Karen Benson claims never happened.

"He doesn't think he's got a chance," your lawyer tells me on the phone. "And to be honest with you, Chris, I'm starting to wonder if he isn't right."

"You've investigated the girl?" I ask.

"And drawn nothing but blanks. Look, John wants a polygraph test. He's frantic for proof, any kind of proof, that he's telling the truth."

"Have you told him how rocky it can be, getting polygraph results into court? Have you sounded out the D.A.?"

"Not yet. I will. The important thing right now is John's own peace of mind, his faith in himself."

You arrive at my office haggard but grimly set on the test. After I've interviewed you, I'm as sure as you are of what the results will be. They prove out. I tell your lawyer on the phone. "He not only didn't rape the Benson girl, he's never been guilty of sexual misconduct in his life. Get the district attorney to admit this evidence, and John Thomas has nothing to worry about."

But the district attorney refuses. I suggest he have his own polygrapher test Thomas. Negative. I suggest the Benson girl be tested. Again negative. After all, the prosecution has nothing to gain from such a test and everything to lose—because someone is lying

18

in this case, and it isn't you. I'm annoyed and frustrated but not surprised. I've seen it happen too often, where a district attorney is more interested in a conviction than in justice. And it isn't that this district attorney doesn't know the value of polygraph tests. He uses them all the time. But under the law, he can block their admission as evidence when it might go against him. In your case, he won't even listen to the word *polygraph*.

Things never looked worse for you. Then suddenly you get a break. And crazily enough, it is Karen Benson who gives it to you. She files a civil action against you for fathering her baby girl. And in paternity suits, polygraph tests are routine. So are blood tests, but in your case, with blood type O, ordinary and expectable, these prove nothing. The district attorney's office agrees to polygraph both you and Karen Benson. By a fluke, I am assigned to test the girl. I would love the chance, but I can't do it.

"Conflict of interests," I say. "I already examined John Thomas. Get somebody else. And don't have him talk to me—not until after he's finished with the girl. I don't want him to know what I learned. It could bias him."

It's a tense day for you. You ring up my office every hour on the hour. I can't convince you there's nothing to worry about, and some of your anxiety rubs off on me. My secretary leaves at five. I'm tired, but I wait another half hour. Then, just as I'm switching off the lights and closing the door, the phone jangles. I know the caller's voice. He's a polygraph operator, and a good one.

"The Benson girl lied," he tells me. Something in his tone suggests he has more to say. He waits. I ask:

"That's all?"

"No. She's confessed. The father of her baby is a married man who lives next door to her parents. She didn't want to get him into trouble."

"So she picked on a total stranger," I say.

"A rich one," he says. "She could tell by the car."

I hang up and dial your number. You snatch up the phone before the end of the first ring. I give you the news. Your shaky laugh of relief is one of the best sounds I've ever heard. I hope it's not premature. There's still that hard-nosed district attorney to worry about. It costs me some sleep—but for nothing. In the morning,

19

your lawyer telephones: The D.A. has dismissed all charges against you.

So it's over. It's cost you thousands of dollars. It's made you ill and it will be a long time before you stop waking in the middle of the night, covered with cold sweat. But it's over. You don't have as many friends as you used to. The tension at your office will be a long time easing. The city to which you always gave so willingly of time, energy, money, imagination, will never be quite the same place to you. But it's over. You can try to forget. . . .

No, you're not Jerry Smith or John Thomas. But they are real men. I've changed their names but that's all. What you've read about actually happened. And if it weren't for the polygraph, both men could have gone to prison. What jury would have believed Smith against the word of ten eyewitnesses? What jury would have believed Thomas when pretty young Karen Benson, in tears, pointed a finger at him from the witness stand and swore that he had raped her?

But, it's fair to say, both Smith and Thomas had luck on their side, as well as the polygraph. The real supermarket bandit turned up. Karen Benson got greedy. It's true. And sometimes you need all the luck you can get. Men who didn't have it are sitting in jails today, trying to convince anyone who will listen of their innocence. Some may well have taken polygraph tests and passed them. But polygraph evidence was all the proof of innocence they could offer at their trials—and their lawyers couldn't get the prosecution, or the judge, or both, to let them bring the test results into court.

4

The Actor and the Teenagers

Yet it's far from true that you always need luck in order for the polygraph to get you out of trouble. Take the case of Doug Cooper. You know him. He's been in your theater time and again. He's a handsome, gray-haired, well-set-up man in his late fifties. Sometimes he's a kindly doctor, sometimes a frontier banker, now and then a priest or minister, a college professor in a lab of glittering test tubes, or a judge in black robes. He's none of these things in reality, of course. He's a movie actor. Not a star, perhaps, but one of that group of faces as familiar to us as our own, though we can rarely put names to them. I'm not, of course, using his real name here.

When he walked into my office with his family and his lawyer one warm spring day a few years ago, I felt as if I'd always known him and liked him. It's true that he wasn't carrying himself with the confidence that marked him in his roles on the big screen. He moved heavily. His shoulders sagged. His eyes, which could be proud and fierce when the role called for it, were dull and bloodshot. Doug Cooper was in a grim and humiliating mess.

His lawyer had told me the story. A few days before, Cooper had been telephoned by a friend, another movie actor, who had just moved into a new apartment in Hollywood. He suggested that Cooper come by to see his new place. Cooper left his own home in the San Fernando Valley and drove into Hollywood along the freeway. He didn't know his friend's neighborhood, and couldn't locate the street right away. He made several turns around a large high school before he got his bearings. He spent an hour with his friend and the friend's wife, drinking coffee, laughing over old times, discussing their prospects for new movie parts. Then he left and drove home.

Later that afternoon, the doorbell rang. Cooper's wife went to answer it. A moment later she came into the wood-paneled den where Cooper was sitting, studying a script. Something about her silence, the way she stopped in the doorway, made him take off his reading glasses so he could see her face. She wore a puzzled frown. He laid down the script and rose from his deep leather armchair.

"What's the matter?" he asked.

"I don't know," she said. "Two policemen are here. They want to talk to you. Doug, what in the world—?"

But Cooper was looking past her. The officers had followed her to the den doorway. One of them said, "We'd like you to come to the station with us, Mr. Cooper, please. We've had a complaint against you, and—"

"A complaint?" Cooper blinked. "Who by? What about?"

"Well, sir—" The officer was young and very blonde. He glanced at Cooper's stunned wife and his face turned red. "I think—I think we'd better talk about it downtown, okay?"

"I'm sure we can straighten it out," the other officer said. "You want to come with us now, please?"

Cooper shrugged, cocked a disbelieving eyebrow, shook his head. "If you say so." He took a step toward them. His wife reached out. He took her hands, kissed her forehead. "It's all right," he told her. "Some wild mistake." He followed the police officers. She watched them go down the curving brick path between bright flower beds to the dingy patrol car. Before he bent to get inside, he turned and gave her a smile and a reassuring wave.

But he didn't feel reassured when, in a shabby room with scarred walls at the police station, they read him his rights and asked him to explain what he'd been doing near the high school that morning in his car. He told them. He gave them the name of the friend he'd visited. Had he parked on a street near the chain-link fence that shut off the high school athletic fields from the street? No. Definitely not. Why? He hadn't sat in the car, kicked open the door, and displayed himself masturbating to some girls taking gym class out on the field? Now it was Cooper's turn to grow red in the face. He stood so suddenly his chair clattered back against the wheezing air conditioner in the window.

"Absolutely not! What do you take me for?"

"It happens," said the sour officer asking the questions. "Four of the girls say they saw you."

"They're lying," Cooper said.

"Why would they do that, Mr. Cooper?"

"I don't know," Cooper said, trying to control his voice, his outrage. "But it's a lie. Yes, I drove around the school grounds. I told you, I was trying to find that address. I'd never been there before."

"Okay." The officer stood up. "That's all for now. But don't go anywhere, Mr. Cooper. Not till we tell you."

If he'd been the kind who runs away, Cooper couldn't have got far. The police were back for him within seventy-two hours, this time with a warrant for his arrest. He was fingerprinted. More importantly, he was photographed. He was released on bail. He didn't have to appear in a lineup. But the police working on the case shuffled his picture in with half a dozen others and showed the assortment to the girls. Only two of them had been able to give any description at all of the man who'd exposed himself to them from a parked car, and those descriptions were vague. But they all stopped at the same photo—Doug Cooper's.

"That's the man," they said.

"They'd seen him in a movie," I told his lawyer.

"That's what he thinks," the lawyer said. "And he did go around the school twice. Which must have been how they got his license number. Hell, he doesn't even remember seeing any girls. And he never stopped except at cross streets. He swears he never parked. He wants a polygraph test to prove those girls are making a mistake.''

"Send me the arrest report," I said, "and anything else you think I ought to see. Type up whatever you know about him. Give me a couple of days to investigate on my own, all right? And I'll see the two of you here Friday morning at nine.''

The arrest report was discouraging. The girls all told an identical story. The man had prowled in his car very slowly past the high school playground, watching the girls through the fence. Then he'd parked, opened the car door, and gone through his indecent-exposure act. But there was no reason to suppose the girls hadn't simply agreed on their stories beforehand. And couldn't they have made the whole thing up? I didn't like their not being able to put into words what the man looked like, what he was wearing, any details. And Cooper had absolutely no past record of any kind of wrongdoing. He didn't smoke, he didn't drink, he'd been married to the same woman for thirty-five years. And in a business where talk travels thick and fast, there'd never been any mention of other women.

I drove to the school neighborhood. There were the white buildings, the lawns with kids sprawled on them in the shade of old California pepper trees. Down the side street the chain-link fence began, closing in the football field, the bleachers, and broad acres of patchy grass stretching into a dusty baseball diamond in a far corner. Girls in shorts were kicking a soccer ball as I drove along the street that backed the high school grounds. Like Cooper, I was looking for the street where his friends lived.

Phil Mason was on location in the Mojave desert filming a movie about dirt bikers. He had a bit part as a small-town sheriff. But his wife was at the new apartment. She was upset about what had happened to Doug Cooper—particularly since it had happened as a result of his coming to visit the Masons. She said they both felt as if somehow it was their fault. I told her that they mustn't blame themselves, that this sort of thing can happen to any man, any time, unbelievable as that might seem.

"But to Doug Cooper, of all people," she said. "You don't

24

know him, Mr. Gugas. Phil and I do, have for twenty-five years. He's a real he-man, no question about that. But on the subject of sex, he's strictly nineteenth century. He not only won't tell an off-color story, he won't listen to one. It still shocks him to hear a man swear in front of a woman.''

"The code of the Old West,'' I said. She'd brought me a cup of rich, steaming coffee. We were sitting in a pleasant, sunlit room, all newly furnished. Outside the windows were green treetops. "That's not a type you expect to find in the acting business.''

"No, but people respect him for it, surprisingly.''

Edith Mason's story of Doug Cooper's visit to her and her husband tallied exactly with Cooper's account. But as I left, I was nagged by doubt. Wasn't Doug Cooper a little too good to be true? Friday morning came, and I had him alone in my examining room. I had him sit in the chair beside the desk into which my polygraph instrument is built. I pulled up the only other chair in the room, facing him, and began to talk about what had happened to him and why. How did he feel about this kind of behavior? Did he know it was common? I'd examined hundreds of men accused as he'd been accused—men of every age and background, from truck drivers to doctors. And more than a few had been guilty.

He shook his head. "I can't believe it.'' And he meant it. He leaned forward, lowering his voice, as if it were a shameful thing to talk about, even between us. "What would make a man do that, expose his private parts? Gosh, do you know—my wife has never even seen me naked. That's the way I was raised. The good old-fashioned American way. My folks were Bible-reading, God-fearing pioneer people, the kind that made this country great. You just—you just don't expose your naked body.'' He grinned sheepishly. "I guess that sounds prudish but that's how I am. And that's how I raised my own kids.''

"You must have had quite a time in school,'' I said. "What about showers after gym classes?''

"I turned my back,'' he said. "And when I was in the Navy in the war—that was something else. I'd hold my bathroom wants till two-thirty in the morning so there wouldn't be anybody else in the head because there were no doors on the toilets.''

"What about those long trough latrines?''

25

He grimaced. "I can't even urinate if anybody's there. My dad was the same way. And I respect that. There's a lock on the bathroom door. I make my kids use it."

I asked, "You've never had a sudden urge to let somebody see this piece of anatomy you've kept so private?"

Color flared in his face. His hands clenched. "No!" he choked out. "Listen. I'll tell you the truth. Once in the eighth grade, in the boys' room, a kid saw my penis and laughed. He spread it all over school, how small it was. I was so ashamed I couldn't rest till I got out of that town."

"Is it true," I asked, "or was he just making trouble?"

"It's true," he said. "I'd never let anybody laugh at me about it again. No—I'd never show it off. There's nothing to show off. It makes me sick to think about it."

We ran the test. He was the farthest thing from an exhibitionist any man could be. And the reactions that showed up on his polygraph chart made that absolutely certain. Doug Cooper had been through a grueling time in that examination room but when I showed him the charts, explained the results to him, and told his attorney I was sure his client was innocent, his shoulders straightened again, and relief showed in his eyes. His wife and two of his three grown youngsters had come with him and waited nervously outside the examining room. They shared in his happiness. They went away smiling.

I wasn't smiling. We had the truth from Doug Cooper. That still left four witnesses who said he was lying. Maybe they were making an honest mistake, maybe for some twisted, adolescent reason they had concocted the story out of their imaginations. For excitement, with no idea of the wreckage they were going to make of a man's life. They'd told the police they would recognize the man anywhere, day or night, if they ever saw him. This gave me an idea. I telephoned his lawyer and told him what I had in mind.

I want to talk to those girls," I said. "and I want Doug Cooper with me when I do."

"Chris, that means contacting prosecution witnesses. You could end up in jail."

"I don't care," I said. "I believe the polygraph. I don't know

26

who those girls saw, if they saw anybody—but it wasn't Doug Cooper, and I'm going to prove it. All I want is your permission to go ahead."

"You've got it," he said. "Good luck."

But I didn't need luck, not this time. I telephoned Cooper and asked him to meet me on Sunday morning. We were going to the homes of each of those girls and hear what they had to say. "Dress casually," I said, "and remember to wear your driving glasses." His operator's license specified that he needed lenses when he was at the wheel of his car. But like most actors, he didn't want to appear in glasses when he didn't have to. He kept them in the glove compartment of his car. And he hadn't worn them when the police photographed him after his arrest.

Jill Rosenberg's family lived in a modest stucco bungalow on a quiet Hollywood side street. A small dog barked and jumped at the screen when Jill's father opened the door. He was in T-shirt and jeans, and a section of the Sunday paper dangled from his hand. I carried a briefcase. Big Doug Cooper loomed behind me on the step. Rosenberg, a small, boyish-looking man, going bald, seemed surprised to see us, but not unfriendly. I explained that I was an investigator doing a follow-up on the indecent-exposure charge made by his daughter. Rosenberg unfastened the screen and let us in. While the dog sniffed at our shoes, I introduced Doug Cooper as my associate and asked Rosenberg to call Jill, saying that I wanted to talk to her.

She came in from the kitchen carrying a canned soft drink, a slight girl, looking younger than her fifteen years, big dark eyes in a thin face. She wore shorts and a red and yellow striped tank top. She dropped into a chair and Rosenberg nodded to us to sit down on the couch. I set my briefcase on the rug that was strewn with other sections of the Sunday paper. My thumb flicked a switch that activated tape reels inside the case. Then I asked Jill Rosenberg to tell me what had happened on the school grounds that day. She told it exactly as it was in the arrest report.

"And the man," I said. "What did he look like?"

"The police had a picture of him," she said.

"I haven't seen that," I said. "Can't you describe him for me?

27

Did he look like me? Did he look like your father? Like Mr. Jones, here?'' I jerked my head at Cooper, who sat silent beside me on the couch.

She studied him, shook her head, drank from her can of soda. "No. He looked like the picture, that's all.''

"Did he wear a hat?'' I asked. "Glasses, sunglasses?''

I don't think so,'' she said.

"But you could positively identify the man if you ever saw him again, right?''

"Oh, absolutely. I'll never forget that terrible face. And what he was—what he was doing.''

"I'm sure you won't,'' I said. "Thanks, Jill. Thanks, Mr. Rosenberg. Sorry to have broken in on your Sunday.''

"It's okay,'' Rosenberg said, and picked up the little dog to keep it from running out when he opened the door for us. "I'll do anything to help you find that pervert.''

"Good Lord,'' Doug Cooper said when we were in my car again and headed for the second girl's house. "What would happen if I'd been accused of murder?''

Denna McLain was a pudgy girl with fluffy blonde hair. But her blue eyes looked as blankly at Doug Cooper as had Jill Rosenberg's. It was plain from the interview that she'd never seen him in her life—not even in a movie. And I had the interview on tape in that briefcase. Anita Gomez gave us a description of the man in the car. It didn't match Cooper's appearance. No, Anita said, as she breezed out the door on her way to mass—the man didn't look anything like my associate. Jackie Slater's mother was a blowsy blonde in a housecoat that hadn't seen a laundromat in a long time. She'd plastered on green eye shadow and thick lipstick, but not accurately. I suspected the glass in her hand held more vodka than tomato juice. No, she wasn't letting anybody talk to her daughter. The poor kid had been through enough. What were we trying to do—blame her for what happened? That was how the cops always acted. "Men!'' She slammed the door.

"It doesn't matter,'' I told Cooper on our way down the scaly stucco outdoor staircase. "Three out of four is plenty. You've got nothing to worry about. Not anymore.''

"Wait till I meet with the prosecutor,'' Cooper's lawyer laughed when I phoned him that afternoon. "I want to see his face when I play him those tapes."

I wanted to be there too, and the attorney and I had a tough time keeping straight faces as we rode the elevator up to the prosecutor's office the next morning. At first he stared at the tape machine as if he couldn't believe his ears. But as the interviews with the three girls rolled on, he first grinned, then broke into laughter. He waved his hands hopelessly at the recorder.

"All right," he said, "enough already. Turn it off. I believe, I believe." I brought the shiny plastic reels to a stop. The prosecutor was on his feet, rounding his desk, holding out his hand to me. He was still chuckling. "Chris," he said, pumping my hand, "if I ever get into any trouble, I want you to know you'll have me for a client."

Doug Cooper didn't laugh. Even for an actor, laughter didn't come easily after the weeks of horror he'd been through. The mistake those four high school girls had made had aged him, cost him a lot of money in lawyer's and investigator's fees, and made him the subject of some pretty vicious gossip. Happily, the actors, directors, and producers who knew him had backed him all the way, and he was soon working again.

But if the Coopers weren't able to summon a lot of merriment at Doug's escape—his wife and grown sons looked drawn and shaken when I brought them the good news—they were grateful. I know. A few days afterward, a small package arrived in my office mail. Inside, in a handsome leather jeweler's box, was an expensive wristwatch, a gift from Cooper's wife. Now and then I wear that watch—to remind me of another polygraph test that cleared an innocent man. And at meetings of the local bar association, I still hear the story of my investigation, with more fantastic and hilarious additions to the legend every year.

5

The Silent Witness

The town was an ancient seaport I'll call Saronicus. From where I leaned on a ship's rail that morning, out on the sparkling Mediterranean, the buildings of the city looked like a tumble of squared white stones between hills green-striped by vineyards, where the silver leafage of gnarled olive trees shimmered against a hot blue sky. Out in those same hills, among the broken, tumbled pillars of ancient temples, shepherd boys tended flocks of white goats, just as in the Greece of legend. But this was far from the Greece of legend. It was a Greece ravaged and battered by modern war, trying to stagger to its feet again after brutal years of Nazi occupation.

I'd been assigned by the American military mission in Europe to help countries we were aiding in other, better-publicized ways, to rebuild their depleted and demoralized police departments. I'd asked to be sent to Greece. It was the country of my mother's birth. I spoke the language. It meant something special to me. I was young, but I'd had police training in college, in the Marines, with the Los Angeles County Sheriff's crime lab, and in the L.A. City Police Reserves. I believed I was equipped for the job. I wanted to help.

It startled me a little to be met at the dock by three police cars, and to be driven with red lights and sirens up through the narrow, crooked streets, straight to police headquarters. The place was neglected and run-down. So was that part of the city I'd come through. There's no mistaking poverty when you see it. So the plush office I was given disturbed me. I didn't object, though; that would only have hurt feelings. The U.S. was their benefactor. I represented the U.S. Only the best was good enough. And it turned out that this attitude went far deeper than repainting a set of rooms, bringing in new furniture, and washing the windows.

No one was going to ask me to do a thing. What did I wish to correct first? They would have to give me their ideas of what needed to be done, I replied. It was all polite and diplomatic. I smiled a lot. They smiled a lot. I was wined and dined. I drank gallons of thick, sweet Turkish coffee. But I couldn't get anyone to tell me what I could do to help. I was brought stacks of files and records. I was shown anything and everything I asked to see. I worked twelve and fifteen hours a day. But I was getting nowhere. No one of importance got to his office before ten in the morning. Every office stood empty and silent in the hot summer afternoons. At around four, when the wind blew a little cooler off the sea, work resumed. I got used to this after a while. But I had to start things happening.

Finally, I asked if everyone wouldn't enjoy seeing some films about the latest U.S. police procedures. I knew the answer I would get would be polite, and it was. A meeting room was swept clean of dust and cobwebs and I set up my projector. I'd seen enough to prove to me that nothing had changed in police methods here in a long, long time. Attitudes and procedures had been handed down without change, decade after decade. A hundred law-enforcement officers from the district showed up for my films and the lecture I gave to accompany them. They murmured in the shadows at the

31

startling and shiny images on the screen. I sensed that many of them could hardly believe what they saw. Time had stood still here while it rocketed ahead in my own country.

But the chief of police in Saronicus asked me right away to set up a training program in the new methods for his department. Could I arrange to get some of this marvelous new equipment for them? Could I teach them to use it? I could and I would. I was overjoyed that at last I'd cracked the politeness barrier and things were going to start happening. I wasn't pleased when the chief told me that the first thing he wanted his men to learn was modern interrogation methods. I privately thought they needed a lot of other basic training before they got to the complexities of interrogation. But I wasn't about to do anything to dampen the enthusiasm I'd finally stirred.

I set up a demonstration of the polygraph. There was a danger that these officers might get the mistaken idea that the instrument was the answer to all the tricky problems of questioning suspects and witnesses and getting the truth out of them. It wasn't. It isn't. But if a display of its possibilities could help jolt this one police department into the twentieth century, misunderstandings didn't much matter—they could be cleared up later. And if my demonstration worked as I was sure it would, word would travel quickly, not just through the district but through the whole country. What I'd been sent here to make happen would start happening at last. I'm anything but a stage magician, but I planned a show that would have that kind of effect.

When the crowd had assembled in the cramped meeting room, I chose three men at random. "I want one among you to play the part of a pickpocket. You're going to steal a wallet. I'll leave the room while you commit your crime. When I come back, I'll run a polygraph test on all three of you and I'll tell you which one of you stole the wallet." I can remember the silence in the room. I can remember how the other officers sat forward on the edge of their chairs, listening and watching as I questioned each of the three men in turn. I didn't want yes and no answers from my make-believe suspects. I wanted silence. I wanted their breathing and skin resistance alone to indicate on the chart who was lying. I didn't even fasten on the blood-pressure cuff. I was sure I wouldn't need it. And I was right.

32

But to keep the show as dramatic as possible, I detached the men from the polygraph without saying which of them had stolen the wallet—though of course I knew. The charts were easy to read but I meant to save the result for the climax. Next, I chose another three men. These I asked to agree privately on one of five colors. It took no more than the time needed to run down the list of colors for me to see the jittering polygraph lines of the one they'd decided on. I kept this to myself for the time being. Then, as the men went back to their seats, I turned to the police chief.

"Suppose I tell you your mother's name," I said.

"You don't know it," he said.

"The polygraph instrument will," I said smiling.

He turned down the corners of his mouth. "Impossible. I'm too tough to be tricked by a machine."

"Let's try and see." I handed him a slip of paper and a pencil. "Write down your mother's name and give this piece of paper to anyone here you choose. Then sit down in this chair, and we'll see what happens."

With a shrug, he wrote down the name, folded the slip, handed it to another officer, gave me back my pencil. Then he rose with an amiable but skeptical shake of his head, and sat in the chair beside the polygraph. He joked with the watching officers as I fastened the tube around his thick chest and attached the electrodes to his strong hands. I switched on the polygraph and began reciting to him common given names of Greek women. Puzzlingly, I got two marked responses, but one was sharper than the other and I settled on that name. I rattled off a few more, then took the chest tube and electrodes off. Rising, the chief asked:

"Well? And what about your marvelous machine? This time it has failed you—no?"

I frowned, pretending to be uncertain. "Well—" I said.

"You see?" He turned triumphantly to the men on the rows of chairs. "It is just as I predicted. I am too tough and wily. The Nazis could get nothing out of me. How could I be intimidated by a few dials and knobs and wires?" Nodding his head in smug self-satisfaction, he took his seat again. "What about these others?" he asked me. "You have not told them the results of your wonderful tests."

I pointed at a young fellow in uniform seated halfway back in the room. He was easy to pick out in this crowd because he had fair hair. I motioned him to stand up. With an amazed expression, he got his lanky body out of the chair. He looked around at his friends with a sheepish smile.

"You're the one who stole the wallet," I said.

He nodded speechlessly. Laughter broke out. I'd been right. Quickly I picked out the three men I'd chosen for the color test. I looked each of them in the eye.

"The color was red," I told them. "Wasn't it?"

"Yes, sir." They glanced at one another, awed. "Red. That's right."

This time there was a murmur of superstitious astonishment. The eyes fixed on me were round with amazement. I didn't waste it. I looked at the chief, who was still preening himself on having beaten what he called the lie machine.

"Your mother's name is Helena," I said.

His bulky body came half up out of the chair in shocked disbelief. It was plain to everyone that I was correct. Laughter sounded once more. The chief looked pale. He opened and shut his mouth as if he couldn't get his breath. Finally he blurted, "But I was sure I tricked you. I thought only of the name of my grandmother!"

"Oh, I know that too," I said carelessly. "It was Maria, wasn't it?"

For a stunned moment he could only blink. Then he got his color back—and his sense of humor. He joined in the laughter. He lumbered to the polygraph instrument and bent over it, wagging his head. He looked at the crowd. He looked at me. "It is everything you said it was. It is more."

"It is magic!" a voice shouted.

"It can read minds," called someone else.

Clearly, it was time to get serious. For the next hour of that sweltering night, in a press of too many bodies in a crowded room, I did my best to teach as much as I could to the eagerly questioning men about how the instrument worked, what produced the lines on the charts, and at what point blood pressure and pulse rate, breathing rate and skin tension, indicated that a lie was being told. I gave them a set of simple rules for questioning. It wasn't only the heat that had me sweating. I was trying to cram into a hectic hour what I knew took grueling weeks and months to teach. But I had to make the most of this chance. And however lamely, I knew I was doing the right thing.

Sure enough, I was asked to teach on a regular basis. I kept the number of men at each session to forty. They came from all over the district. They learned not only basic polygraph technique but the use of the newest camera equipment designed for crime fighting, and of wire and tape recorders as well. After I had seen some pretty crude and brutal interrogation techniques used on witnesses and prisoners, I asked for a chance to question them myself. Threats of disgrace, even of beatings and the lock-up, only made witnesses tight-mouthed and suspects sullen and contemptuous. It was counter-productive. The Saronicus detectives were getting nowhere.

I used a wholly different method. There were three unsolved cases; a shooting, a rape, and a robbery. I studied reports. I looked into the backgrounds of the incidents. I found out all I could about the men and women I was going to talk to. When I was face to face with them, I made sure they were as comfortable as possible. I invited the local officers to sit in on the questionings. Their jaws sagged in disbelief when I gave the prisoners coffee and cigarettes. I not only didn't lift a nightstick at them, I never even raised my voice.

Within an hour, I had a full confession from the rape suspect, and the young tough who had done the shooting had told me all about it. The robbery suspect, though, was older and tougher. There were bruises on his face that I was fairly sure came from rough handling by the same men I had invited to sit in chairs across the room and watch my interrogation. These officers liked me, but thought of me as a teacher of newfangled, gadget-ridden police methods. They'd not exactly agreed to let me interrogate these suspects—they'd challenged me. They hadn't said so in words. Their eyes had told me. And they were sneering now.

Plainly, they felt I was wasting time. I asked the man about his village, his family, childhood, wartime experiences. We talked about thievery as a way of life—the morality of it. We talked about the church and God. I heard the bentwood chairs the detectives were sitting on creak as they shifted position impatiently. I didn't mind.

This man who had only spat at the feet of these officers, who hadn't said a word to them except to curse, was talking to me freely. An hour went by. The room was thick with cigarette smoke. Dusty summer sunlight struck in hot through the window high in the wall of the interrogation room. The pigeons that had been noisy through the morning on the tile roof overhead had grown silent in the noon heat. Still the man talked to me. And suddenly he was admitting to the robbery. Before another ten minutes had passed, he gave me details of five earlier robberies that had gone unsolved. I rose, thanked the man, shook his hand, and called a guard to take him back to his cell.

This went down well—with some of the men. I was asked to train all the detectives on the Saronicus force in these interrogation techniques of mine. The young ones were eager and learned pretty quickly. The older ones were resentful and grew more so as less experienced men chalked up confession after confession with the new methods, and they kept failing with the old ones. No one voiced open hostility, but I began to be leaned on by senior officials and department heads. They wanted me to fail at something. Not that I hadn't been careful always to ask advice and consent from every commander before I made the smallest change. But I was making changes. And this had to mean that the methods on which these men had built their careers were less than perfect. It was only human for them to feel threatened.

They threw at me every sort of police problem, from traffic to narcotics to ballistics. Even if I'd had less training and experience, there was almost no way I could have failed. Neglect and stagnation were the causes of most of the problems. Time, energy, and common sense were the basic tools anyone needed to solve them. That in the U.S., where I'd had my training, a lot of new answers had been found to questions still being attacked in outdated ways here, made coping fairly simple for me—even though to those watching, what I did may have seemed wizardry. On my side, I felt that to have made things worse would have taken real genius.

But I didn't get much rest. By now I was setting up training programs for police agencies, civilian and military, all over the country. Word of the work I had done in Saronicus and the surrounding district had reached the Minister of the Interior. With his encouragement and his orders that field commanders and police executives from every district attend my training sessions and then set in motion similar programs for their own men when they returned to their posts, I felt I'd done what I was sent to Greece to do. But I'd had to drive myself. I hadn't taken a day off since I arrived. Now I began to make myself stay away from the office on Sundays and relax.

It was the end of summer. The sirocco blew, a strong south wind, like a blast from a furnace. I'd darkened my rooms and was making as few movements as possible: The *Libas*, as they called that wind in Saronicus, can kill. I stripped and stretched out on my bed with a damp cloth on my forehead. Then the telephone jangled. I let it yammer a long while before I pushed to my feet with a groan. The floor was of glazed tile and usually it felt cool—but not during the Libas. As I moved to the phone through the humid shadows, the soles of my feet warmed. The telephone receiver was warm when I lifted it. Could I come to headquarters, right away, please? It was a serious matter, a matter of the highest priority.

I showered, flapped into a crisply starched shirt, a fresh uniform that was limp by the time I reached the police building. Two detectives met me, men I had trained. Their bloodshot eyes and beard stubble said they'd been working long hours without sleep. In voices hoarse with weariness they explained. A wealthy man, a very wealthy man, an important man with much influence, a former holder of a powerful political office, was raising hell with the department. He had gone so far as to phone the interior minister, a personal friend, to complain.

"Of what?" I asked.

"His wife has disappeared. She simply vanished. Two days ago. Into thin air. We cannot find her."

"What about ships?" I asked. "Trains. She's rich—she could have gone by air. Nobody vanishes, you know that."

They grimly shook their heads. "We have checked the ticket offices, the travel agencies. She is a well-known lady. It would have been impossible for her to go anywhere unrecognized for long—even if she took a false name."

"What about friends?" I asked. "Especially women friends. She may have told one of them."

"They are as surprised as her husband," one of the detectives said. He wiped sweat from his forehead. His eyes begged me. "Tell us what to do."

"I don't have any complaints about what you have done," I said. They'd followed the same pattern of investigation I'd have followed. "What does the husband say? Was there difficulty between him and his wife? Did they have an argument? If so, what about?"

The detectives looked at each other bleakly. Neither of them wanted to make the admission. One of them broke the deadlock of silence by leaving the room. I heard the bubbling of the old-fashioned water cooler in the hall. I looked questioningly at the other detective. He shifted in his chair. He scratched his dark beard stubble. Finally, with a despairing look toward the door, he told me in a voice not much more than a whisper:

"We haven't questioned Mr. Petroklos."

"What?" I could hardly believe him.

"Well, you don't understand. He's—he's not the kind of man we could go to. Not in that way. I mean—" He spread his hands helplessly. "He is—well, Petroklos."

"In what way?" I asked. "What do you mean?"

From the doorway, the detective who'd gone for a drink of water said, "He is important, influential."

"Above suspicion," I said. "Is that what you're telling me? Well, who says you're suspecting him of anything? He's a witness, that's all. He reported the crime. He should have been the first man you talked to. You know that."

They nodded dismally. They knew that. "But he might be offended. He is not an ordinary man."

Plainly, they were scared stiff of Petroklos, his money and his clout. They were afraid for their jobs if anything they did or said rubbed him the wrong way. Their solution had been to steer clear of him—and it was no solution at all. But I didn't say that. Maybe I was wrong in thinking they ought to have been braver. I knew of cases in my own country where wealth and power had the same effect. And, of course, that was the answer: I was a foreigner. I couldn't be gotten at in the way these local men could. That had been why they'd called me.

"Would you like me to talk to Petroklos?" I asked.

"Oh, yes. Please, Major. Please. You talk to him." They were as relieved as if I'd just proved to them there is no Devil. They grinned all over their tired faces. They pumped my hand. One of them pushed the telephone toward me. "His number." He fumbled a slip of paper from a pocket. "I have it right here."

I dialed. A servant answered. I gave my name, said I was assisting the police in the search for Petroklos' wife, and would like to speak to him. He didn't sound friendly when he came on the line, but he agreed to see me. The detectives had readied a police car for me, with a driver. They meant for me to go alone, and it took some persuading on my part to get them to follow me out of the building into the hot sun. The two of them sat silently in the car with me as it climbed into the hills. They were as dejected as if they were on the way to their own funerals.

Tall wrought-iron gates swung open to let our car pass through. White gravel crunched under our tires as we followed a curving drive between dark cypruses to Petroklos' handsome villa. I pushed the doorbell and turned to gaze at the sparkling blue sea below. The place had a beautiful view. The detectives, however, weren't enjoying it. They looked pale and shrunken in their rumpled suits. A maid opened the door. My uniform made it obvious to her who I was— the American military officer. She motioned to me to enter. The detectives hung back. I jerked my head at them and reluctantly they followed me inside. Once the door shut behind us, the high-ceilinged entry hall was cool. An indoor fountain splashed.

Petroklos sat in a long salon whose only light filtered in at a hot slant through the slits of jalousies that covered french doors. But as my eyes grew used to the dimness I could make out the furnishings—handsome antiques. On the white walls hung impressionist paintings. These contrasted in the best possible taste with a few ancient Greek marbles. Petroklos himself sat at the far end of the room. In his hand was a glass that looked as if it held white wine. He was a lean man, with a head of splendid iron-gray hair. There were strong lines beside his mouth. He rose to shake my hand and, with some indifference, those of the Saronicus detectives. He waved us to chairs. He asked me what I wanted.

"Only the answer to one or two questions," I said. I'd brought a small tape recorder. I told him that its use would save him time in the long run. He didn't waste words. He simply nodded. I switched the machine on and began.

"Does your wife enjoy travel?"

He lifted bony shoulders in a dismissive shrug. "We are comfortably situated here. She could find no more picturesque surroundings anywhere in the world. Why should she wish to travel?"

"Perhaps she has relatives she went to see?"

"She was an only child and her parents are dead."

"Perhaps she went to Paris to shop? I understand she is a lovely woman and dresses beautifully."

"She has never been to Paris," he said shortly.

"Have you looked at her appointment book? That might tell us where she's gone."

"She kept no appointment book," he said.

"The servants," I said. "She wouldn't have told her maid where she was going?"

"I have questioned the servants. They keep nothing from me. They know nothing."

"I wonder if I might look at her closet with her maid. Perhaps she can point out to me the clothes your wife took with her when she left."

"I'm afraid that's impossible," Petroklos said. "Major Gugas, just what is your purpose in coming here and asking me these questions? What possible good could it do you to examine my wife's wardrobe?"

"You asked the police to make every effort to locate your missing wife," I said. "The American military mission has appointed me to work with the police here in Saronicus—to help modernize their methods."

A corner of his mouth twitched. "Through the use of that little machine? Through guesswork about my wife's couturier?"

"Do you and your wife get along well?"

He stared at me, frozen-faced.

"Did you have a quarrel before she disappeared?"

He stood up. "This interview is at an end," he said. "Good day, Major. Good day, gentlemen." He left the room. In a moment the maid appeared and showed us out.

40

The detectives were as quiet on the ride back down into Saronicus as they'd been on our way to see Petroklos. This time their reason was different. They thought I had failed and they were embarrassed for me. I asked them what they thought about the interview. They were noncommittal. It had been interesting, they said—but that was simply politeness. They hadn't registered what had happened in that beautiful, dim room. Or, rather, they'd registered only one thing, and it made them worry. Mr. Petroklos had been annoyed.

"Ask yourselves why," I said. "Husbands and wives quarrel. Everybody knows that. Why not admit it if they had some misunderstanding and she marched out? Why not let me look in his wife's closet? What's he got against our finding clues that might lead us to her? He claims he wants her found. I wonder if he does."

"He has a mistress," one of the detectives said. "That's the rumor."

"That wasn't what he was trying to hide," I said. "But maybe she can tell us what it was. Who is she?"

He didn't know. But I knew where to ask: at the city's most expensive restaurants. The third maitre d' I talked to, in a hush of heavy white linen tablecloths, deep crimson plush, and glittering chandeliers, gave me the name of Petroklos' kept woman after I'd folded a bill into his fat, perfumed palm. Her last name was Martin and she spoke with an accent—French, he thought. She was tall and blonde. It so happened that she lived in the same apartment block as he did. He told me how to find it. Petroklos kept her well. It was a handsomely furnished flat with a view of the bay. Three silver-gray Persian cats slept on cushions in the heat. She was slender and elegant and stupid. We'd talked only a few minutes when she told me with a laugh of sour contempt:

"He is jealous of her. Imagine! That dark, dowdy little—how do you say it?—*antiquaille*."

"Frump?" I asked.

"She dresses like a peasant," said Mlle Martin. "She has a mustache like a pirate. Yet he is forever imagining that this man, that man, the other man is pursuing her with amorous intent. He cannot be away from her for half an hour before he is imagining that she is sleeping with someone else." She laughed again, and stroked one of the cats. "As if any man would look twice at such a hen. She came from a farm. She will always smell of the barnyard."

I took a call when I returned to the police building. It was Petroklos' attorney. His client was upset. He said I was accusing him of foul play. Was that true? I answered that the thought hadn't crossed my mind. I'd only been after facts that could help us locate his wife. Well, I must not annoy Mr. Petroklos again. Any questions I had I was to direct to the attorney. I promised I would, hung up, and went to find the two detectives.

"Where is Madame Petroklos' family farm?" I asked. "That would have come into Petroklos' control when he married her, wouldn't it?"

"Yes. It is very remote." The detective smiled. "Who called it a farm? It is a large estate. No one lives there anymore. The Germans billeted soldiers there during the war but it has been abandoned ever since."

"Take a camera," I said. "Get me photographs of the place: the house, outbuildings, the grounds, everything."

"It is a long distance," he said. "I will need a car, a large allowance for petrol."

"I'll see to that," I said. "I want you to start right away. I'll clear it with your department head. And please get back here as quickly as you can."

He was puzzled. "What good can photographs do of an old abandoned estate? It will be nothing but weeds and creepers and broken windows."

"Maybe," I said. "But take pictures of everything—from every angle. I'll see you day after tomorrow."

I spent the time questioning Petroklos' neighbors, with little success. He was a private man, cold and close-mouthed. No one had ever caught more than a glimpse of his wife. When he went out, it was always alone. Ordinarily on business, they supposed—except in the evening of course. But he rarely took out either of his expensive automobiles after dark. I questioned women who were said to be Madame Petroklos' friends. They rarely saw her, in fact; less and less in recent years. Her husband kept her virtually a prisoner. He was frightfully jealous of her. She seemed, lately, almost terrified of him, when these friends spoke with her by telephone.

No one knew anything about Madame Petroklos' disappearance. But that seemed very unlikely. Someone had to know. My instincts said that the someone was Petroklos himself. My suspicions grew stronger when his attorney showed up at my office making threatening noises. Why was I going about the city asking questions of everyone about his client? The police were supposed to be searching for his wife, not blackening his name and reputation, casting suspicion on him. I shrugged. If he wanted us to stop, all he had to do was cooperate with us.

"He called the police in the first place," the lawyer said. "You can't call him a criminal."

"I never did," I said. "Look, he claims to know nothing about his wife's whereabouts. If that's true—"

"Of course, it's true," the lawyer snapped.

"Of course." I made my tone ironic. "So why doesn't he let me give him a polygraph examination? He's telling the truth. The results can clear him of any part in the mystery. As a lawyer, you can see the value of that."

"I can. And I will speak to him." The attorney rose. His expression was glum. "But I doubt that he would consider it. He would regard it as an indignity."

"More of an indignity," I said, going to open the door for him, "than being suspected of getting rid of his wife?"

The lawyer turned on me. "Watch what you say."

"It's not what I say that matters," I answered. "I have an open mind. But other people are saying it. You know that. That's why you came here today."

He glared at me for a long moment, then turned on his heel and walked out. In less than an hour I had a phone call from the American consulate. In fifteen minutes I was in the Consul General's office. There were no aides present, no secretaries; nor was I asked to sit down.

"You were brought here," I was told, "to train the Greek police in modern methods. You were not brought here, Major, to join the Saronicus force and conduct investigations into the behavior, criminal or otherwise, of Greek nationals. Do I make myself clear?"

"Petroklos has been pressuring you," I said.

"He's a big man, a powerful man, a respected man."

"And his wife has disappeared," I said, "and I will bet you my month's pay that he killed her. Sir."

"If he did," the consul said, "it's not your business."

"The local police are afraid of him," I said. "What do you want to happen here? Do you want him to get away with murder? Murder isn't Greek business, or American business. It's human business."

"You keep out of it," the consul said. "If you don't, he'll turn this into an international incident. Washington will make *you* disappear, Major."

I shook my head. "Petroklos is guilty as hell, and if nobody else knows it, he does. He couldn't stand the attention an international incident would focus on him. He's only making noises, hoping you'll call me off. And if you cooperate with him, you'll be as guilty as he is."

The consul's eyes hardened. "I'm warning you, Major."

That was good. He wasn't ordering me. At least, I hoped he'd chosen the word deliberately. "Yes, sir," I said.

"You may go," he said. And then, as I pulled open the door, he added, "And you'd better be damned sure you're right about this. You've got a fine reputation. But a mistake in this case and you'll be finished forever."

"When you report to Petroklos," I said, "will you just tell him you talked to me as he asked? Then give me twelve short hours."

When the detective who had driven the two hundred kilometers to the family estate of Madame Petroklos and back laid on my desk the photographs he'd taken, my hands shook, picking them up. There were two dozen. They were crisp and clear. I shuffled through them, then got a magnifying glass from a desk drawer and studied them inch by inch. The detective leaned over my shoulder.

"What do you expect to find?" he asked. "The place is like a forgotten graveyard."

I looked up at him. "Maybe not so forgotten." I reached for the telephone and dialed Petroklos' attorney. "I have new evidence in the case of Madame Petroklos," I told him. "I'd like to have Mr. Petroklos look at it. I think it will help us clear up the case."

"He wants you off the case," the attorney said.

"I promise to get off it—if he comes and talks to me."

"He has nothing to say to you," the attorney said.

But Petroklos appeared. I had thought curiosity would bring him—curiosity and fear. He looked glummer than ever. He was even more tight-lipped.

"Mr. Petroklos will answer no questions," the attorney said. "He will examine the evidence, but that is all. Just what is this evidence?"

"Photographs," I said, "of his wife's family estate."

"What?" The attorney snorted and started to get up from his chair. But Petroklos caught his arm and pulled him down again. I'd been watching him closely. Something had changed in his eyes. I told him:

"You want to see them, don't you?"

He held out his hand.

I shook my head. "Not here," I said, and stood up.

"What are you talking about?" the attorney said. "Why not here? What sort of games are you playing, Major Gugas? We have warned your American consul that if you—"

"He spoke to me," I said. "I have a polygraph instrument in an interrogation room down the hall. If Mr. Petroklos will allow me, I'd like to seat him there, to measure his breathing rate, his blood pressure, his pulse, and so on while we discuss the photographs."

"He will discuss nothing," the attorney said.

"His physical reactions might suggest to both of us information he has about his wife's disappearance which he has overlooked or forgotten," I said.

Petroklos, his face frozen, was watching me intently. I picked up the batch of pictures and shuffled through them, careful to keep the backs to him. He watched my every move the way a rabbit watches a snake.

The attorney rose again. "He will answer no questions."

I raised my eyebrows at Petroklos. "No questions," he said.

"All right," I said. "I won't ask any questions and he doesn't have to give me any answers. But in return for that courtesy, I must ask that he allow me to take the measurements with the instrument I mentioned."

The attorney looked down at Petroklos. Petroklos dragged his fascinated gaze from my hands. He gave the attorney a grim nod and stood up. I dropped the photographs into their envelope and led the

45

way down the hall. I motioned Petroklos into the chair next to the polygraph instrument and he obeyed stiffly and wordlessly as I directed him so that I could fasten the corrugated tube that checks respiration around his chest, the blood-pressure cuff on his arm, the electrode thimbles to his fingertips. I switched on the instrument. I moved quickly, afraid he would change his mind at any moment. But he simply had to see those pictures. I didn't really know why. I had only a hunch to go on. But that hunch had started out ugly, and he was making it uglier by the minute.

I wanted to check the machine's responses, but I'd promised to ask no questions. I had to chance that he was reasonably healthy, reasonably sane, and that the machine was in good working order. I took the pictures from the envelope and put the first one into his hand. He stared at it without the flicker of an eyebrow and handed it back. His respiration was quick—there was evidence on the moving graph paper that he was under severe stress—but those things would figure in the circumstances. I handed him the next photograph, and the next, and the next. And then, abruptly, the pens began jiggling sharply. When he handed that photograph back, I glanced at it, but only for a split second. Then I went on showing him the rest of the photographs.

"Well?" he said, when the test was ended.

"I'll have to analyze the results," I said. "That will take me until morning. I'll be in touch with you." I shook his hand, and I shook the attorney's hand. "Thank you very much." I was tempted to say, "I think we've got the answer to your wife's disappearance." I didn't say it. Something told me it would be more than reckless—it would be deadly. But as soon as I'd escorted Petroklos and his attorney out to the waiting limousine, I rushed back inside. I found the detective, looking worn-out from his long drive, slouched half-asleep over a cup of that thick, syrupy Turkish coffee.

"Come on," I said. "Round up four men. Get a second car. Throw some spades in the trunk."

"Spades?" He gaped at me blearily. "Car? Trunk?"

"We're going back to Madame Petroklos' estate," I said. "Right now."

"But"—he gestured at the window—"it will soon be dark.

Those roads are treacherous. Anyway, what can you do when you get there? It will be midnight.''

"So bring flashlights," I said. "And be sure the batteries are fresh.''

Shaking his head, he pushed away his cup and got groggily to his feet. The look he gave me said that the crazy American major had really lost his mind this time. But he went off to get things started. Maybe the country we passed through, driving as fast as the narrow, crooked roads would let us, was beautiful. I saw only as much of it as the beams of the headlamps lit up when we passed. The car was old. I was shaken up and bruised by the time we reached the ivy-covered pillars that flanked the driveway leading to Madame Petroklos's girlhood home. Parched weeds and briars edged the drive. Dry grass between the wheel ruts brushed the underside of the car. The untrimmed branches of trees scraped the roof. The house loomed up in our headlight beams, windows black and empty as the eyes of skulls. The driver halted the car and looked over his shoulder at me for instructions. I leaned forward, stiff and sore from the long drive, and shook the shoulder of the detective who had taken the photographs. He came awake with a grunt.

"Where is the stable building?''

The lights of the car full of officers that had followed us glared in the rear-view mirror and made me wince.

"The one with the old fig tree at the corner?''

"That's it,'' I said. "How do we get there?''

Its roof had fallen in. Spiderwebs sagged with dust among the broken rafters. There was a smell of decay where once had been the warm, hay-sweet smell of horses. The floor of the stable was composed of slabs of stone. Our flashlight beams showed us that none of these had been disturbed. Beetles scuttled away across the dried and yellow moss. We went outside again. Followed by murmuring men whose spades clanked as they stumbled over the uneven ground, I walked around the rough stone walls of the stable, until I reached the gnarled trunk of an old tree twisted upward at an angle. Overhead was a canopy of large, limp leaves. Clumps of figs, dark and swollen with ripeness, weighted down the branches. Rotting fruit was thick underfoot. It filled the warm night air with cloying sweetness.

47

At a half-crouch, I played the beam of my flashlight on the ground all around the tree. I kept moving outward from the knuckly roots, circling the area a few feet at a time. I knelt. The others crouched around me. I touched the ground and felt dampness. I groped further, on hands and knees. Dry. No rain had fallen for weeks. I raked aside a mat of vine that had held the dampness in this tree-shaded spot.

"Dig here," I said.

The grave was shallow. The body had begun to decay. The smell of death rose from the earth. Men stumbled away into the dark and I heard them being sick. Covering my mouth and nose with a handkerchief, I knelt again and shone my light on the skull. It had been smashed in. I stood and turned away. The detective stared at me.

"How did you know?" he said.

"The polygraph," I said. And I remembered Petroklos' face in the interrogation room hours ago when I'd shown him the photograph of this corner of the stable nearest the old fig tree. I saw again the sudden shivering of the styluses writing their unmistakable message of guilt on the traveling belt of graph paper. The gaunt, gray-haired man's blood pressure had jumped so at that moment, I'd been afraid he would have a stroke.

"But he said nothing," the detective protested. "Not one word."

"He didn't have to," I said.

I made the detective promise me that neither he nor any of his men would ever mention my part in the case. I was dropped off at my apartment in the gray of early dawn, exhausted and deeply relieved. When Petroklos was arrested at his handsome villa, when reporters crowded the police building, clamoring for the story, I was sound asleep in another part of the city. My name was never mentioned. I'd come out right, but I'd still have been in trouble if what I'd done became known. So far as the newspaper people and broadcasters knew, the Saronicus police had cracked the Petroklos affair unaided.

Petroklos was convicted after a sensational trial. To me and to the police, the polygraph had proved its worth. The remaining weeks of my duty tour couldn't have been better, and when it came time for me to move on to another country on a like assignment, two hundred officers escorted me to my train. The truth about the solving of the Petroklos puzzle did come out years later. And I still hear from men who were my students and became my friends about the "black magic" I used to break that case, without the suspect uttering a word.

The Police Spy

Riots and burnings charred Washington, Detroit, Los Angeles, and other cities in the 1960s. For many blacks, Martin Luther King, Jr., moved too deliberately. They wanted change, and it wasn't happening, not quickly enough. Nonviolence seemed only to make whites believe blacks were cowards—or so these urgent young men thought. Action was needed, action now, and if riots, fire-bombings, and killings were the only acts that would bring about the changes so desperately desired, then these were the right means to use.

The line between activists and revolutionaries grew vague—at least to the public's nervous gaze. Paramilitary outfits formed—guns, boots, uniforms. The list of new organizations kept growing. The names have faded now, but they made headlines then. The militants had a lot to say, and they said it in shrill street language.

They were talking about revolution, and their talk scared a lot of people. So did the violence that followed. Not the least shaken up were law-enforcement agents.

A number of black revolutionaries went to prison. There, they stirred up trouble where they could. Sometimes it was lethal. Prisoners died by violence. Guards died by violence. Inmates previously indifferent to politics suddenly became fervent activists. Bloody riots shook San Quentin and Soledad. Men died. Punishment was ruthless. A so-called underground press had come into being to echo the tumultuous fears and hatreds of those years. It rallied against the system that had locked these people up. "Political prisoners," it called them. "Racism," it charged. "Fascism."

Largest of these underground papers was the Los Angeles *Free Press,* and this account of one of the strangest cases I was ever involved in begins on a hot August morning in 1971, when a young black named Louis Tackwood strolled into its shabby offices looking for its political affairs writer, Michael McCarthy. The flashily-dressed Tackwood must have startled the staff, which tended toward bare feet and ragged jeans. He was the wrong kind of black. This one couldn't conceivably be politically conscious. Tackwood didn't let their raised eyebrows bother him. Slim, handsome, with an easy smile and charm to spare, he sweet-talked, he fast-talked. And he reached the man he wanted.

McCarthy, not quite thirty, had spent time in California prisons. He'd become an organizer there, and had been a close friend of George Jackson, who, only a few days earlier, had been shot to death at San Quentin. McCarthy didn't believe the official story that Jackson had been armed and trying to climb a prison fence. This made him more than ready to listen to what Louis Tackwood had to tell him—which was that the Criminal Conspiracy Section of the Los Angeles Police Department had known beforehand of Jackson's break-out plans and had kept hands off. To McCarthy, this meant that the CCS had counted on Jackson being killed.

How did Tackwood know about the inner workings of the CCS? Simple: He worked for them, and for another LAPD elite unit, the Special Investigations Section (SIS). He had been a police informer since 1961. It didn't bother him. He enjoyed the risk, the trickiness, the intrigue. It made him feel smarter than everybody else.

McCarthy listened uneasily. He was willing to believe the police conspiracies against black militants that Tackwood was outlining to him. But what were Tackwood's motives? After all, McCarthy, a vocal and visible activist, could be a police target. So why wasn't Tackwood simply trying to set him up? Was there any way to trust him? If Tackwood had, as he asserted, really given a black nationalist organization guns furnished by the LAPD, then wasn't Tackwood in part responsible for the shooting deaths of two young militants at a recent campus rally? Didn't this make him a very dangerous cat? His claim that he wanted to expose in print the whole antiradical apparatus of law enforcement in California because he was angry at their attempt to "frame" a black activist might be true—but it might not.

McCarthy wanted advice. He went to a scruffy slum by the sea called Venice to talk to Robert Duggan and Marilyn Katz. Duggan, a good-looking young man with a shock of blond hair, had mixed in South American revolutionary politics. Marilyn Katz, small, slim, dark, intense, was a sociologist who had been active in the Students for a Democratic Society (SDS) and was researching what she regarded as an ominous growth in police power and influence. They agreed with McCarthy that Tackwood's revelations, if true, should be printed. With the help of a lawyer called Dan Lund, they worked out a plan to test Tackwood's truthfulness while protecting themselves in case Tackwood was trying to entrap them.

Maybe he was. He certainly reported on them to his superiors at CCS. But he maintained that this was only to set up an excuse for his visits to the Duggan-Katz apartment in Venice, and that the information he gave was false. Meanwhile, he passed McCarthy's truthfulness test by bringing him, Duggan, and Katz information about themselves that he could have found only in police files. In their presence, while they ran a tape recorder, he phoned and talked to an officer at SIS. The conversation left no doubt in their minds that Tackwood had, as he claimed, taken part in undercover operations.

In its next issue, the *Free Press* published the names, addresses, and telephone numbers of agents and informers working undercover for the police against militant black and other extremist organizations. The paper didn't reveal its source, but the source was

Tackwood. He knew them all. It still seems incredible to me that the police could have been so careless as to let one operative have free access to everything in their offices. A shock wave hit the "Glass House"—LAPD headquarters in Los Angeles—and shuddered through the police departments up and down the California coast. The delicate wiring of dozens of secret operations snapped. The agents named were in danger of beatings, even death. The police were furious at whomever had leaked to the enemy. They ought to have been furious at themselves. Tackwood knew that in the deadly game he played, you trust no one. Yet he had conned veteran police officers into trusting him completely. He was delighted with himself: He was smarter than all of them.

The reels of tape stacked up in Duggan's closet. Tackwood talked for hours—and not just to the underground press anymore. A writer had said that the tapes would make a book. Tackwood had signed a contract. A book might make him a celebrity when it came out. He went on talking. In story after story, "those mad dogs in the CCS" were described as undercutting constitutional protections and recklessly breaking every police guideline in the book. These charges fit the notions about law enforcement that McCarthy, Duggan, Katz, and their friends shared, so they found the last story he came up with credible, bizarre as it was.

Tackwood claimed that the CCS and the FBI had set up a joint special unit, Squad 19, to stir up massive violence at the upcoming Republican National Convention, then scheduled to be held in San Diego. They would use Tackwood and agent provocateurs like him inside militant left-wing organizations to turn demonstrations into riots. The leftists themselves would be blamed, of course. Television coverage would send the nation into a panic, and this would free President Nixon to use his special emergency powers to arrest and lock up every radical dissident in the country. Tackwood would stick with Squad 19 "until the dynamite goes off," so that he could feed to Duggan and friends each step in the plan as it developed.

But it didn't work out that way. A couple of days later, Duggan's phone rang. Tackwood told him he had the complete Squad 19 plans for San Diego and was bringing them to Duggan in Venice that night. Duggan hung up in shock: The phone might be tapped. Tackwood was far too slick to say what he'd said. This could be a trap. Duggan gathered up Katz and McCarthy and drove to attorney Dan Lund, who drew up an affidavit stating that Louis Tackwood, working for the Los Angeles police, meant to frame Duggan on a charge of receiving stolen documents.

But Tackwood didn't keep his date. Something else was wrong. He dropped from sight. He had missed appointments by a few hours before, but never until now for whole days at a time, never without checking in to explain. Perhaps the phone call had been on the level but the tap had been on and the police had learned Tackwood was double-crossing them. Duggan felt that Tackwood was probably "in the Los Angeles river with several .38 slugs in the back of his head." And who would be charged with the murder? Duggan and friends flocked back to Lund's office. Letters went out to the Los Angeles district attorney, the state attorney general, the attorney general of the United States. Tackwood's disappearance must be investigated. "We believe his police superiors have found it necessary to conspire in the kidnapping, or worse, of Mr. Tackwood."

Next, Duggan and friends contacted the Los Angeles *Times,* the Washington *Post,* and *Newsweek* magazine. If nothing had yet happened to Tackwood, his story in print, nationwide, might keep anything from happening. Jerry Cohen of the *Times,* Leroy Aarons of the *Post,* and Karl Fleming of *Newsweek* came to Duggan's Venice apartment. They listened to McCarthy's, Duggan's, and Katz's accounts of their relations with Tackwood, then heard Tackwood's own voice on tape, unreeling story after sensational story. They left very late, agreeing that there was terrific copy there—if Tackwood could be believed.

Doggedly, systematically, they checked him out. In detail after detail he had told the truth. Police records showed it: Times, dates, everything jibed. If he said he had been at a given place at a given time with given persons, he had been. Prisoners he claimed to have been responsible for jailing affirmed the fact. Two Berkeley New Left blacks who had run for City Council seats nodded when asked if Tackwood had worked in their campaigns. He had also admitted to them he was an agent for the State Bureau of Criminal Identification and Intelligence (CII). Tackwood had spoken of a telephone in his apartment with a direct tap from a police division. The reporters found it. The undercover nature of much of Tackwood's work made confirmation of all facts impossible. But everything that could be checked on tallied. Tackwood's story began to look more and more credible—and his disappearance more and more ominous.

Then he surfaced, in the company of his buddy, Sgt. Larry Brown of the LAPD's Special Investigation Section. Brown had taken Tackwood straight to the district attorney, who was agitated about Duggan-Katz-McCarthy's charges that the police had kidnapped the informer. To the DA, Tackwood denied everything his New Left friends had said about him. He had never told them anything. No, he hadn't made any tapes. "Like I told the CCS . . . these are dangerous, tight people," he declared. He specifically denied his story of having furnished arms to a black group, and any knowledge of an informer he had implicated in a police raid on another group's headquarters.

But once he was out of the clutches of Brown and the DA, he went straight to Venice. He had told the DA he'd been in hiding these three weeks, afraid of Duggan, McCarthy, and company. Now he told Duggan that the police had kept him locked up, moving him from jail to jail, threatening to make him stand trial on an old grand theft auto charge unless he gave the DA the answers the police wanted him to give. He hadn't meant anything he'd said to the DA. He was still on Duggan's side. He wanted to shaft the pigs for all the dirty tricks they'd played on dissidents, blacks and honkies both.

But by the time the three reporters got to Tackwood, he was telling a different story. No, he hadn't been locked up by the police. He had gone into hiding at a friend's house, afraid both of the police and of the young radicals: He could end up with a broken neck. And only when he'd gotten into a barroom fight and been afraid of retaliation had he emerged to seek out Sgt. Brown for protection. Yes, the stories he had told Duggan, McCarthy, and Katz about police undercover actions were true. He would stick by what was on those tapes.

The reporters were distrustful. Where did the truth leave off with Tackwood and jive begin? They telephoned me. They wanted Tackwood given a polygraph examination. His was a great story, but they weren't about to rush it into print if it was simply a product of his fast-moving imagination.

I spent a week checking Tackwood out with the help of the three reporters. They brought me what they'd dug up in their own research, and they brought me tapes—including several Tackwood had made of conversations by phone with police officers in CCS and SIS about ongoing clandestine operations against black and other militant left groups. I was shaken. Oh, the use of informers is police routine. I'd polygraphed informers: Tricky, devious, double-dealing, they were still indispensable. I was sure Tackwood had been an informer if only because, in spite of an arrest and conviction record, he'd spent almost no time in prison. He was obviously too useful outside.

I also knew that when they can, police will plant someone inside, say, a narcotics ring, to feed them the facts they need to make arrests. I moved in law-enforcement circles, so I was aware of the alarm the militants were causing there. It would follow that they'd use plants inside such outfits to keep tabs on what they were up to. But Tackwood and those telephone tapes of his were saying more, much more. There seemed to be clear evidence that the police were using illegal methods—planting evidence before raids, furnishing weapons and explosives, setting groups against one another with sometimes murderous results. Why hadn't Tackwood and his bosses on the third floor of the Glass House been indicted for conspiracy and half a dozen other felonies?

Tackwood appeared with the three reporters. He was jaunty, dressed in flashy clothes, and had a wide, winning grin for me as he shook my hand. I had to make a conscious effort to remember that this man's warmth, charm, and good looks were the tools of his trade—and a deadly trade it was. I settled the reporters in my outer office and took Tackwood with me into the inner one. I knew the reporters were eager for polygraph test results that would prove Tackwood either a priceless news source or a worthless liar. So was I. But before I could test him, I had to talk to him.

In fact, Tackwood didn't need interrogation. He talked willingly and well, and never seemed to tire. What he told me—and I put it on tape, of course—was substantially what I already knew. Most of it I've already set down in this chapter. The variations in what he'd told Duggan, McCarthy, and Katz were slight. But the question that was bothering me was why he'd done his sudden turnaround. He'd been a big success at covert operations. The men he worked for liked him so much they'd done him every favor in the book. There was no trouble he could get into that they didn't bail him out of. He was making good money. He was a big shot in his strange world. Even turning in his friends didn't seem to bother him—he'd been at it for years.

"I got sick of all that shit they kept handing out."

"The officers?"

"Blacks and Mexicans and every other minority—to them we are nothing but dirt. They are red-necks, man, bigots. Extremists are what they're supposed to be chasing, right—what they're supposed to be putting down? Well, let me tell you who the extremists are. It's them. You get to know them, there's no way you're gonna be surprised at the kind of shit they made people like me pull against radicals. Those mad dogs believe in fighting fire with fire and to hell with the Constitution and all that bullshit. Oh, yeah, they are dedicated, all right. They live, breathe, eat and sleep covert operations. And they are a law unto themselves. How I know that is, I never saw any big brass, ever, stick their face in the door up there. These maniacs are on their own. If the chief ever found out what was going on up there, he'd piss all over himself."

"And that was why you went to McCarthy?"

"I never went to him. He came to me, man. I don't know how he knew. But he hit the right moment. He says I was the one to blow the whistle on all that dirty stuff, and I says, you know, you're right. I could blow that whole fink operation wide open. What did he want me to do? Get him all the names of police informers and undercover people and what they were working on. It was no trouble. I had the run of the files. I could pick up anything I wanted to in that office and no questions asked. I gave McCarthy, Duggan, and the rest whatever they said. Shit, I even got on the phone to my police contacts and got them to make statements that were violations of every human right you can think of."

"McCarthy and Duggan and Katz are satisfied," I said. "But those reporters out there aren't. And neither am I. Oh, sure—some of what you've told is true. You've embroidered it a good deal, but basically it's true. Those talks with the police bear that out. Some of it. But you've mixed in a lot of lies, too, haven't you? And this I can tell you, that won't go down with the polygraph."

He stared at me, scowling, and sat forward in his chair. "You think I'm lying? Man, are you some kind of fool? What for would I make up lies to get myself in trouble? And you know, I am up to my ass in trouble. Cops on one side, blacks I snitched on, on the other, and those radicals on the other. I'm surrounded, man. Would I make up stuff to get myself killed? No way. It's the truth that's about to waste me."

"You'll survive," I said. "If I ever saw a survivor in my life, it's you."

He grinned wanly. "Okay, let's hitch this thing up and get the show on the road."

"In a minute," I said. "First, let's tear the embroidery off this Republican Convention business. If we do, will there be anything there at all? I doubt it. If you want to know what I think, I think you wanted to cap your act for McCarthy, really shake him and his friends up, give them something really big to get excited about. Hell, you'd already told them about everything from dynamitings to murders. You were going to have a book a co-author was going to write with you. You had to have a last chapter, didn't you, better than anything that went before? That book is going to make you rich and famous, right? So you decided what could be bigger than the police blowing up the Republican National Convention and blaming it on black militants and Weathermen and Yippies? Only you got a little carried away, didn't you? You promised the plans for all this, and then you couldn't deliver, right? So how did you handle it? You disappeared. You'd jumped in a hole too deep to jump out of, so you went to the neighborhood bar and got drunk and stayed that way for three weeks. Isn't that what really happened?"

"A cop in San Diego told me—"

"And that's the little grain of truth in the whole blown-up fantasy, isn't it? What some cop in San Diego told you. How sober was he?"

"He was running a game in his head, is all," Tackwood said. "How sweet it would be to get them all off the streets and locked up good, once and for all."

"But there was no Squad Nineteen, right? There was no sergeant, there was no FBI agent?"

"Oh, they're real, all right."

"But if I were to talk to them about you and your heroic part right in the middle of their elaborate plot?"

"Don't bother," Tackwood said softly. He had begun to sweat. He glanced around the plain room. "Look, man, is it safe here? I mean, I haven't got any friends left, you realize that? They could break in here with machine guns and shoot me to pieces."

"Security is my business," I said. "Nobody's going to break in here."

"They could get to my wife," he said. "Nobody looking out for her." He glanced at his watch and stood up. "I better get back to her."

"The test," I reminded him. "Sit down."

"How long is it going to take?" he asked. "We already been in here for hours."

"Not enough hours," I said. "Did you give police guns to anyone with instructions to shoot anyone?"

He shook his head. He was staring worriedly at the office door. "Money, not guns. I mean—they could have used the money to buy guns."

"And the instructions?" I said.

"To take whatever steps they thought were necessary to stop the black organization from spreading."

"That's a little different, isn't it?" I said. "Now, about that famous raid on their headquarters. You said it was set up by an informer who was a police plant inside the organization. Did you know that before the raid?"

"I knew a fellow," he said. "Hell, yes."

"But not that he was an informer," I said.

"A cop told me," he said. "No, I didn't know before. But"—he glanced warily at the polygraph instrument—"I was told I'm not supposed to talk about those things. Not on the lie detector. They could get me on conspiracy charges, man."

"It doesn't matter," I said. "There's plenty for us to talk about." I sat him down again, attached the equipment, switched it on, and ran preliminary tests to check his reactions. They were normal, but he was far more upset than he showed outwardly. I detached the equipment.

"He needs rest," I told the reporters. "Check him into a hotel.

See that he doesn't take any stimulants or depressants—no alcohol, no drugs. Bring him in early tomorrow morning and I'll run the tests.''

"Well, what did your preliminary examination show?'' they demanded. "You took long enough. Can't you tell us anything?''

"Off the record,'' I said, "he's an opportunist who will work for whoever offers the highest price. He's done some of the things he claims. We'll have to wait for the test results to learn how much of what he says is really true.''

The reporters were counting money among themselves. "What hotel?'' they asked.

"The nearest,'' I said. "He's so nervous he's on the edge of hysteria. It would be impossible to get accurate readings on him now. Oh—and get a detective to guard him.''

They did. But that didn't prevent Tackwood from telephoning. Next morning Duggan, McCarthy, and Katz were in my office with their attorney, Dan Lund, before Tackwood and the reporters even arrived. Lund insisted on going over with Tackwood and me the questions I proposed for the test. He ruled out the touchiest and most telling ones. But by rewording I kept in a few that I felt would help the reporters decide whether to insist that their editors print the Tackwood story, or to scrap it. I asked these questions:

"Did you knowingly lie to the district attorney last week—by direction?''

"Yes.''

"Did an LAPD officer of the CCS tell you they had prior knowledge of the George Jackson attempt to break out of San Quentin?''

"Yes.''

"Did you participate in an FBI attempt to locate a black militant training center near Santa Cruz?'' "Yes.'' This was a reference to a raid on a Marin County courtroom, in which three armed militants and a judge were killed.

Two of the reporters had been unable to wait during my lengthy pre-test questioning and Lund's cautious editing of the queries I might and might not present to Tackwood. But Cohen of the *Times* was still in the reception office. I took him aside and told him that

Tackwood's responses were the truth. But I told him and the McCarthy-Lund crowd that there was no way to get satisfactory polygraph results on a long list of questions all in one day. Tackwood would have to come back. We set an early date for the next morning.

But the radicals had gotten nervous. They were worried, first, that the newsmen were getting cold feet about the story, and second, that the police might swarm down on Duggan, McCarthy, Katz, and Lund and arrest them, along with Tackwood, for God knew what charges. They decided to break Tackwood's story to the public quickly. They arranged for broadcast of a news conference from the studios of the local Pacifica FM station, KPFK, that would reach not only the Los Angeles area, but also New York, Washington, Berkeley, and Houston, through Pacifica outlets there.

Of course, they didn't tell me this. If they had, I'd have advised them to back off.

Still, Tackwood had then left my offices in the company of Duggan, McCarthy, and Katz, laughing and seemingly without a care or suspicion to his name. I shook my head. Tackwood was some kind of actor! Why hadn't he gone with Jerry Cohen? And why did he appear once more in company with McCarthy and friends the next morning? It was baffling. But less so than what happened next. As soon as we were alone in the examination room, Tackwood caught the lapels of my jacket. Rolling his eyes at the door, trembling, he hissed at me:

"Man, I don't know what to do. I got to get away from them. I can't move."

"You don't have to whisper," I said. "This is a soundproof room. I'm not an attorney. I can't advise you. I'm only in this case as a polygraph examiner, Louis. Jerry Cohen, Leroy Aarons, and Karl Fleming hired me to find out whether you're telling the truth. I'm not connected with this case any other way. And I am not about to give you any advice."

"Jerry Cohen!" he said, snapping his fingers. "Yeah. He's powerful. Got the whole Los Angeles *Times* behind him. They *own* this town. What about you get in touch with him? See can he fix it for me to get together with the DA."

I blinked. "But you saw the DA. All you did was lie to him."

"That was different. I don't want to see these people. Man, I've got to talk to the DA."

I got in touch with Jerry Cohen and passed on Tackwood's message. Cohen asked to talk to him. I don't know what was said in that conversation, but when he hung up, Tackwood looked relieved.

"Cohen will call you back," he said.

"Good," I said. "Now, I've lined up questions for you that Dan Lund has approved. Let's get started on the next set of polygraph tests."

"Dan Lund!" he snorted. "He's not my attorney."

"He was yesterday," I said mildly.

"Get me a piece of paper," Tackwood said. I got a sheet of my office stationery and a pen. He wrote on it. *I herewith dismiss Dan Lund as my attorney*. He pushed the paper at me. His signature was at the bottom. He said, "Will you witness that?"

"If you're sure," I said. He nodded. I signed. "Now," I said, "will you please sit in that chair? Let me attach these things, and let's get on with the test."

Then the phone rang. It was Jerry Cohen. "I've talked to the district attorney's people," he said. "I'm down at their offices now. They accept Tackwood's offer. They want the whole story. They'll furnish their own polygraph expert."

"The way he keeps flip-flopping," I said, "the DA had better get to him fast."

"They're on their way," he said, and hung up.

I didn't check my watch, but it didn't seem that five minutes had passed before a big fist was hammering on the door of the examining room. I'd had just enough time to settle Tackwood in the chair and hook him up to the polygraph instrument and turn it on. I unlocked and opened the door. Four hulking men stood there. Beyond them, in the waiting room, I saw McCarthy, Duggan, Katz, and Lund. No—it would be more accurate to say I heard them. They were shouting at the DA's men. They were white-faced, bewildered, scared, indignant, all at the same time. Lund tugged at the shoulders of one of the men.

"What do you mean!" he yelled. "You can't take Louis Tackwood. Where's your warrant?"

The investigator shrugged him off and all four of them crowded into my office. They slammed the door in Lund's face and held it shut. He beat on it from the outside, while one of the investigators identified himself to me as being from the district attorney's office. He had orders to escort Louis Tackwood downtown. Tackwood was staring at the men wide-eyed from the examination chair. I began detaching the respiration tube, the blood-pressure cuff, the electrodes.

"Are you sure you want to go with these men?" I asked.

He jerked a nod. "That's what I want." He stood up.

Lund kept beating on the door.

"What about this?" I handed Tackwood the paper.

He pushed it into a pocket. "I'll give it to Cohen."

"Let's go, Tackwood," one of the DA's men said. The door came open. Lund lurched in. "What the hell's going on here? Who are these men?" The small room was crowded. McCarthy and Duggan jammed the doorway. "You can't take him away." Marilyn Katz's voice was shrill in the outer office. "This is a kidnapping!" The DA's men paid them as much attention as if they'd been a swarm of gnats. With Tackwood between them, they barged toward the exit. I caught the last of them by the arm.

"Listen," I said, "don't rough him up. He's sensitive and smart and chancy. Don't give him any reason to resent you. Treat him right, and you've got a case worth having. Knock him around, and you'll blow the whole thing."

The man only grunted. He followed the others out. The New Left group clattered after them, still shouting. I don't know, for myself, what happened downtown. But in their book, *The Glass House Tapes,* McCarthy, Duggan, Katz, and their friends say that Tackwood signed "every statement" the DA's office "put in front of him." These included accusations that Duggan and Katz had held Tackwood against his will, and far more seriously, had "conspired to receive stolen documents from confidential files." The DA summoned Duggan and Katz.

But the DA's people let Tackwood go on his promise to return the next day and take a polygraph test. When Duggan and Katz returned to the Venice apartment after their session with the DA, they found Tackwood waiting for them, all smiles. "Man, I'm sorry

I signed all that shit, but what could I do? Listen, it doesn't matter. You know what's going to happen now?"

"We go to jail?" Katz asked bitterly.

"No man. The DA has called a press conference to break the story about you bad-ass radicals tossing the nice police-mans that been so busy protecting and serving, you know? Only he called his press conference for the same time as yours—right?—the one you got set up for me at KPFK?"

Katz and Duggan nodded numbly.

"And I ain't going to be with the DA, now, am I? I am going to be with you. At KPFK. To tell it all, just the way it happened. All about the CCS and the SIS and the FBI fucking over the black people of America. Right? You better believe it."

They didn't. They knew better than to trust Louis Tackwood anymore. But he surprised them. He could always be counted on to do that, all right. He did show up for the KPFK press conference. It was heard all over the United States. Television carried the story. So did newspapers, here and abroad. Tackwood had what he craved—the limelight. He stood in the middle of it, grinning, for a whole week. The DA hastily dropped the charges against Duggan and Katz. Nothing whatever was done about the covert operations units at the LAPD.

And nothing more was ever heard of Louis Tackwood.

7
A Touch of Arson

J oe Keller winced in the hard light that glared off the blue water of the marina. It was painful. He yanked shut the curtains. Shivering, he flapped into a bathrobe. He hated living here. No matter how bright the sun got, it was cold. A damp wind always blew off the ocean. And the place had cost an arm and a leg. But Helen, Susie, and Matt had nagged him till he'd sold the old house in West L.A. and moved down here to Bahia Island, where the rich people lived. He wished to God he'd remained a truck driver. They'd never been poor. He was good, could have his pick of jobs at top rates. But they could live like people, not like those shiny, imaginary beings in TV commercials. He should never have gone into business for himself. Plastics! He wished he'd never heard of them.

Grimly he left the bedroom and stumped down the hall. Smells reached him of breakfast: coffee, bacon, toast. His gnarled little hand gripped the bathroom doorknob. It wouldn't turn. Through the door, he heard the splash of a shower. Susie—late for her first lecture, as usual. How blessed could a father be in his children? Bitterly, he made for the other bathroom. But that door was locked too. Who by? He scowled to himself. Couldn't be Helen—she was cooking breakfast. He rattled the doorknob.

"One second," came a deep male voice.

"What the hell are you doing home?" Joe Keller called.

"I got here late last night." The knob turned, the door opened. "Didn't want to wake you up." The youth who appeared startled Joe Keller. He himself was jockey-size, spindly, with leathery skin and hard black little eyes. His son Matt was big and beefy. His hair hung to his shoulders, he wore a scraggly mustache, and the thick lenses of his wire-rim glasses blurred and softened his watery eyes. Joe couldn't get over having produced this monster. It might not have been quite so disappointing if the kid, with his size, had any aptitude for sports. To look at him, he should have been an NFL center, a home-run slugger, the white hope of the heavyweight boxers. He was none of these things. He was even clumsier than he looked, slow-footed, nearsighted, accident-prone, always hurting himself. No, all that interested Matt was arguing. That was why Joe had decided the only job for him in life was as a lawyer. Awkwardly, Matt edged past him, barefoot in a terry-cloth robe. He was trying to dry that long hair of his. The towel hung over his face. His father called after him as he lumbered toward his room:

"Is there something wrong with my calendar? I thought your term still had a month to run."

Matt said something through the thickness of towel but Joe couldn't hear it. He had to use the bathroom. He could wait to talk to Matt. As he gave a twist to the bathroom lock, he told himself grimly that, as far as that was concerned, he could wait forever. Twenty minutes later, showered, shaved, dressed, he found Helen and Susie in the window glare of the eating area off the kitchen. Susie was just leaving the table. She was speaking to her mother, who, coffee cup halfway to her mouth, was staring gray-faced, bulging-eyed, at the television set. It was all she ever paid any attention to anymore. She'd romanced about the boats and the gulls and the whitecaps before they moved here. Now she never gave them a second glance.

"Good-bye, Daddy." Susie, bare midriff, jeans so tight only the color said they weren't her skin, pecked him with a kiss on the bare skull he'd carefully combed strands of hair across. In big dark glasses and some kind of crazy exaggeration of a boy's cap, she flounced out of the kitchen. He called after her:

"See if you can open a book today, for a change."

Not that he'd opened a book in his life. But he'd had no father to spend thousands on his education.

"Good morning," he snarled at Helen.

She twitched and very slowly turned her head and looked at him. Her mouth, cigarette dangling from the corner, smiled mechanically. "Good morning, dear. Oh, listen." To his stunned surprise, she rose and turned off the television set. As she bent above him to fill his coffee cup, he noticed that her housecoat had egg dribbled down it. He winced. The damned thing had come from some Beverly Hills boutique where they charged ten prices. Why couldn't she look after it? She wanted to live among the rich. Why couldn't she show a little class? She smelled, too, and not just of bacon, but of sweat. She said, "Matt's home. Now, don't lose your temper with him, Joe. It's all a misunderstanding. It can be cleared up. He can go back."

"What?" Joe Keller watched her set the glass coffee urn on the warmer. "What's a misunderstanding?"

"At the college. That professor had it in for Matt right from the start. And now—"

A pain shot down Joe Keller's left arm. He almost dropped the coffee cup. It rattled and sloshed in the saucer as he set it down. He clutched the arm. He felt very hot. He tugged at his freshly-knotted necktie. He was a dapper man. He liked knife-sharp creases in his suits, crisp collars, natty ties. That was another thing that disgusted him about Matt—those unironed workshirts he wore, those bleached-out Levi's with torn pockets. He didn't seem able to get his breath. He shut his eyes and panted.

"Joe, what's the matter?" Helen's voice came dimly to him.

"Nothing . . . All right in a second," he whispered. "it will pass. It always does." And after another few seconds, it did. It left him damp with sweat and shaky, but the pain was totally gone, as if it had never struck at all. He drank some more coffee. Helen set eggs and bacon in front of him on an expensive ironware pottery plate, hand-decorated in a design he hated. He began to eat. He never got fat but he always had a good appetite. He bent low over his plate and shoveled in the food.

"Your father's not feeling well," Helen said.

Matt plunked his bulk down heavily on one of the dainty-looking white wrought-iron chairs at the glass-top table. Joe darted a glance at him—the way you look quickly at some awful accident and turn as quickly away. The kid wore a greasy leather-fringed vest. An ecology flag had been decaled to it and was flaking off. The hair on his fat chest was pale, like unhealthy grass. His father said:

"They've kicked you out of Pacific too, right?"

"Old Hickman had it in for me. He never liked my master's thesis idea from the start."

"Then you should have changed it," Joe Keller said.

"I'm not there to please him," Matt said, a big hand pawing a piece of toast off his father's plate. "I'm there to get an education. I was researching—"

"I know, I know," Joe Keller cut him off. "The legal rights of teenage unwed black welfare mothers in Watts. I know, I know."

"You know but you don't give a damn," Matt said with his mouth full of toast and imported English marmalade.

"It's not going to help you run Keller Plastics."

"Who needs Keller Plastics?" Matt sprayed crumbs.

"It's paying your way through law school."

"I'll pay it back when I get out and get working."

"You're going to work for the poor," his father said. "Remember? You're going to *be* poor, remember?"

"What's being rich got you?" his son asked.

Joe Keller stood up. "Let's settle this now," he said. His arm started to ache but not with those shooting pains. This was a dull ache—like the pain Matt gave him. "You don't want anything to do with Keller Plastics, right?"

68

Matt rose to pour himself coffee while his mother dished out his breakfast from fancy red enamel skillets. "You got it."

"Starting now?" his father said. "Yeah, let's have it that way, shall we? Starting as of this moment, you have got nothing to do with Keller Plastics. And that means no more checks, buddy. You got it?"

"I'll pay it back." Matt looked pale. "I have to get my degree. I have to pass the bar."

"But not so you can take over the plant," his father said.

Stubbornly, eyes swimming loose and foolish behind the thick lenses, the boy shook his head. "Never. I've always told you that."

"I thought you'd outgrow it."

"Get stupider as I got older, you mean?" Matt said.

"Is that what you think I am?" Joe said. "Stupid? To have built that business from nothing? To have bought you all this? Are you forgetting the spider bikes, the surf boards, the motorcycles, the cars—whatever you and Susie asked for? Christmas every day?"

"You did your best." Matt shrugged big, lardy shoulders and sat down to a heaped plate. "You meant okay, I guess. But your values are all screwed up. Nobody respects that materialistic crap now. My values—"

"Oh, shut up!" Joe Keller swung on his heel and made for the door to the carport. "Take your values off to Hippie Land, will you? Where they belong." He yanked open the door. He shouted over his shoulder, "I don't want to smell them around here when I get home. Understand me? I'm through with you." He went out and slammed the door.

Getting out of his car in the plant parking lot, he ran a suspicious eye over the rows of employee cars. He knew every one. Lately there'd been cars from neighboring businesses occupying some of the slots. He'd raised hell with a dozen firms. Now the slots reserved for the second shift stood primly empty. He'd rearranged their punch-in time so their arrival wouldn't coincide with the day shift's departure. It had been costly and a headache. The damned police had forced him to do it. Keller employees were jamming nearby freeway ramps and causing traffic tie-ups at five o'clock. That was the price of success. The police made you out a criminal.

He pushed through the glass doors into the reception area and jerked to a halt. He had hired a black woman as receptionist. The government made you hire blacks whether you wanted to or not. Now there this one sat above the blinking lights of the slope-fronted console telephone on her broad, glossy desk—wearing a platinum blond wig. He walked up to her. She looked up, smiling with large, handsome white teeth.

"Good morning, Mr. Keller."

"Take that goddamn thing off," he said. "This isn't a Las Vegas nightclub. It's a business, remember? If I'd wanted a clown for this job, I'd have wired Ringling Brothers."

He seethed, riding up in the elevator. But his troubles weren't over. They were only beginning. When he pushed through the paneled double doors marked with his name above the word PRESIDENT, a tall man rose from one of the deep, crushed-velour chairs in the outer office. He had close-cropped white hair and steely blue eyes. He smiled and held out a hand. With a baleful glance at his secretary (why couldn't she have lied, said Keller was in Rio or Anchorage?), the plastics manufacturer took the hand and shook it. But not with enthusiasm. This was Bob Anthony, chief fire inspector. His last report had listed twenty nit-picking violations in the Keller plant. Estimates by contractors of the work needed to bring the old buildings up to standard had outraged Joe Keller. He'd shoved them away under *File and Forget*. Now the day of reckoning was here. Where had the year gone? Gloomily he waved Anthony toward his office and asked the girl to bring them coffee.

"You haven't put in those roll-down fire doors in the three hallways in Building B," Anthony said. "You've still got those fiberboard partitions around those tanks. Acetate. That stuff is highly flammable. I asked for cement block there, cinder block, brick, poured cement. You haven't made a single correction."

"Have you seen Europe?" Joe Keller asked.

Anthony smiled and shook his head. "The city doesn't pay salaries that allow for that kind of vacation. I have three kids in college. Maybe after they're on their own."

"My wife and I," Keller said, "planned to go this summer but she's going to have to have some surgery that will keep her down for months. I've got the tickets and travel arrangements all laid out. I wonder—wouldn't you and your wife like to do the tour? Every-place from Turkey to Leningrad—Paris, Amsterdam, Rome, London? I mean, the reservations are no good to us now. You might as well have the fun out of it.''

Anthony's smile had vanished. He unrolled a set of plans on Joe Keller's desk. He began pointing. "I've marked the places where the changes have to be made," he said in a cold voice. "I wouldn't delay, if I were you. A fire in this place could kill every employee you've got. With all those volatile chemicals you're storing, no one would stand a chance of getting out alive.''

"I offered you an all-expenses-paid trip," Joe Keller said. "Didn't you hear me?''

"I'm doing my best to believe I didn't," Anthony said. "And I'd suggest you never mention it again. Now, look here. This staircase has wooden doors top and bottom. Those will have to be replaced with metal. Double fire walls here, here and here . . . ''

At noon, Joe Keller winced again in the sun glare off the blue water. The restaurant was expensive, hung with fishnets, heaped with tarry kegs. He was eating an avocado stuffed with shrimp and grousing to himself about its tastelessness. He'd had a couple of Wild Turkeys on the rocks—better than 100 proof. But instead of picking him up, the whiskey had made him headachy, logy. Philips, the man across from him in the St. Laurent suit, looked cheerful. But then, he was young. He had the world by the tail. No place for him to go but up. He'd jumped from one international conglomerate, to a second, to a third, always to jobs better than he'd left. He spent his life jetting from the Middle East to Japan to Switzerland. If you wanted to talk about work, as Joe Keller understood work, he had never done a day's work in his life. Lucky bastard.

"So, what's on your mind?" he asked Joe Keller now. "This is pleasant, isn't it? Nice the way they're tarting up these water-fronts.''

"I want to take up your offer," Joe Keller said bluntly. Bluntly was the only way Joe Keller knew to say anything. "I'm ready to sell out.''

Philips looked startled, and breathed a little apologetic laugh. "Now? But that was eighteen months ago when I came to you.''

"I said I'd think about it," Keller said. "Didn't I?''

"Yes, you did. That's right, Joe." Philips lit a long, slim, brown cigarette. There was ice-melt in the bottom of his martini glass. He sipped it, put the glass down, turned it by its stem. "But a lot of water has gone over the dam since then. I'm afraid you thought too long."

"Nothing's happened to plastics," Joe Keller protested. "Business is up almost twenty percent over last year."

"I'm ready to believe that." Philips pushed at the short-rib bones on his plate. "Our forecasts showed that was what would happen. That's why we wanted your plant."

"So—now you can have it," Keller said. "And to make the deal sweeter, you can have it for your original offer, even though it's worth more now."

Philips shook his head sadly. "Joe, I'm sorry to say this, but my people couldn't wait. We wanted in to plastics, we couldn't get you to move, we went elsewhere."

"So you bought one plant," Keller said. "To an outfit like yours, what's one more plant in one more country?"

Philips breathed his little laugh again. "It's what we wanted. Diversification means just that, Joe. Light aircraft is what we're after right now."

"You mean you don't want Keller Plastics anymore?"

"I'm afraid that kind of sums it up." The young man reached across the table and squeezed Joe's hand. It was a faggoty kind of gesture. He knew it wasn't supposed to be, anymore. Men were hugging each other, patting each other on the butt, even kissing, these days. Even in sports. It made him sick. He withdrew his hand quickly. "I'm sorry, Joe," Philips was saying. "I wish you'd been in touch. We decided you weren't interested. Look"—he picked up the tab from beside Joe's elbow—"this lunch is on me, right? God knows, it's little enough. Hey, I'm really sorry to disappoint you. What a misunderstanding. Wow." He reached to squeeze Joe Keller's hand again but Keller put the hand away. "Well, look, it's not the end of the world. I see a lot of people in a lot of places. If you want me to, I'll let them know you're looking for a buyer."

"Sure," Joe Keller said bleakly, "thanks."

On the beach in the dark, Joe Keller hunched his scrawny shoulders inside a fleece-lined car coat. He tugged at the woolen Irish hat the wind kept trying to blow off. That same wind, bringing fine salt spray out of the night surf where it broke on the rocks, was cold, cut at the thin cloth of his trousers, made him shiver. He pushed his hands deeper into his pockets and walked on. Another man, heavy, with a thick midriff, walked beside him on the dark sand. This man had a phlegmy wheeze of a voice. It said:

"Hell, it'll be the easiest assignment they ever got."

"I'm not interested," Joe Keller said, "in whether it's easy or hard. I'll pay. I want the job done right. I don't want anybody to be able even to suspect"—he turned and caught the thick man's sleeve and jerked on it fiercely—"even to suspect the fire was started on purpose."

"I've told you," said the man with the phlegmy voice, "these guys are the best in the business. They don't make mistakes. And with all those chemicals in that plant of yours, they could leave footprints like elephants. There won't be anything that isn't burned to a crisp."

"You're sure, now?" Joe Keller asked.

"They burned down three plants of mine, didn't they?" the wheezy man asked. "And I didn't even have a can of cigarette lighter fluid in the place. Just dresses, cloth. The insurance didn't bat an eye. They paid off like they were sorry for me. Oh, they're good, these guys."

"They better be." Joe Keller tramped onward. He stopped. "What do they want?" He moved on again.

"Cash. Half up front," the wheezy man lumbered after Keller. "Half when the job is done."

Joe Keller stopped again. He unbuttoned the car coat and from an inner pocket pulled a wad of something and pushed it into the hand of the bulky man. "That's the first half. Now, I'm leaving town tomorrow. They burn it tomorrow night, after the last shift leaves at midnight. I don't want anybody hurt."

"What about you?" said the wheezy man. "You sure you want to do this? I mean, you're doing great. Profits up every year. It took a long time to build this business. Nobody's on your tail for debt like with me."

"They're on my tail for everything else," Joe Keller said

grimly. "Hell, it doesn't mean anything to me anymore, Manny. Just a pain in the ass. I hate it. I hate my whole goddamn life. My workers hate me. My wife hates me. My kids hate me. What's the good of working anymore? Taxes. Regulations. Unions. Police. Fire. Insurance doubling every year? Well, I'm going to get that back, at least. Honest, Manny, it will be a load off my mind. I can relax. No more hassles. No more bullshit."

"What about the kids?" Manny said.

Joe Keller only snorted. "Come on," he said, "let's get off this beach before we both get pneumonia. I want to live to enjoy that insurance money." He started for the dull glow of town lights inland over the palisades. "And I'll meet you here, same time, Monday night, with the rest of the payoff, right?"

Breath coming noisily, Manny followed him. "Right."

The Keller Plastics fire was spectacular. Fed by huge stores of chemicals, the flames leaped and crackled hundreds of feet into the black sky of early morning. Their red glow made square miles of factories and warehouses look like a vision of the world's end. When dawn came, Keller Plastics was a trio of burned-out brick shells. Wisps of smoke rose from the heaps of charred rubble, the scorched and twisted cadavers of machinery. Fire fighters, grimy-faced, plodded wearily in their rubber boots across drenched paving that mirrored their yellow slickers, the shiny red of the fire engines. As the last lengths of hose were wound up and the big machines rumbled away, four men climbed out of automobiles, crossed the wet paving, and began probing the rubble. One of them was Bob Anthony. Two others were fire department arson experts. The last was an insurance company claims investigator.

It wasn't any of these who called me, but they were the reason I was called. I'd just reached home and was having a drink before dinner while watching the six o'clock news. Keller Plastics was flaming up anew in the phosphorescent colors of the little screen, when the phone rang. The voice at the other end was that of an attorney I knew, Les Bernstein. I'd administered countless polygraph tests at his request over the years. I knew him to be sensitive and ethical, that rare kind of lawyer who genuinely cares not only about his clients, but about right and wrong. He talked to me about

Joe Keller. The plastics manufacturer was being given a bad time by his insurance company over the fire. Police and fire inspectors were backing them up. They were accusing Keller of having burned down his own factory.

"Now, Joe Keller is not the kind of guy that makes it easy for you to like him," Les Bernstein said. "He's got a very short fuse. He's tough. He's worked hard. He came up from nothing. He's a perfectionist. The people who work for him hate his guts and he hates theirs. But you can't destroy a man just because he's got a lousy personality. And that's what they're trying to do."

"Les," I said, "I hate to disillusion you, but it's nothing unusual these days for people to burn down their businesses to collect insurance."

"Not Joe Keller," Bernstein said. "He was winning. He had so many contracts, he was turning them down. He'd worked twenty-five years to get where he was. Beautiful townhouse at Bahia Island, ten-thousand-dollar cars for him and his wife, new cars for the kids—one in college, the other in law school. And it was only going to get better. So why would he set fire to it?"

"The Arson Squad is sure it wasn't spontaneous?"

"That's what they say. The inspectors had found all kinds of fire safety violations. Bob Anthony was in only a couple of days ago. Joe says he was demanding work that would have cost a hundred thousand dollars. Anthony said the place could go up in flames any time. But now he's changed his tune. Arson, he says."

"If his employees hated him," I suggested, "why couldn't it have been one of them?"

"It could," Bernstein said. "But you know unions. They're not going to let their members be polygraphed."

"So that leaves Keller himself?" I said.

"You're going to love it," Bernstein said. "Like shaking hands with a rattlesnake. But they're after him, Chris, they're determined to get him. A polygraph test will help me fight them off."

"If he passes it," I said.

"If I didn't think he'd pass it," Bernstein said, "would I have called you? He didn't set that fire. Hell, he wasn't even in town. He didn't know anything about it until today."

"Get me the insurance reports on the fire," I said. "And I'll want to talk with the arson inspectors and the other fire people. Maybe they missed telling you something important."

"Don't go yourself," Bernstein said. "Send investigators. I don't want the prosecution to know what my strategy is going to be. I don't want them to know a polygraph examiner is in on this— okay?"

"They won't," I promised. But I thought as I hung up that Bernstein wasn't as sure of Keller as he said. If he'd thought Keller was going to pass the test, then he'd already be planning to allow Keller to be polygraphed by the district attorney, with an agreement that his client be freed of charges if the DA's test results agreed with mine. Law-enforcement agencies often take this way out if their evidence is weak or circumstantial. If it's not all that bad they may still, on the strength of polygraph evidence, let the suspect plead guilty to a lesser charge. Innocent suspects sometimes refuse this way out—though it saves time and money. And for their righteous stubbornness, a lot of them end up in jail. I didn't know where Keller was going to fit into this scheme of things. But after I'd read my investigators' reports on him, I concluded that Les Bernstein should have been less optimistic about his client's chances than he'd seemed on the phone. Keller ran his shop and his life ruthlessly. He drove himself fifteen hours a day. He drove hard bargains with everybody he dealt with. And he cut corners, maybe because he was impatient, maybe because he was crooked.

"I'm not here because I want to be," he said to me when he entered my office. "Bernstein's idea. I don't like it. He says I have to prove I didn't set that fire. I don't have to prove anything."

"Arson's a serious charge," I said. "You're lucky no one was killed or injured. Les is only trying to protect you. He's not just your attorney. He's your friend."

"Yeah, for thirty years. While the going was smooth." Joe Keller grimaced. "Now, when it gets a little rough, right away he doesn't trust me." He stood up abruptly. "Hell, I don't need this. I'll get another lawyer."

"He'll want you polygraphed too," I said, "if he's any good. It's your only defense. The arson people found unmistakable evidence that the fire was set. You're in a position where you have to show them that, whoever set it, it wasn't you."

"I wasn't even in L.A.," he said. "I was in Tahoe. Ask the airline."

"I already did," I said. "That checks out. But it doesn't say you didn't pay to have the fire set. There are professionals who do that for a fee, you know."

"What kind of creep do you take me for?" Keller said. "I don't hang around with criminals."

"If you didn't have anything to do with that fire," I said, "that fact will show up on the polygraph chart." I explained to him how this could work in his favor with the district attorney, how it could get him off completely, or at least give him the chance to plea-bargain.

"Lesser charge!" he exploded. "I'll be damned if I will. What are you, Gugas—in collusion with the cops, the fire department? Who's paying you?"

"You are," I said. "Only you. I'm not in collusion with anybody. I'm completely neutral. That's my job. Les Bernstein thinks you're innocent. A polygraph chart that shows that will be his weapon for getting the police and fire insurance people off your back. Now, why don't you just calm down? I'll switch on the tape recorder so we can have an accurate record. I'll ask you a few preliminary questions about the fire and your knowledge of it, we'll settle between us which of the questions will be best for the test, then I'll seat you in that chair, hitch up the instrument, and the whole process will be over in a few short minutes."

"It looks like the chair they strap you into in the gas chamber," he said. "I don't like it. I don't like the whole setup. Why should I go through it? What have I done? Paid my taxes, right? You want to see my tax bill? No, you don't. You'd pass out. I pay for the courts. I'll take my chances with them." He left the examining room.

"Hold it," I said. "Come on. It's nothing like the gas chamber. That's childish. You didn't set that fire? Fine. All I want to do is prove it. There's nothing to get emotional about. Why are you so excited?"

"Who's excited?" He turned back, hand on the knob of my

outer office door. "Hell, I get accused of burning down a couple million dollars' worth of plant and equipment every day, don't I? What have I got to be upset about? What a question! I'm getting out of here."

"Don't leave," I said. "I'm going to have to tell Bernstein. He didn't doubt you. When he learns how you've acted here this morning, what's he going to think?"

"Let him think what he goddamn well pleases." And Joe Keller left, slamming the door. I went into an inner office and telephoned Les Bernstein. My advice was simple and straightforward: Tell Keller to cooperate with me. I wouldn't work with him if he fought back. The process was too delicate for that. Too much time could be wasted, and the results wouldn't be any help to him or anyone else.

"Do you think he's guilty?" Bernstein asked.

"You know better than to ask me that," I said. "I don't draw conclusions. I let the polygraph do that."

For a moment, when Joe Keller showed up the next day, I believed that my cautions to Bernstein had gotten to him and convinced him it was for his own good that he take the examination. But the impression didn't last. He was acting too much out of character. Either he'd taken pills to slow him down, or he was hiding something. He seemed smug, self-satisfied, as if he'd put something over on me. He even twitched a little wry smile at the polygraph instrument as he sat down in the examining room.

"What's happened?" I asked. "Charges withdrawn?"

He shook his head. "No. But they will be."

"Why?" I said. "Bernstein didn't call me."

"He doesn't know yet," Keller said. "I passed a lie-detector test."

"What!" I stood up. I felt my hands make fists. "You took a lie-detector test where? Who gave it to you?"

"Some kid doing police studies at college. He came a lot cheaper than you do."

I wanted to throw Keller out. Instead, I pushed the telephone toward him. "That's all right with me," I said, "but you'll need Bernstein's approval. And I doubt it's going to be all right with him.

The reputation of the man behind the polygraph is what counts in these cases."

"It's my money," Keller said, "I'll spend it the way I want to. I don't owe him for this. I paid for it myself."

"What's this kid's name?" I asked.

The youngster was doing polygraph testing to earn a few bucks. The fact was, he didn't even use a polygraph instrument—only a device to record skin resistance changes. No blood pressure, pulse, or respiration rates had been recorded. Worse, he'd asked Keller fifteen questions. The normal number is four—sometimes five. Fifteen questions would make nonsense of the examination. No wonder Keller felt so sure of himself. I felt surer than ever that if his neck was to be saved, he needed a legitimate test.

I ignored the college kid's existence. I ignored my own feelings. With Keller's grunted permission I switched on the tape recorder and got to work. Keller kept balking. Why was I asking all these questions before he was even attached to the instrument? The other examiner hadn't wasted all this time. I was just trying to gouge him for a higher fee. At the same time, he kept shifting away from the fire. He seemed to want to talk about everything else. I heard about his slovenly wife, the luxurious townhouse he hated, his flunk-out son, his discotheque daughter, the way the police and fire departments hounded him, the insane demands of the unions. I kept steering him back to the fire. This process wasn't going to work, for me or for him, unless he understood that I was in charge. At last I had enough answers to enable me to go ahead with the test. Now I had to get him to respect the polygraph.

I gave him a test meant to show whether or not the subject is going to be satisfactory, but I also meant for it to show Keller I could catch him in a lie. I held out a handful of coins and asked him to choose one and seal it in an envelope. He did this while I looked away. Next, I told him to answer all questions I asked him with a no. He did as I said. I smiled grimly to myself as I saw what the pens were scribbling on the chart. He'd tried to make nonsense of the test by choosing three coins. I told him so, flat out. I also named the coins. He paled.

"Jesus," he said. "You know what you're doing."

"It's nice to hear you say so," I said dryly. "Now, what do you say we get on with this?"

He agreed. But only with his mouth. His first chart was a disaster. He did everything he could to foul up the process. He took deep breaths, he coughed, he kept shifting in the chair; worst of all, he wouldn't confine himself to yes and no answers. He talked. I stopped him. I told him I knew what he was doing, that he must be doing it because he was afraid of the polygraph, and that his fear made him look guilty.

"You keep claiming you're innocent. Les Bernstein believes it. Well, now's your chance to prove it. Take the test, and take it the way I tell you to."

He settled down. His attitude puzzled me, because the responses of that tough, shrunken body of his to my questions about his involvement in the fire showed plainly that he was guilty. I couldn't figure him out. What had all his snapping and snarling been about? Hadn't it been his version of righteous indignation? I shuffled the questions and ran the test again. The results left no doubt. Joe Keller was lying. I took the tube from around his narrow chest, the cuff from his arm, the electrodes from his hands.

He stared. "That's all?"

"Sit over there where you'll be more comfortable," I said. When he'd done so, watching me warily, I told him, "You paid someone to set that fire."

"And they did a piss-poor job," he said bitterly. "It's as easy as that, is it?"

"Who do you want to tell about it, me or Les?"

"I can't tell Les," he said gloomily. "He believed me when I said I didn't have anything to do with it."

"I'll have to tell him," I said.

"Go ahead. I'll still deny it." He barked a laugh that didn't have any joy in it. "I thought by going to that college kid, I wouldn't have to face you. I had you checked out. They all say you're so good it's scary. So you're busy. I figured if I told you this kid had already run me through and I'd come out clean, you wouldn't want to waste your time, and Les would be satisfied."

I shook my head. "The DA wouldn't have bought it."

"Maybe not. Ah, the hell with it." Keller gave me a wry, tired smile. "I don't mind going to jail. Let the government pick up my check for a while. I've footed the bill for them long enough."

"You think you're joking," I said, "but you won't like prison. Nobody does, not even the ones that go back again and again. Take my advice, tell Les everything that happened. He may find a detail that will make things go easier for you."

Keller snorted. "You mean five years instead of ten?"

"It could make a difference," I said.

"I'm not admitting a thing," Keller said. "I'll tell you if you want, but I won't tell him." He told me, much the same things he'd told Manny on the midnight beach. It had taken him a long while to find a conglomerate interested in buying Keller Plastics. Then he'd waited too long. The conglomerate had lost interest. He'd have to hunt years for another buyer. His son didn't want the business. Taxes, regulations, insurance rates, union demands, harassment by building, fire, and police inspectors—it was nothing but aggravation. He was fed up. He wanted out. Now.

"I phoned Manny Manfredi. Garment business. He'd told me how he'd been running this arson game for years. I remembered. I asked him to meet me on the beach. He was still in touch with the guys who'd burned him out. They'd want ten thousand for the job and they were experts." Keller gave a sour, silent laugh. "Some experts. Anyway, I gave Manny five grand to hand over to them for openers. I said do the job Saturday night when the last shift goes off at twelve. I'd be out of town. I'd pay the rest off after it was over." He'd been eyeing the polygraph. Now he asked me, "Can I see my charts? What do they look like?"

I laid them out for him on the desk. I started explaining the sets of irregular lines running side by side on the long graph paper. I was using the blunt end of a ball-point pen to show him where the reactions of the styluses jibed with his responses to each numbered question, when suddenly the pen wasn't pointing at anything. Keller had snatched up the charts and was shredding them. I shouted. He backed off, ripping the paper straight across. Before I could get from behind the desk, the charts were scraps, lying on the floor at

Keller's feet. I was speechless. I stared at them. I stared at him. He took out his wallet and tossed a pair of hundred-dollar bills on the desk.

"They were mine," he said. "I'm paying for them. It's up to me what I do with them."

"That was stupid," I said. "They couldn't be used against you. But your confession to me is going to stand with Les Bernstein."

Those hard black eyes looked straight into mine. A smile twitched Keller's mouth. "Forget it," he said. "He won't believe you. You're a fake and I'll tell him so."

"Tell him what you want to," I said. "I'll tell him what I have to. I don't have any choice."

I was glad I didn't have any more appointments that day. Keller had shaken me up. I downed a martini at a bistro near my office, then rang Bernstein.

"Are you positive?" he asked. "Maybe you misinterpreted the charts."

"You don't really think so," I said.

Bernstein groaned. "No, I'm sorry. But—but this is a shock, Chris. I know he's a hard man to like, but I can't believe he'd get involved in anything like this. I'll—I'll talk to him and get back to you."

I went back through the velvet dark, the soft music, the laughter, to the leather stool at the bar, and ordered a second martini. Bernstein was like a lot of decent men—he couldn't believe that others didn't have his high standards. To him, Joe Keller was that salt-of-the-earth American archetype, the self-made man. He might be tough, he might run roughshod over anybody that got in his way, but he was honest, blunt, with the courage of his convictions. It was all right as a stereotype, I thought glumly, turning the olive in my drink, but I'd had a long career examining people close up, every pore, every blemish. I hoped it hadn't made me cynical, but I knew it had made me skeptical. And nobody was a stereotype. People were complex and contradictory. There wasn't one of them that couldn't surprise you—and as often as not, the surprises were unpleasant. I was sorry, but Les Bernstein was about to get one of those.

"I don't know what your point was," he said on the phone the next day, "but it wasn't smart to lie to me, Chris. Keller never confessed to you."

"You're forgetting," I said calmly. "You gave me permission to tape-record him. He's forgetting—he gave the same permission."

"And"—I heard Bernstein gulp—"and you've got his confession on tape?"

"When do you want to hear it?" I asked.

It took almost two hours that afternoon. I didn't like to watch Les Bernstein's gentle face. The color ran out of it. He was white to the lips. He stared at the turning reels. He stared at me. Shock was in his brown eyes. You're a fake, the tape said, and I'll tell him so. Then all that came from the loudspeaker was hiss. I switched off the machine. Bernstein sat there staring. I stepped to the door and asked my secretary for coffee. I had to shake the lawyer's shoulder to rouse him. He stared at me blankly. He saw the coffee. He accepted the cup numbly.

"Take a drink of that," I said.

"No." He got out of the chair, leaving the cup on the desk. "Oh, Chris. Oh, my God. I am getting out of this. That lying son-of-a-bitch. What he tried to do to me! Give me that phone. I'm telling him right now. No more! Not one blessed minute more!"

"Easy," I said. "That's not professional, Les, and you know it. Sit down. Think for a minute. You're not the first lawyer a client ever lied to. It happens every day. It's happened to you, yourself. You know that."

"But I believed the bastard!" he choked. "And I swallowed what he told me about you. I've known you for years. I know you wouldn't lie." He held his hands out to me. There were tears in his eyes. "Forgive me? I'll never doubt you again. I swear it. I'm sorry, Chris. Really sorry." He left quietly a few minutes later. I felt sorry for him. He'd aged that afternoon. I hoped he hadn't turned bitter. But he had—at least toward Joe Keller. He ignored my advice and withdrew from the case, handing it over to another firm.

In the end, as it turned out, that didn't matter. Before the date set for his trial, Joe Keller woke in the night with chest pains. Susie hadn't yet come home, but Helen, clumsy, weepy, stumbling and falling, managed to get him into her car. She drove him to Bahia

83

Island Hospital. After they moved him out of intensive care, the room where he lay breathing oxygen through plastic tubes was expensive. That meant its windows faced the bay. And the hard light, glaring off the blue water, was in his eyes as he died.

The Thieving Witness

Twenty-five billion dollars would be a hefty robbery haul. It's a figure too large for most of us even to imagine. But that's the loss figure shown by American business and industry every single year from employee theft. Who makes up the loss? It is passed on to you and me in the form of higher retail prices. The story I'm about to tell is a strange one, yet it repeats itself daily in hundreds, even thousands, of factories and warehouses all across this country. I'm not referring to the odd box of paper clips or rubber bands every office worker walks out with now and then—though these account for their share of that $25 billion figure too. No—I'm concerned with items meant to sell, costly in material and wages to build, and whose loss in large enough quantities can and does destroy whole businesses.

Arrow Drugs, as I'll call it here, is one of the largest retail chains in America, with big, shiny stores in cities and towns from coast to coast. They sell everything from aspirin to aquariums, from cigarettes to house plants, from trusses to tricycles. Their headquarters and main storage and distribution center is in Ohio. It sprawls over so many acres that it took me some time to locate the office I was looking for. And from that office, a secretary pointed me to a big meeting room whose windows looked across the curved, silver roofs of countless huge warehouses beside interlacing railroad tracks. Those warehouses and what they contained formed the major preoccupation of the dozen men assembled in the room.

Some of them, wearing Arrow Drugs warehouse workers' coveralls, were private security officers. Six were polygraph experts—a couple of whom I knew well, all of whom I had met. They came from the far corners of the map. They were all topflight men. As I suppose I must have, they looked a little scruffy from jet flights they'd left at the airport to come directly here. The last man in the room was a lieutenant of detectives from the force of the city where Arrow had its headquarters. The chief of plant security introduced himself to me and laid out the problem.

"These warehouses are being stripped," he said. "There's a lot of sloppy inventorying. It looks to us as if nearly everybody concerned is either stealing or covering up for the ones who do."

"We went in," said one of the men in coveralls, "thinking we'd spot a handful of workers getting out with a carton of film there, a tripod there. It isn't like that."

"It's a plague," another of these undercover investigators said. "So many people are ripping off Arrow, you can hardly believe it." He was bald. His shiny scalp caught the sunlight and reflected it as he shook his head. "New employees, old employees—it's fantastic."

"That's why you're here," said Luke Marshall, the head of plant security, who had telephoned me at my office in Los Angeles yesterday. "It's a touchy situation, a tangled situation. We don't want to accuse anybody of stealing when they're innocent. We want to get the bad apples out of the barrel, though. And we want to do it fast, before it can spread any further."

"The union?" I said. "You know they're not going to let you accuse anybody of stealing."

"They've got to be handled very carefully," Marshall agreed. "That's why I got you, why I got the rest of these polygraph men. You've, all of you, had plenty of experience. You understand the problem. You'll be delicate and you'll get the results we need."

"If the union digs in its heels," said the police lieutenant, "you can dump the whole thing in my lap. I've told you that."

"We don't want to do that if we don't have to. We don't want to make criminals out of these people, or give them the chance to come back at us for rousting them. We'd like to handle it quietly, with no newspaper sensations, no trials, no jails. We don't want to hurt anybody. We simply want an end to the rip-off."

"Who have you talked to?" I asked.

"Talking to the employees didn't get us anywhere," Marshall said, and nodded at the men in coveralls. "That's why we brought in a special undercover squad, gave them badges and time cards, put them to work on forklifts and in every corner of every warehouse we could slip them into without it seeming odd. They've got names and details." He shuffled papers on the desk. "And I'm assigning each of you a few of those names, employees to talk to, to give lie-detector tests to—right?"

"We'll need dossiers," I said.

"Right here." He patted a stack of manila file folders at his elbow. "And offices have been cleared for you in the personnel department. They know as little about this as we could manage. The chief knows, of course. So let's keep it that way—right?"

I was assigned five Arrow employees. One of them was union steward in his warehouse on his shift. George Grady was around forty, about five ten, stockily built, with thick shoulders and hands that showed he'd done hard physical work all his life. His red hair was thinning. He had freckles. His red-brown eyes were watchful. I had chosen to interview him first, because if he got recalcitrant, he could muzzle the others. I wanted the hardest job out of the way right at the start. If I could handle him, the others should be easy. I settled him in the little box of a room assigned to me, saw that he had a tall, ice-filled Coke from the machine down the hall, and talked to him man to man.

"Arrow is dropping tens of thousands of dollars," I said, "because workers are stealing stuff. They're walking out of your warehouse with carton after carton of color film, cameras, lenses, tripods—you name it."

"Who says so?" he wondered.

"You haven't heard anything about it?"

He shook his head and swallowed some of his Coke. Then he gave a shrug of those tough shoulders. "Oh, hell. Sure, I've heard rumors. The guys talk. But I don't know of anybody actually ripping anything off."

"It's happening," I said. "And it's getting worse. Naturally, Arrow wants it stopped. Naturally"—I smiled—"they figure that old employees like you will want to help them stop it."

"Right," he said, "what can I do?"

"First of all," I said, "clear yourself of any suspicion that you might be involved. You can do that by taking a polygraph examination."

"You're kidding," he said. "The union doesn't allow them. They talk about it at our meetings all the time. Union polices itself. If some member sees another one stealing or something like that, he's supposed to go to his local. They'll look into it. If the guy is guilty, they kick him out. I mean, it figures, doesn't it? It could wreck the union if they didn't, right? Anyway—lie detectors are out. They don't work. All the owners use them for is to scare the workers, make them admit stuff they never did."

"They work," I said. "And the union knows it. I could show you a list of twenty-five, thirty union locals that use polygraph examinations themselves. Everything from Teamsters to Optical Workers, just in the Midwest alone."

"You're kidding," he said. "What for?"

"Thefts from the unions," I said. "Labor-management disputes. You name it. But that's not the point here. Nobody is being accused of anything, least of all you. If there are thieves, isn't it better to find out who they are by asking a few quiet questions, than smearing everybody working here, whether they ever stole anything or not?''

"Hell," he said, "I don't mind." Polygraph equipment sat on my desk. He smiled at it. "I don't believe in the thing, but if it will get me out of here and back on the job, let's go.''

"You're volunteering," I said. "And that's the way it has to be. Nobody's going to be tested who doesn't ask to be. Does that sound fair?''

"Sure. Let's go ahead.''

I began connecting him to the instrument. "I'm going to ask you flat-out questions," I said. "Don't think I'm accusing you of anything. It's just the way the instrument has to be used in order for it to do its work.''

"Ask me anything," he said.

We ran four tests. The man must have meant what he said: He didn't believe in the polygraph, because he lied easily and often. Had he ever seen anyone without permission remove from the warehouse anything worth more than one hundred dollars? "No." But the pens on the traveling graph paper said he had. Did he himself ever take without permission anything from the warehouse valued at more than one hundred dollars? "No." But the pens on the graph said he had. I mentioned particular items from a list of the hundreds missing from recent inventories—cameras, flash equipment, light meters. I'll admit I was shocked. He'd stolen all these things and more. Repeatedly. My own unwillingness to believe this was happening was what made me run so many tests. Yet no matter how I rearranged the questions, his breathing, pulse, and skin responses jarred the instrument in exactly the same way each time.

I detached him from the machine. My mind was racing. He was damp with sweat. Plainly, what he'd felt inside as I asked the questions over and over again wasn't all that easy for this man to contain. I thought George Grady was essentially honest. That conviction hadn't changed because of the tests. In fact, it was reinforced. He was about to crack up. Or was he? If I told him now what the polygraph charts showed, how would he react? He could go straight to the union and they could stop me and the other six polygraph examiners cold. Then the police would take over. The company couldn't keep the matter in the family, then. And there was more than a little danger that Grady and a lot of others wouldn't simply lose their jobs and reputations, but might well end up in prison.

I gave him a cigarette and lit it for him—judging from the shaking of those big, freckled hands of his that he couldn't do it himself. The ice rattled in the flower-printed wax-paper cup when he drank from it. I sat down at the other side of the green steel desk that had his personnel file open on it. His record showed no black marks. His life had been ordinary, simple, law-abiding. He had the same wife he'd started out young manhood with. There had been children. He owned his own modest home. I glanced at him again. He looked drained. His eyes were turned toward the polygraph instrument, but he wasn't seeing it. He was looking at something dismal in his mind. I said:

"George—you weren't quite truthful before. You know about these thefts. When I named certain items, you made those pens jump around." The fact was, every piece of merchandise I'd named had triggered a sharp reaction. "Who's doing this stealing? How are they getting away with it? This plant has a security check system. How do they get around it?"

He looked at me. He tried to say something. He couldn't get the words out. He began to cry. It wasn't a dignified performance, but he was helpless to control it. I got up, turned my back, and stood staring out the window while the hoarse sobs jerked out of him and finally, gasping and snuffling, he got charge of himself again. I turned back. He was wiping his nose and eyes awkwardly on the sleeve of his white coverall with the Arrow Drugs logo over the heart.

"Sorry," he mumbled at me. "I can't name them. It's every-body. Worse than that—it's me."

"I thought it was," I said. "How?"

"The company rule is you go out certain exits. Only those are checked. But nobody obeys the rule—not if they want to take some-thing home."

"Home?" I said. "What do they want with it? Do they resell it? Is there some fence that buys it? We're talking about five figures worth of stuff, maybe six."

90

"Home?" he said. "I don't know. I meant, out of the plant, is all. It's easy. Nothing to it. It's a crime how easy the company makes it."

"Sure," I said. "It's their fault."

"It is," he said grimly, "and you know it."

"Tell me the method," I said.

"It's been going on for years," he said.

"I know that too," I said. "That's not what I asked."

He let his shoulders slump. He sighed. His nose ran. He wiped it on the back of a hand. "There's no control over parking. You park near your work area—see? And at lunch time or a coffee break, you walk out the warehouse doors over to your car and put whatever you swiped into the car, right?"

"Isn't there a guard to prevent that?"

Grady's smile was crooked, bleak, and didn't last. "I don't think he sees too good."

"The manager," I said. I riffled through papers I'd been given for the man's name. He had thirty people to oversee. "Don't tell me he's blind too."

"His office is at the back. It's glass on three sides. But the way cartons and stuff are stacked up in there, he doesn't have a line of vision. He can't see what's going on. Anyway, he's up to his ass in paperwork."

"Do these workers pay off the guard?" I asked.

"A warehouseman doesn't make the kind of wages you can pay blackmail out of." He shrugged again. "I don't know. Probably they give him part of what they steal—or let him in to steal whatever he chooses."

"Are all the guards and security people corrupt?"

"If they're not, they're sure as hell a lot dumber than they ought to be. The company could stop this any time it wants. You want to know the truth? The whole damn work force ought to be fired. They all steal. You can't tell me management doesn't know that. Like I said, how many years does it have to go on?"

"Name me dollars and cents," I said. "How much would all the stuff you know about being stolen add up to?"

"God, I don't know. At wholesale?" He simply lifted his hands and let them fall again. "Over all these years? It could be like you say—twenty-five, fifty thousand? I don't know. I never thought about it that way. But you figure it. Guys are walking out of these warehouses with stuff every day—and I mean every day.''

"It's not an organized theft ring? They don't pass the stuff on to some crooked dealer who pays them a little for it and markets it to retailers who aren't too particular about where they get their stock?''

"No. They swap stuff. I mean, I'm in Warehouse Nine, right? That's cameras, film, photographic supplies. Somebody else is in, like Fifteen—sporting equipment, okay? He needs some film and I need tennis balls for my kid. So we trade, see? But, no, there's no ring. Not that I ever heard of. It's mostly everybody for themselves.''

"You're underestimating the cost,'' I said.

"Yeah, I guess it would be more like a hundred thousand, wouldn't it? I mean, you figure thirty guys to a warehouse and all those warehouses—'' He broke off and shook his head. "You don't think of it that way. I mean—all those mountains of cartons of stuff. Out of all that, who's going to miss one box of film, even a camera?''

"Is that what you took?'' I asked. "One box of film? One camera?''

"Do I have to answer that?''

"You don't have to talk to me at all,'' I said. "But Arrow Drugs is paying me. I have to turn in my evaluation of those polygraph charts.''

He looked at the floor. He clasped and unclasped his hands. He looked up at me, grim-mouthed. "My basement's full of stuff. None of it's used, though. Never been out of the boxes. I'll give it back.''

"Good,'' I said. I flapped at him the sheaf of inventory reports of missing merchandise from Warehouse Nine. "Can I see it? Check it off against this list?''

"Hell, yes. Anything. I just want to get it over with. I been living with it for years—all that junk I didn't have any right to. I don't know.'' He shook his head in numb disbelief. "Every day I kept thinking, they're gonna catch up with you, George. Every time a patrol car came down the street, I felt sick. But I couldn't stop. It's crazy, a bad dream.'' He smiled at me feebly. "And now it's over. And you know what? I'm glad.''

"Sign this slip," I said. "We'll go in my car."

Grady's wife stared at me with washed-out blue eyes. She wiped her hands on an apron before she shook my hand in a kitchen that smelled of floor wax. The house was an old frame one, on a side street of houses just like it. She appeared anxious to keep it shiny, but not quite able to do so. The floor gleamed but the thick old yellow enamel needed washing down. There were traces of greasy cobwebs in the ceiling vent over the stove.

"I've tried to tell him to give it all back," she said to me in an unsteady voice. "I've begged him not to bring any more home."

"It would take a truck to haul it back," he said.

"Now what's going to happen?" she asked me.

"I don't know," I said. I tried to smile reassuringly. I didn't do it with a lot of conviction. The best Grady could hope for would be a suspension without pay—which, from the look of the place, he couldn't afford. At second best, he'd be fired without separation pay, without whatever pension the company had set up for him. At worst, the police could be brought in, he could be arrested, tried, and imprisoned. "That will be up to Arrow Drugs. I don't have any say in the matter. What are they like to work for?"

Grady shrugged. His wife said, "They've always been pretty fair to us."

"Fairness isn't always to everybody's advantage," I said. "Mrs. Grady, why don't you go to the telephone right now and get in touch with a lawyer. You may need one."

She looked into her husband's face. He gave her a glum nod. She left the kitchen. "Come on," Grady said to me. "Let's get this over with. Have you got the inventory sheets?" I had them. He opened a door, flipped a light switch and went ahead of me down narrow, unpainted wooden stairs into a cellar lighted by a sixty-watt bulb hanging from a ceiling of naked studs and boards. He'd been right about needing a truck. Cartons were stacked around us head high. They were thick with dust. There were so many of them only a narrow passageway was left between the foot of the steps and the furnace. Looking around me, I gave a low whistle. He said, "This isn't all."

It wasn't, either. The attic groaned with cartons. Bedroom closets spilled boxes of film at our feet when we opened the doors.

93

Years of steam had molded and mildewed film jammed into the little cabinet under the washbasin. I straightened up. "What did you plan to do with it all?"

"I don't know." His hands hung helpless. "I haven't taken a photograph in twenty years." The bathroom was small. We stepped out of it again. "I gave my mother-in-law a camera, once. Maybe somebody else, I forget. That's all, though. The rest of it is still here."

"A lot of it is too old to be returned."

"Yeah, but you're going to take it, aren't you?" He looked scared that I might be going to let it go on cluttering up his life and conscience. "I don't need it."

"You never did," I said.

In the end, I phoned for that truck I'd thought he was joking about. It took a long time to load it. And all over the city, other vans labeled ARROW DRUGS were carting off the contents of other cellars, attics, closets. Because George Grady was far from being the only Arrow employee who had hoarded away stolen merchandise. In all, by means of polygraph examinations and simple confessions, our team of investigators turned up twenty-five people on the payroll of Arrow Drugs who had been taking away those bright new cartons over months and years.

The depot we decided on for the reclaimed merchandise was the police department. That didn't work. There was too much—far too much. As for checking off those inventory loss sheets—even with help, the job took us days. And not every thief had tucked away his loot as George Grady had. Some had sold and made presents of it. What we were able to account for, the stuff actually stacked in mountains around us, totaled out at more than three hundred thousand dollars' worth. When we figured out, with the help of the people who'd stolen it, the value of the goods dispersed and unreclaimable, and added this to the other tally, the loss to Arrow Drugs topped half a million—wholesale!

The good news was that the other examiners and I were able to clear, by means of polygraph tests, a number of employees whom those coveralled plant security men had tagged as thieves—as well as other workers who had stayed honest while the rip-off disease infected all around them. The company couldn't keep news of the bizarre story from the papers and television, so that not only were jobs, pensions, and futures destroyed, but reputations too. A good many of the company thieves stood trial and went to jail. There was a strong backwash that swept supervisors, even managers, out of their jobs. Arrow Drugs was badly hurt as a company. Not much later, that huge complex where the thefts had been uncovered was forced to close.

Those managers and supervisors who were dismissed hadn't themselves stolen anything. They'd simply been slipshod. But so had top management. It irked me to see people down the pay scale punished, while the vice-presidents in charge of operations went unscathed. Later on my final night I sat in my motel room, batting out on my portable typewriter an angry letter to the board chairman of Arrow Drugs. A decent security system could have prevented this disaster. Arrow's screening of job applicants was an invitation to the untrustworthy. I pointed out half a dozen areas in which top management was to blame for what had happened.

I'd never expected to hear from Arrow Drugs again. To my surprise, a week later I was summoned East again to meet with the men in charge of overall operations, from purchasing and shipping, right down to the retail level. They asked me to map for them a real security program. They had dropped tens of thousands in inventory loss, attorney fees, investigator charges, court costs. They didn't want it to happen again. They'd learned the hard way that money spent on security is money saved—for management, for shareholders, for customers. Arrow Drugs tottered but it survived—in part because of a changed security program, beginning with a new system of screening applicants that included a polygraph examination, which prevented thieves caught and fired by other companies from finding their way into jobs where they could steal again.

9

Sabotage in the Plant

It was almost three in the morning. The moon had set. The stars were hard points of light in a hard black sky. A cold wind blew, a Texas plains wind, gritty and relentless. Inside long rows of wooden barracks soldiers slept. Here and there in the darkness a sentry stood half asleep, rifle clutched in numbed fingers. In a broad fenced area beyond the barracks stood the transport vehicles, shapeless in the night. The curved canvas tops of troop carriers loomed against the sky.

Cal Brewer moved among them quietly. He stooped at each, unscrewed the cap of the gas tank, bent to pick up a heavy square can from the rutted ground, and from the can emptied something into the tank, something that glittered white in the starlight. He set the can down again, screwed the top back on the gas tank, moved on to the next truck. He rubbed his hands on his fatigues and smiled to himself. That took care of the trucks. Now, on to the jeeps. He hurried in his clumsy boots and the can clanked against a bumper. The noise was loud and sudden in the silence.

"Who's there?" came a sharp voice. Footsteps sounded on the hardpan. Brewer crouched. The voice demanded, "What the hell's going on out here?" The steps came nearer. Brewer watched from the shadow of a jeep. The man was only a silhouette, but Brewer realized he wasn't some kid sentry. He knew the man's bulk. It was Technical Sergeant Lawrence, the noncom in charge of the motor pool. His voice whip-cracked again: "Come on. I know you're there. Step out where I can see you." He stepped closer. His shirttails were out. They flapped in the wind. Then, suddenly, he gave a sharp grunt and crouched, out of the line of Brewer's sight. But not out of hearing. "Sugar!" he said. And he was on his feet again. "Come on out, you sabotaging son of a bitch. I'll bust your ass." He made straight for the jeep.

Cal Brewer realized it was too late to run. But it wasn't too late to defend himself. He hated Lawrence. Lawrence was the one to blame for Brewer's losing his corporal's stripes yesterday. He groped inside the jeep and his hand closed on a hammer. He crouched, tense, heart thudding in his ears. Lawrence came around the front of the jeep. "All right, soldier. Straighten up. It's all over. What are you, crazy or something? You know what you're going to get for this?" He stepped forward. Brewer sprang, swinging the hammer. It connected with Lawrence's skull. The sergeant fell against the next jeep in the line, then slumped to the ground. Brewer turned to run.

The beam of a flashlight hit him in the eyes. The sentry. "Hold it!" Brewer winced but he didn't move. He couldn't see anything but he knew the kid must have a rifle pointed at his belly. He also knew the kid was nervous. He could tell from the pinched sound of the voice saying, "Drop the hammer, soldier. Right now!"

And Brewer dropped the hammer. . . .

Brewer glared down at the skinny woman behind the desk. She was fifty if she was a day. Her hair was dyed bright red. She wore dresses off the Young Misses rack and her ears, her scraggy neck, her bony fingers glittered with cheap costume jewelry. She wore too much lipstick, too much eye shadow. Her desk, in the greasily glassed-in walls of the mezzanine office at the auto parts shop, was a dumping ground of papers. She was holding one of them out to him—an order form, in triplicate. And he was saying:

"What the hell do you mean we haven't got a Pinto distributor rotor. We've got a goddamn *hundred* Pinto distributor rotors. Who told you—Peterson?"

"Yes, Mr. Brewer." He thought for a split second that nobody around here called him Cal anymore. "But I didn't take his word for it. I went and checked, myself."

"You!" Brewer snorted. "What the hell do you know about the stockroom, for Christ's sake? You're blind as a bat anyway, you old fright. You couldn't see it if it fell on you." It was true. She was vain about her looks—looks that had left her years ago, if they'd ever been there. She refused to wear glasses. It was a joke in the shop. Everybody laughed about the way she held orders and letters up to her face to read them, how she bent squinting over her type-writer as she worked. If he'd been the owner of this business instead of only the manager, he'd have fired her long ago. He stepped around the desk, grabbed her spindly arm, and yanked her up out of the chair. She gave a squeak of fright. "Shut up. I'm not hurting you. But I am going to teach you this business, if I never do anything else around here. Come on." He dragged her, protesting, after him, out the office door and down the stairs.

The lower half of the door to the stockroom was a counter. Old Ike Peterson leaned on it, using a stub of pencil in knobby old fingers to note a figure on a clipboard holding a ruled form. Brewer reached for the door latch, rattled it. Locked. Peterson looked up, startled, but not in time to get out of the way. Brewer put a hand in the middle of the old man's chest and shoved. Peterson staggered backward, stumbled over a stack of boxed spark plugs, and fell. Brewer paid no attention. He ignored Lily Grant's protests. He reached over the counter, unlocked the door and pushed through it, dragging her after him. Peterson lay on the cement, legs up over the cartons. He was wincing, clutching the back of his head, moaning.

"Shut up," Brewer said. "You're not hurt. Get up, you old square-head. The phone's ringing."

Stepping over the old man, he jerked Lily Grant with him down the long, crowded aisles of shelves. He eyed the boxes lined up on the shelves as they passed. He snorted. Half the time, it looked like, the labels on the shelves had nothing to do with the merchandise stored there. No wonder the woman's desk was stacked up the way it was. No wonder they could never catch up. No wonder nothing ever got done on time around here—and what did get done, got done wrong. No wonder stuff kept coming back. The big surprise to him was that any customer ever got the part ordered. He came to a halt. He jabbed a finger at a shelf label. He jerked Lily Grant's arm.

"Look!" he said. "What the hell do you see there?"

She whispered shakily, "I can't read it."

He pushed her at the shelf. He let go of her arm, grabbed the back of her skull, and shoved her face at the words crudely lettered by Peterson on the strip of tape. "Pinto Distributor Head Rotors!" he roared. "Can't you read that?"

"Let go of me, Mr. Brewer!" she cried, and twisted away from him. "Of course I can read it. But they're not there. Look for yourself."

He looked. She was right. He glanced along the shelf. He had a quick eye and a good memory. He knew from the shape, color, and pattern of the boxes alone what each contained. Thousands of them. That was why he'd come up so fast in this place. He had the whole catalogue in his head—thousands of items, tens of thousands. And she was right. There wasn't a box of Pinto rotors in sight. He began grabbing boxes and flinging them off the shelves, the contents bursting them open and scattering on the floor. He went along the shelves, cursing, and with big sweeps of his arm bringing everything crashing down. Peterson came running.

"My God, Mr. Brewer," he shouted, "what are you doing? Stop that. We'll never get it sorted out." He lunged at Brewer, clutching, trying to grab his arms. Brewer didn't stop. He'd never stop. This place was chaos, anyway. He'd show them. Goddamn it, there would be order here if it killed him and everyone else! He flung the old storeroom supervisor off. Peterson careened backward along the aisle and fell again. Lily Grant threw herself at him.

"You stop that!" she shrieked.

He swung at her as well. Her red wig tumbled. Under it her matted hair was streaky blonde and black. He laughed wildly and kicked at her. He stretched out both arms and dragged clean another shelf. And then there stood Hooper in the doorway, white-faced, gaping at him—Hooper, who owned the shop. Red seemed to swim in front of Brewer's eyes. He was sweating. His hair had fallen over his face. Somehow he'd ripped his suit. Some greasy product had spilled down his front. He stopped, panting, clumsily pawing at his soaked and darkened tie. He looked at Hooper. The round little man was speaking but there was some kind of roaring in Brewer's ears and he couldn't hear. Lily Grant was clinging to Hooper, crying. Hooper was looking at old Peterson, staggering to his feet among the ankle-deep parts in the aisle. Gently Hooper put the old secretary aside and came along the aisle, reaching out to help Peterson up. Then he was standing face to face with Brewer. And now Brewer could hear him.

"Get out. Get out of here and never come back . . . "

Redwing blackbirds whistled in the hot noon air. They were far off across the vacant land, perched and swinging on tall reeds, where a trickle of water kept things green. Brewer hoped the customer didn't notice. He pointed out to her instead the immense gas storage tanks a mile off to the left, squat and glinting silver in the sun. Far along in the other direction factory buildings crowded together. Trucks, big eighteen-wheelers, hurtled along the cleanly paved strip of roadway where he'd parked Mrs. Esther Robinson's car, a sleek new maroon Seville.

"It seems ideal," she said. She took off her dark glasses for a moment but the brightness of the sun made her flinch and she put the glasses on again. A flock of crows flew over, noisily cawing. She looked up. She looked at Brewer. "It seems strange no one has picked this land up before. She waved a long hand toward the storage tanks, and turned to wave the same hand toward the factories. "So near. I'd have thought—"

"It wasn't open for development till recently," Brewer lied. It never had been. It never would be. It turned to swamp when the rains came. That little thread of water over there where the blackbirds were quarreling spread clear out to the roadway here. The land where the building had gone on was twenty feet higher. But why should he tell this sleek widow with six million dollars to

drop the plans to expand her late husband's highly successful elec-
tronics manufacturing business? She'd find out for herself, in time.
"But as I said, it's already set up for you—nearness to railroads, an
airport, road brought up to standard for heavy trucking. As you say,
Mrs. Robinson—it's ideal. I'll go further. I'd say it was just made
for you. Those plans for the buildings you showed me—I can see
them standing here now."

"What are those birds with that strange whistle?"

"Redwings," he said. "You seen enough?"

"I'll be coming back again and again," she said, and in her trim
slacks, headed back for the car, Gucci handbag swinging, Gucci
heels puncturing the raw earth. Without bothering to turn her head,
she called to him: "When can you bring me the papers? I'll want to
arrange to give you a certified check."

He opened the car door for her. "I'll have them ready tomorrow
morning, if that's convenient." She climbed neatly in and he closed
the door. He got into the car on the driver's side. As he slammed his
own door, he thought to himself that with his commission from this
sale, he could have a car just like this. Two if he wanted. The
warning buzzer sounded from the dash. He smiled at her and fastened his seat belt.

She said, "Tomorrow morning will be fine. Perhaps you'll join
me for some breakfast by the pool. My cook does marvelous things
with crepes in the mornings."

"Thanks." Brewer started the car. "I'd like that."

"I think you will," she said. "I'm sure I will."

He did. But he didn't like anything that happened thereafter.
The crepes were good. Sleeping with her was even better. Better
still was the million-dollar check she handed him as he left at noon.
But from there on, it was all downhill. No, that wasn't the right
expression. It was a crash from a great height. When he picked
himself up, months later, he'd been tagged a crook and had lost that
hard-won Realtor's license he'd thought was going to let him use
Cadillacs the way other people used paper cups. But he was only
bruised, not broken. Esther Robinson must have liked him in bed as
much as he'd liked her—and more, emotionally. She didn't go to
attorneys. The real estate firm fired him. The state took away his
right to fleece people with condemned land. But there hadn't been

any publicity. And he had enough honest money in the bank to start again . . .

Brewer Auto Parts ran with slick efficiency. It was the exact opposite of old Hooper's shambles of a shop. It got the parts. It filled the orders. There was speed. There was accuracy. People got to work on time and did their jobs. Anybody who couldn't or didn't got carried out with the day's trash. One warehouse became two, and two expanded to three. Brewer Auto Parts had it made. Cal Brewer bought a lavish, low-roofed ranch house under handsome old oaks in an expensive corner of the San Fernando Valley. He installed in it a lovely young wife—not that one woman's loveliness was ever enough for him. He lunched at the best restaurants, danced at the posh discos, ran a glossy white power launch out of the marina.

He met Glen Morris, Harvey Snyder, and Tom Oates—young men going somewhere, young men of his own kind. Or that was how he put it to himself. It turned out he was wrong, but that wouldn't matter until later, much later. Morris had been an Air Force test pilot, Snyder was an expert on aircraft engines, Oates a gifted technical designer. Brewer could add to their partnership management and money skills. Together they could get rich. They founded Sunset Air Parts. In ten years' time, it was grossing millions.

Then things started to go sour. That was when I got a phone call from Will Terrell, the plant manager. The small factory, located near an airport, was attractive. Its handsome landscaping set off the sand-color, flat-roofed, one-story structure, giving it a look both friendly and efficient. Indoors, things were bright and neat: off-white walls, planters, curtains and carpeting in tweedy yellows and oranges, upholstery to match. Through the wide picture window back of Terrell's desk, light aircraft in butterfly colors took off and landed against a background of sunlit mountains. The place struck me as an unlikely setting for the dark story which began unfolding that morning and was to become even harder to accept as time went on.

"Somebody's sabotaging us," Terrell said. He was a blond young man who looked more like a high school senior than the gifted business administrator he was. Anyway, there were pictures on his desk of two young children who couldn't have been anyone's but his. "Wrecking machinery. If we can't stop it, it's going to stop us. We're already running behind on orders."

"Competitors?" I said.

"What we make nobody else makes." He shook his head. "What have you done?"

"Put in undercover investigators," Terrell said. "They didn't like the actions of a couple of newer employees and I let them go." He made a face. "It wasn't them. The sabotage went right on. We put in closed-circuit television scanners. No results."

"What about guards?" I said.

"We had two. We put on four. Nothing stopped. I don't know. What have we got—forty employees? We've never had one instance of troublemaking. They like the place. We make it as pleasant as we can, starting with the shop. For example, nobody stays too long on one machine or one operation. We switch them around to avoid monotony. We put in a pool, a rec room. We don't make static about coffee breaks—not if the work gets out. Cost of living raises. Never a word from the union. I know these people. Maybe three-quarters of them have been with Sunset for years—right from the start, longer than I have."

"There was a devil in paradise," I said.

Terrell gave a wry laugh. "All right, yes. They don't like Cal Brewer."

"Who's he?"

"One of the four owners, one of the four who started the business. He handles the dollars and cents end." He named the other partners. "They're the creative ones. You couldn't ask to work for a nicer bunch of guys."

"Except Brewer," I said.

Terrell shrugged. "Oh, Cal's all right. Most of the time—if you don't cross him. He's a demon for efficiency. He wants everybody to measure up to the standards he sets for himself. And sometimes we ordinary mortals have off days, you know? It's only human. He doesn't make allowances for that. I try to steer him away from contact with employees. If he wants to fight, let him fight with me, or the other partners. Or his wife. Wow, do they ever fight!"

"It's not his wife you got me here to give polygraph tests to," I said. "It's the workers. Does that mean you think Brewer made an enemy out of one of them, when you were looking the other way?"

"I don't know what to think," Terrell said. "You come highly recommended. You tell me."

For the rest of that day, and all evening at home, I went over the personnel files of Sunset Air Parts workers, present and past. I found nothing that even suggested any of them might take to wrong-doing. The next morning I did close checks on the three Terrell had fired on suspicion. They came out as clean as the others. I checked out Terrell himself. I checked out the partners. Everything seemed in order. I returned the files. The only thing left for me to do now was give polygraph examinations to the workers. I told Terrell this, and he called to an interview room in the personnel department three who had been with Sunset Air Parts since it opened.

"Lie-detector tests!" exclaimed a raw-boned, white-haired man of close to sixty. "You take me right back to Nazi Germany. No. If you don't trust me, fire me."

"We trust you, Mr. Gottschalk," Terrell said. "As a matter of fact, we trust everybody in the shop. That's why they're there. But somebody doesn't deserve that trust. Somebody's wrecking machinery. You know that."

"It is no call to go prying into a man's life, when he has done nothing wrong." This was another expert tool and die man, also from Europe, stocky, with a brush haircut. "I come to work. I do my job. That is where your interest in me begins and ends." He rose, the other two with him. "It will be sad to me to leave. But I will leave if I must before I will permit myself to be subjected to"—he glared at me—"Gestapo tactics."

"Come on, boys," said the third man, already opening the door. He eyed Terrell reproachfully. "I never thought I'd see this day. Not around here."

Muttering, they filed out. Terrell looked pale.

" 'Gestapo tactics,' " he said. "Wow, that's heavy." Pain was in his boyish blue eyes. "I didn't deserve that."

"Don't feel bad," I said. "They don't understand the polygraph—almost nobody does."

"They'll understand it," he said grimly, and reached for the phone. "I'll order them to take those tests, and anybody who won't—as far as I'm concerned, they're guilty."

"Hold it," I said. "You can't do that. Not in California. The labor laws won't let you."

He let the phone rattle back into its cradle. He stared at me. "Well, then, what do we do?"

"Contact the police," I said. "Crimes have been committed. Get them to administer the tests. They're allowed to do it. You aren't—not as an employer."

He dialed the local police. He spoke to them, I spoke to them. They turned us down. Forty people were too many for them to handle with their short staff and heavy workload. Terrell hung up, defeated. I said we weren't beaten yet. I asked for a chance to speak to the whole crew. Did they have an assembly room? Get them together there at break time and give me ten minutes with them.

"What will you say?"

"First, that I won't ask any questions except about the damage to the machinery. Second, that the polygraph can protect them all from suspicion by nailing the one who wrecked the machines. Third, that unless the sabotage stops, the plant will have to shut down—and that will mean an end to their jobs. You stay with me and back me up on that."

"Right." Terrell reached for the phone again. "I'll arrange for the meeting."

It went well. I brought in three more examiners. With their help, all forty employees were tested without creating gaps in the work force that would further slow production. I myself ran tests on the three men fired by Terrell on suspicion. As their personnel files had suggested to me earlier, like the luckier shop people who had kept their jobs, not only hadn't they taken part in any machine wrecking, they knew nothing about it. I showed Terrell the charts, going over with him in detail just the questions asked and the responses they'd produced.

"I can't believe it," he said.

"Believe it," I said. "None of these workers had anything to do with the sabotage."

"Somebody did," Terrell said stubbornly. "You've made a mistake."

And of course he was right. I'd forgotten the security guards. We tested all of them that day. None of them was connected with the incidents. That left Terrell and the partners. The plant manager was guiltless. Morris, Snyder, and Oates proved as amiable as Terrell had described them. They accepted the fairness principle with easy good humor, and took the tests with interest and intelligent curiosity about the process and its results. Of course, they passed. Then came Cal Brewer's turn. He had objected that he was too busy to take time off from his desk to participate in "electronic games." The pilot and the two engineers had found the polygraph fascinating. Only the technically untrained Brewer showed contempt for it, calling it a fake when I spoke with him by phone to set up a time for us to meet.

Morris had advised me, "Don't let Cal get to you. He's good people, underneath. That abrasiveness is something he's developed as part of his technique for making things happen. He's topflight as a businessman. Hell, this company would be nowhere without Cal."

The others had listened without comment. I judged they put up with Brewer because they felt they needed him, but that if they'd ever liked him, that time had passed. It wasn't my business to form an opinion one way or the other. This didn't prevent my having a negative reaction to the man. He was lean and suntanned but he didn't give an athletic impression. It was nerves, not outdoor exercise, that kept him thin. He was tense. I couldn't see his eyes because he wore dark glasses, but stress sounded in his high, grating voice. This could be laid to the crisis caused by the sabotaging of the business he was responsible for, of course. That was logical. But his hostility toward me and my reason for being at Sunset Air Parts jarred with that. The prospect of the polygraph test was what was making him edgy this morning. He smoked incessantly. He laid his cigarette pack and lighter on the corner of my desk as we talked. The cigarettes were MORE. The lighter was engraved with the logo of a Las Vegas casino . . .

He closed the casino office door quietly behind him and his hands shook as he slipped his checkbook back inside his jacket. His shirt was damp with sweat. He wiped his forehead with a handkerchief and moved along the hushed, deeply-carpeted, dimly-lit corridor toward the faint sounds at its end—the whirr of roulette wheels, the click of chips, the muffled tumble of dice on baize. He'd dropped another five thousand tonight. How the hell was he going to explain that to Miriam? He reached the doorway and stood glumly surveying the plush room with its murmuring players. There were the blackjack tables. He took a step. No—he'd had enough. Or rather, they'd had too much. He swung away sharply, heading for the bar, and collided with a man. He mumbled apologies and tried to step around him. The man smiled and caught his arm.

"Mr. Brewer?" he asked. "Mr. Cal Brewer of Sunset Air Parts?"

"Yes." Brewer hadn't seen this man before. He was dark, mustached, about forty. He smelled of expensive cologne, his shirt looked tailored, and his suit had run him at least three hundred dollars. His handshake was firm, and those handsome white teeth of his gleamed friendliness. Brewer said, "That's right. Who are you?"

"My name's Delgado," the man said. "I'm in manufacturing myself. Can I buy you a drink?"

A drink was what Cal Brewer needed. He went along. It was late. Most of the bar stools were empty. It was quiet in this corner. They were virtually alone. "Something on your mind?" Cal Brewer asked.

"I'm interested in Sunset," Delgado said. "Would you consider selling?"

Cal Brewer shook his head. He tasted the Glenlivet. "I've got partners. We're doing fine. They wouldn't dream of selling."

"But you?" Delgado cocked an eyebrow. "You've been dropping a lot of cash at the tables."

"You noticed." Brewer said it wryly, but it gave him a cold feeling to realize this man had been watching him. "Yeah—but, like I said, Sunset's doing great. I don't drop what I can't afford."

"Your wife doesn't think so," Delgado said. He dropped the remark indifferently, looking away. "She thinks you're compulsive. She made you see a shrink." Delgado had big soft brown eyes with long black lashes. He blinked the lashes at Brewer in a look totally innocent. "Isn't that right?"

"That's pretty goddamn private business." Brewer got off the stool. "What the hell are you after?"

"Take it easy," Delgado said. His voice was smooth, soothing. "I said I'm interested in Sunset Air Parts. I've done some investigating, that's all. It's natural. You'd do the same. Sit down." He patted the bar stool. "Let's talk."

"You think I'm in financial trouble?" Brewer heard the false truculence in his voice and told himself that was stupid. The man obviously knew the truth. He gave a short, joyless laugh and got back on the bar stool. "Well, you're right." Mouth twisted, shoulders slumped, he drank from the thick, stubby glass.

"And you can't climb out," Delgado said. "Not with anything less than your share in Sunset Air Parts."

"It's not that bad," Brewer said doggedly.

"My accountant says it is. He says you could sell your Cessna, your boat, the Bugatti and the Bentley—and you'd still come up short. Real estate values are way up, of course. The house might get you in the clear. But you'd be standing around naked. Where the hell could you go? You've got a funny background, remember?"

Brewer eyed the sleek man. "I don't like you."

"I'm just making you a business proposition," Delgado said. "Let's not indulge in personalities, Mr. Brewer."

"What the hell are you doing?" Brewer asked.

"Pointing out the facts. Is it my fault if they're not very pleasant, not very encouraging? You've been trying to wipe out your own future. I only want to give it back to you."

"Thanks," Brewer snorted. "I'm sure it's altruism on your part, pure philanthropy."

"You could look at it like that." Delgado smiled.

"It's no use," Brewer said. "My partners won't sell. Why should they? We've got a unique thing going. We outclass anyone else in the quality of our stuff. That's not bragging. That's a fact."

"I already know that—hand craftsmanship, all of it. That's why I want your plant and not somebody else's."

"It's not just a business to those guys," Brewer said. "It's their life. They're proud of it. You couldn't offer them enough money to give it up.''

"What if business dropped?"

Brewer eyed him. "The charts are all going the other way. Up. You know that too. You're bound to."

"Right." Delgado signaled the bartender for another round. "But what if something went wrong? What if the machinery broke down?"

"We'd fix it," Brewer said. "We've got a top maintenance crew."

"I'm talking about serious damage," Delgado said. "Wreckage." The bartender set down new drinks and took away the glasses that held nothing but ice. "You could lose weeks, right? How many weeks could you afford?"

Brewer said, puzzled, "Not too many. We run pretty close on time. There's a heavy demand. It's not easy to keep up, not when you insist on our kind of quality."

"So if there was a breakdown, your profitable little operation would show losses pretty fast, wouldn't it?"

Brewer narrowed his eyes. "Are you threatening us?"

"I'm trying to do you a favor, trying to get you back on your feet."

"Are you suggesting that I—" Brewer let the words fade out. He watched fascinated as Delgado brought a wallet from an inner pocket and with his thumbs spread it open. By its corner, he pulled up half an inch of a single bill among perhaps twenty that made the wallet thick. It was a one-thousand-dollar bill. Brewer moistened his lips. He said faintly "—that I sabotage my own factory?"

"How much did you drop at blackjack tonight, Mr. Brewer?" Delgado asked. "About five thousand, wasn't it?" He looked into Brewer's eyes. "That's quite a loss for a man with as many debts as you've got."

"It wasn't a lucky night," Brewer said.

"Oh, I think it's going to be a very lucky night." With a faint smile curling the corners of his mouth, Delgado slipped one, two, three, four, five of the crisp bills out of the wallet. He put the wallet away. He studied the bills in his hand. He looked at Brewer. "To answer your question—no, I'm not suggesting anything. All I'm saying is that if something were to happen at Sunset Air Parts to cripple production, perhaps your partners wouldn't be so keen on hanging on to the business. Perhaps they'd consider selling out."

"You're dreaming," Brewer said.

"Oh, of course, one little breakdown wouldn't do it. But if it went on for a while—" Delgado let the suggestion hang unfinished.

Brewer got off the stool. "You're crazy," he said. "I can't believe any of this. It can't be happening. Look—thanks for the drink. Nice talking to you, I guess. It's late and I'm hallucinating. Good night." He started to walk off.

Delgado caught his arm. He said, "It's happening. Does this make it more real?" He pushed the five thousand-dollar bills into Brewer's breast pocket. "And if I said that once that first breakdown happens, there'd be another five of those for you—would that help make it more real?"

Brewer's legs felt weak. There was an empty booth of buttoned red leather. He sat down. Delgado sat across from him. He went on, "And if I said that when your partners decide they've had it with a business plagued by breakdowns and agree to sell out, there'll be fifty thousand cash for you, plus a silent partnership in Sunset Air Parts—would you still think you were hallucinating?"

Staring into Delgado's face, Brewer's hand went to the bills in his pocket. His fingers told him they were real. His fingers counted them. He moistened his lips. His voice came hoarse. "I'll see—" He cleared his throat. "I'll see what I can do."

Delgado gave him a gentle, encouraging smile. "I thought you would," he said . . .

"All right," Brewer said to me as I removed the polygraph attachments from his chest, arm, and hand. "The little parlor game is over with. How did I do?"

I kept my face expressionless. "I'll have to have a little time to study the charts," I said. It wasn't true. If ever I'd seen test results that didn't need a second glance, Cal Brewer's were it. "I've asked everyone the same questions. Nobody reacts quite the same. I want to be as accurate as I can."

"When Terrell told us he was bringing you in," Brewer said, "I voted against it. That was a big enough waste of time and money. But to suspect the owners of a business of wrecking it themselves—'' He jerked into his jacket. "That tears it. It takes some kind of nerve to ask to get paid for anything that ridiculous.''

"Thanks for your time,'' I said. "I'll get back to you.''

It was plain to me that Cal Brewer had knowledge of the sabotage—how it was done, who had done it. But he wasn't the type to break down and confess just because his nerves had jumped when I'd asked him three or four questions. I needed more to confront him with—if there was more. I got on the telephone to a couple of trusted investigators and asked them to run to earth everything they could find on Cal Brewer—no matter how far in the past. They got me the answers even more quickly than I'd hoped.

Brewer had been discharged from the Army as mentally unstable after pouring sugar into the gas tanks of Army vehicles and striking a noncom with a hammer. He'd lost his next job, at an auto parts distributorship, for abusing other employees, even though the owner had made him manager only a few weeks after hiring him. He had done well selling industrial real estate, then lost his job and his license for cheating a client on worthless land. I remembered the Las Vegas cigarette lighter. My men brought me photostats of checks Brewer had written to ten casinos. Totaling the amounts of his losses put them well beyond what he made as a shareholder in Sunset Air Parts. Another set of checks written to pay rent on a Westwood apartment turned up a young woman Brewer was keeping. His wife knew about it, as she knew about the gambling. She'd made Brewer start therapy in the hope of saving their marriage . . .

Morris, Snyder, and Oates frowned. The documented proof of Brewer's checkered past lay on Morris's desk. He was president of Sunset; Snyder and Oates were vice-presidents. They stood beside Morris's desk, as I did. They looked disgusted but not surprised. Seated behind the desk, Morris pushed the papers away from him.

"I'm sorry you did this,'' he said. "It just turns up a lot of rocks without getting us anywhere.''

Snyder dropped lankily into a chair. "It just proves what I've thought about Cal for a long while—that he was some kind of creep. When he offered to sell out to us, we should have accepted.''

I said, "When was this? You didn't tell me."

Oates said, "It didn't come up. Yeah, a few weeks ago. When that didn't work, he said the company was in trouble and why didn't we dump it before we had to go into bankruptcy? We couldn't stop the sabotage. We were taking so long filling orders customers were canceling. We could still get a good price but if we waited too long, we wouldn't have any goodwill left."

"Why didn't you take his suggestion?" I asked.

"It wouldn't be selling a company," Snyder said. "It would be selling our lives. We care. Not about money, about aircraft. We built Sunset with our own hands, our own ideas. We do what we do better than anybody else."

"The word for it is pride," Morris said.

Oates touched the papers on the desk. "Anyway, here's the reason he made the suggestion. His bank statement. He needs every dollar he can lay hands on. What an idiot."

"None of this makes him a saboteur," Morris said.

"He has easy access to every part of the plant," Snyder said. "He could walk in and out of any entrance with nobody questioning why."

"So could all of us," Morris said.

"But we don't work overtime the way he does—he could be here after everybody else left and no one would think twice about it. Whoever saw him wouldn't even remember."

"And he did sabotage those Army trucks," Oates said.

"That was a long time ago," Morris scoffed. "Hell, he was no more than a kid. Kids do crazy things. I flew under a bridge on a dare. I could have killed not only myself but the girl with me."

"That's not quite the same," I said. "There was nothing malicious about that—it was just thoughtless. Look, Will Terrell brought me here to try to solve this sabotage problem with polygraph tests. They've cleared everyone else, yourselves included. You've accepted that. Why won't you accept that Brewer's charts don't clear him? They show he knows about the sabotage."

"Knows what?" Morris asked.

"Everything," I said. "Now, what do you want to do about it? Shall I confront him or not?"

The three looked at each other. They'd worked together a long time. They didn't need words. Morris sighed. "All right. I guess I'm outvoted. You go ahead. But I sure hate to think you're right."

"I know I'm right," I said.

But I wasn't prepared for the Cal Brewer who entered my office that afternoon. The arrogance was all gone. He looked pale, washed-out. A nerve kept twitching at the corner of his mouth. I couldn't see his eyes back of those big-lensed black glasses, but from the weak smile he gave me as he dropped into the visitor's chair, and from the tiredness that sounded in his voice as he tried for insolence and missed, I judged something bad had happened to him. This wasn't the way I'd thought he was going to act. I'd figured him for the kind who would fight right down to the end. Had one of the partners, after promising me to say nothing to Brewer, been unable to keep silent? I couldn't believe that. Then what had happened?

"Okay," he said, in a bad imitation of his old self. "So I failed your gimmicky little test. What do I have to do—stay after school?"

"Maybe years," I said. "You know who wrecked the machinery in your shop. When you answered no, your blood pressure and your breathing answered yes."

"The miracles of modern science," he said.

"You paid someone to do it," I said, "or you did it all by yourself."

"Why?" He fumbled a long brown cigarette from its pack and lit it with trembling hands. The flame of the Las Vegas lighter wavered. "Why would I do anything so crazy?"

"Because you're drowning in debt," I said. "You've gambled away all your own money and every dollar you could borrow. You're in a corner." I picked up and dropped back on the desk a file folder that held the records on Brewer my investigators had gathered. "It's all in here. It makes pretty sad reading, the story of your life. You act like a winner, but the fact is, you can't cope. You never have, you never will. And people who can't cope get frantic and do crazy things. Like sabotaging their own factories so business will fall off and partners who didn't want to sell will have to sell.

"Christ," he said softly.

"Have I got it right or not?" I asked.

"I asked them to buy me out," he said. "They wouldn't. I didn't have any choice. Asking them to sell Sunset was like asking them to cut off an arm. What could I do?"

"What did you do?" I said.

He told me about that nightmare night in Las Vegas, about Delgado and the five thousand dollars—all of it as I've told it to you. But there was more. After the first jamming of the machinery—he'd done it after midnight, slipped into the shop when the watchman was in another part of the building—Delgado had folded into his palm a second set of thousand-dollar bills. Somehow Delgado had known exactly what had happened. Production was brought almost to a standstill for two days. Brewer then damaged two more machines. Losses jumped. But this time, Brewer had almost been seen. He'd sweated what he was doing. The second time, it had made him physically sick. Speeding home along the midnight freeway in his expensive car, he'd had to stop to throw up. He took a plane to Las Vegas. When Delgado showed up for their appointed meeting, Brewer had handed back the last five thousand dollars.

"Take it," he'd said. "I want out."

Delgado's smile was regretful. "This is only half."

"I'll get you the rest. I swear it."

Delgado gave his head a little shake, and again tucked the big bills into Brewer's pocket. "You haven't got anyplace to get the rest. Only from me. You go on with what you're doing. You're very good at it. Stop worrying."

"I don't like it. Those guys don't deserve it."

"We'll pay a fair price," Delgado said, "better than fair. They can't take too much more. Throw some more scrap iron in the works. They'll buckle."

"It means too much to them," Brewer said.

"Stop thinking about them," Delgado said. "Think about yourself. Where are you going to be if they keep refusing to sell?"

"I'll manage somehow." Brewer tried to hand back the money again. "Look, I want to call it off, I said."

Two men loomed up beside the table. Brewer thought he recognized one—a welterweight he'd watched years ago. The other was lean, with eyes "like a snake," to use Brewer's words. This one

114

opened his jacket. The handle of an automatic stuck out of his waistband. Delgado said:

"These are my associates. If you try to get funny, Mr. Brewer, they'll turn you into something that has to be kept alive with machines in a hospital."

Brewer said to me, "He rings me up every night. Every night. I have to be at a phone booth in the shopping center near my house. I've explained how Terrell called you in, how you're getting too close. And last night, they were waiting for me by the phone booth. The big one hit me in the kidneys. I couldn't get up off the blacktop for ten minutes. I'm pissing blood. They'll kill me."

"Not now," I said. "You'll be where they can't get at you. This is on tape," I said. "Do I wipe it, or do I play it for Morris and Snyder and Oates?"

"You son of a bitch," he said.

"I can wipe it," I said. "But it won't change things."

"No," he said. "Go ahead. Play it for them. What the hell can I do?"

No one could locate the man from Las Vegas who called himself Delgado. But Cal Brewer went to prison anyway. I had been wrong about one thing—they got at him there. He was beaten in the laundry room to within an inch of his life. He's living out what's left of it in a small desert town, just about able to hobble down to the general store and back. His wife divorced him and moved to another state—to escape the threatening phone calls that kept coming once her husband went to prison. As for Sunset Air Parts, it still stands sunnily in its pleasant landscaping, backed by the little airport and the green mountains. And for Oates, Morris, and Snyder, business has never been better.

10
Digby and the Federal Court

The chunky youth in the UCSD-stenciled sweatshirt squinted in the hot Mexican sunlight. The sweatshirt was minus its sleeves. His shorts were made of Levi's torn off raggedly halfway up his thick thighs. He wore faded blue tennis shoes. He wiped a sweaty hand through his long straw-color hair. He was aggravated.

"Come on, Will. What's the matter with you?"

"Look—I didn't come down here to buy grass, man. I came to buy that French perfume."

"Yeah, at one-third cost, I know." The chunky lad gestured at the street of shops. It swarmed with tourists and with little boys and skinny old men in *serapes* trying to sell everything from postcards to their sisters. "Only nobody here ever heard of it. Now, let's get some weed and go home." A blast of *mariachi* music came from a loudspeaker over the door of a record shop. He winced and raised his voice. "I hate this dump. I hate the smells, I hate the food, I hate the music."

"But you love their dope," the boy named Will said. Well, okay, go get it. I'm going home. And I'm going home alone—because I don't want to get busted at the border. You can sit in a Mexican jail for life, you know. They throw away the key, Don."

"Who's going to get busted?" Don scoffed. "Guys do this every weekend. You know that. You smoke their grass without worrying, I notice."

"Forget it," Will said, and turned away.

"How you going to get home? It's my car, remember?"

"I'll walk till I can catch a Greyhound," Will said.

Cars were lined up with their motors idling in the harsh glare of midday at the border gate, waiting for inspection so they could cross back into the States. Will trudged past them. He was disappointed. He'd hoped to go home with a gift for his mother. But that was the way it was with rumors. You got someplace and found they weren't true. The good news was he could pass the customs men with a clear conscience. For some reason he remembered the prayer book verse, *We brought nothing into this world; it is certain we can take nothing out*. And then the blare of an auto horn broke his thoughts. His name was shouted. He looked around, shielding his eyes with a hand. An arm waved from one of the cars standing in line.

"Hey, Will, come here!"

He trotted over. The driver of the car was Ken Hoffman, a dude he took a couple of classes with. "Hey, man. What's happening?"

Leaving the engine running, Hoffman opened the door. "Man, am I glad you came along. I've got The Revenge. I have to hit the men's room, and I do mean now! Look, drive my car across, will you? I'll meet you on the other side." He dodged in among the pack of sidewalk tourists with their newly-bought straw sombreros. In a minute, he was out of sight. With a wryly amused shrug, Will slid behind the wheel of Hoffman's car. The cars ahead had inched forward. He rolled the car after them. At the gate the uniformed man in dark goggles asked him the routine questions in a bored voice. Then:

"All right. Will you get out of the vehicle, please, and open the trunk for me?"

Will obeyed. The man bent to paw around in the trunk. There was a sandy, tar-stained sleeping bag, a pair of ski boots, a bicycle wheel. There was something else—a shaving kit. The officer, a map of sweat on the back of his neatly starched uniform shirt, zipped it open and emptied out razor, toothpaste tube, spray can deodorant—and a small plastic envelope holding white powder. He held this in his hand and looked at it. Something in his stillness alarmed Will. He started to take a step backward and the man caught his arm.

"Come with me, please," he said.

The man back of the desk in the small, hot office said, "This is heroin. Four or five grams. Don't you know anything? You can't take heroin across the border."

"It's not my car," Will said, "and it's not my heroin. I don't know anything about it."

"Come on," the officer said.

Will told him what had happened.

"Wonderful. Where did he go?"

"I don't know. He said he had diarrhea. So then he'd go to the nearest john, wouldn't he? Only it was a lie. He sucked me into driving the car so he wouldn't get caught. He's probably across the fence waiting for me. Go find him. Go ask him."

They found Hoffman without trouble. But he said:

"No, man, we came down here together to score and we scored. Will told me he had the deal lined up. It was his idea. He had the money, he had the contacts. All he didn't have was the car. So we had to use my car. Shit—now look what's happened!"

What had happened wasn't all that unusual. But the case of *William Digby* v. *United States* grew into a landmark episode in the history of the polygraph. I came into it this way. James Garcia of the Federal Defender's office in San Diego telephoned me in Los Angeles. I listened to his description of what had happened to Will Digby with less than complete attention. It was too familiar, and I was deep into several complicated cases at the time that were keeping me jumping.

"There are good examiners in San Diego," I said. "What do you need with me?"

"They've already tested him," Garcia said, "And he came out

118

fine. But I want to take the charts into court. You're court-qualified, and they aren't."

"Oh, no," I said. "I don't like courtrooms."

"Hell, you've done it before. Lots of times."

"And you know how it goes," I said. "You're a lawyer. You've probably done it yourself. First the defense sets you up. They make you give your qualifications till you sound like you ought to be able to heal the blind and raise the dead. Then the other lawyer zooms in and tears you up for bragging, and makes you look like you can't tie your own shoelaces, or worse, like you steal pennies from little children. Sure, you live through it—sometimes you even win—but no way can anybody say he likes it."

"It's very important," Garcia said. "Digby is a good kid, Chris. A fine, decent boy. All he wants is a chance to go to college. If he loses this case, his whole future goes down the tubes. And he's innocent. You test him. You'll see."

"It's not a major case," I said. "Why is a federal judge going to admit polygraph evidence on a simple case like this one?"

"Because we're moving heaven and earth to make him," Garcia said. "If I didn't think we were going to, would I have called you?"

"I'll be there," I said, and hung up with a sigh.

The plane trip to San Diego is a short one. Up out of the morning overcast in a wide, lazy swing over the blue Pacific and the channel islands, then down to Lindbergh Field. It takes all of twenty minutes, and the last are a little bit breathtaking. I can't think of another approach to a major airfield where you seem literally to fly down the main street of the city. I didn't look on this particular day, though; I was deep in books and papers. My lap was stacked with them. Because while this was in name going to be William Digby's trial, what would really be on trial would be the polygraph.

This meant that I would be the prosecution's main target. If they could put me in a bad light, throw me by tricky cross-examination, make me answer with the wrong words, shake my concentration, not only could Digby go to prison for buying and attempting to smuggle heroin, but polygraph evidence might not get another chance in federal court in the West for a long time. A lot depended on me, and I wanted to be sure no question came my way that I didn't have an answer for. Between now and the date set for Digby's

119

trial, I was going to put myself through polygraph school all over again.

Garcia was busy. The telephone kept ringing. Clerks kept hustling in and out with armloads of heavy law books that they stacked up on a table with legs of tubular steel obviously brought in for the purpose. Garcia's desk was already overloaded. He hung up the phone and smiled apology at me.

"You're really going all out for this case," I said.

"It's a classic," Garcia said. "The outlines are perfect. If we can't get polygraph evidence admitted this time, we never will."

"What outlines?" I said.

"Digby drove another boy's car. The border patrol found heroin in the trunk. Digby didn't know anything about it. The other boy, Hoffman, says Digby bought it and put it in the trunk and the whole thing was his idea. He turned state's evidence to avoid prosecution."

"For what?" I said.

"Being a party to attempting to smuggle heroin."

"If he's so innocent, why is he acting guilty?"

Garcia pawed among the papers on his desk. He had to stand to reach across the stacked law books and hand the file to me. "He's a user," he said. "Three previous busts. Digby never used anything stronger than pot."

I leafed through the file. Garcia's investigators had done a thorough job. I felt better now. He was young, but he had a grip on this case. He was burning a lot of energy, but intelligently and efficiently. He meant to go into court and win. Nothing less was going to satisfy him, and if he couldn't get Digby cleared in San Diego, he was going right to the top, to the U.S. Supreme Court if necessary. I liked him and was pleased he'd called me in. The phone rang again, Garcia snatched up the receiver, and I had a few minutes to read through what the investigators had learned about Digby. That pleased me too. When Garcia hung up the phone, I said:

"Send Digby to Los Angeles, will you? I want to examine him in my own office on my own equipment. I don't want any noise, any distractions."

"He doesn't want to miss any more school than this has already cost him," Garcia said. "Saturday all right?"

"Fine with me," I said.

William Digby had an earnest look about him. He wore the jeans and T-shirt that are the high school uniform of today. His hair was long. He had the normal golden tan of the San Diego kid who spends time on the beach. He was no scholarly drudge. But what Garcia's investigators had found out about him said he meant business about getting a good education and ending up a lawyer. Now he stared at me, unbelieving.

"You want me to what?"

"Have a urinalysis," I said, "at the medical lab on the next floor in this building. It will only take a few minutes. It's not painful. Did you think it was painful?"

"I know what a urinalysis is," he said.

"And do you know why I want you to take it?"

"To see if I've been shooting up," he said. "Wow! I can't believe this. Did you tell Jim Garcia you were going to do this to me?"

"Have you been shooting up?" I asked.

"No!" he shouted. "I don't use narcotics. Didn't Jim tell you that? I drove Hoffman's car to the border station. His car. Not mine. They found heroin in his car. This is crazy."

"It's standard procedure," I said. "This is a narcotics case. I was hired by Jim Garcia to clear you of any suspicion if I can. What you say and what Jim Garcia believes are none of my business. My business is to prove the truth. It's called objectivity. It's called the scientific method. It doesn't imply anything against you or for you. If you have been using narcotics, the polygraph tests I give you will be all bent out of shape. If you haven't—and I have no reason in the world to think you have—then I can go ahead with the tests, and you can get on PSA and be back in San Diego in no time."

"The lie-detector dudes in San Diego didn't make me take any urine tests."

I looked at my watch. "Shall we go now?"

He hadn't been shooting up. But his resentment toward me for making him take the urinalysis showed up on the preliminary tests I ran on him. It was righteous indignation, but it threw off his reactions. I had to calm him down before we could get on with the tests themselves. When I had him willing to crack a smile again, it wasn't

121

long before I could free him from the polygraph attachments. His spoken reactions matched his physical ones exactly. His account of what had happened in the hot noon Mexican sunlight at the border that day was true.

"If it had come out I was lying," Digby told me, "it would only mean polygraph tests are worthless."

"I think this one will be worth plenty to you."

A shadow crossed his young face. "I hope so. Jim says they don't like admitting lie-detector evidence."

"If anybody can make them," I said, "he will."

I drove him to the airport. In the bustle of the PSA terminal he shook my hand. "I'm sorry if I was rude," he said. "You were only doing your job."

When he'd left, I went to a booth in the bar and telephoned Garcia. He was pleased but not surprised. He'd had no doubts about William Digby. He'd been absolutely sure my tests would clear the boy and confirm those already given him by the San Diego examiners. "I'll want your written report as soon as possible," he said. "And when can we get together? There's a lot to talk over. I'll be honest—I'm worried about your attitude toward testifying."

"I don't let it show," I said.

"I've never seen you on the stand," he said.

"I've been there," I said. "Don't worry. I'm as keen about this as you are. I won't wreck it for you."

We met where we wouldn't be bothered by ringing telephones and reviewed the case every step of the way. Garcia had boned up on the polygraph. There was little or nothing he didn't know about the instrument and the legal ins and outs he was about to go up against. We were on identical ground. I'd swilled a lot of midnight coffee, doing my homework for this case. It had left me tired, because I'd been carrying a heavy workload in my office and in the field—sometimes twelve or fifteen hours a day. But I was ready. Nobody felt stronger than I did about the viability of the polygraph. I was grimly determined to convince the court of its accuracy and usefulness.

"I want to put on a demonstration," I said.

Garcia blinked. "In the courtroom?"

"I've done it in a hundred places," I smiled. "Why not in a courtroom? That's where it will make a difference."

He looked doubtful. "I don't know, Chris. I've got F. Lee Bailey coming to testify. He's bringing his own polygraph expert, Zimmerman. Lynn Marcy will be here, and Robert Brisentine from D.C."

"That's an impressive lineup," I said. "But what they say will carry more weight after the polygraph has been shown in action. You know what the prosecution will do—try to prove it's not accurate, not reliable, that there are too many human factors involved."

"Suppose your demonstration misses?" Garcia said. "We'll be finished before we even start."

"It won't miss," I promised.

But I was nervous when the youthful Garcia approached Judge Samuel Sullivan at the high bench to ask him to permit something to happen that had never before taken place in a federal court. I had some doubts as to whether I could keep down my breakfast, the little of it I'd been able to swallow. The judge gave his permission. Then I was too busy to worry about my nerves. A bailiff was assigned to be the subject of my demonstration. When I'd fastened on the respiration tube, blood-pressure cuff, and electrodes, I asked him to think of a color, then answer no to every question I asked him. After a few questions, I was able to tell him the color he'd picked—yellow. Then I had him choose a coin, without telling me which one of the handful he'd taken. Again he answered no to all my questions, as I'd instructed him to do, and I was able to tell him he'd chosen the nickel. A courtroom is a quiet place normally, but the stillness in this one as I gave the tests was as if no one was even breathing. That stillness cracked when the test was finished. There were gasps and murmurs. I saw smiles. I breathed again.

My hours on the witness stand went the way Garcia and I had carefully planned them. I first had to account for my experience, my training, my background. Then I had to detail how the polygraph worked in establishing whether a suspect or witness was telling the truth or attempting to use deception. I cited some of the statistics I've given earlier in this book on the reliability and accuracy of the polygraph in laboratory and field-work testing. Then I had to face the prosecuting attorney for cross-examination. She had done careful research and her questions were probing and skillful. But when I left the stand at the end of the court day, exhausted as I felt physically, I was certain James Garcia and William Digby had a very good chance of coming off winners. On the plane ride back to Los Angeles, I dropped into the first easy sleep I'd had in several weeks.

"They brought on a good local polygraph man," Garcia told me on the telephone the following evening. "He had it all laid out as to just why the courts have been right to ban polygraph evidence all these years. But I don't think he impressed the judge. You did. Zimmerman and Marcy and Brisentine did."

"You're sure that's not just what you want to think?" I wished I'd been able to be in that courtroom to see and hear for myself, but I had too many cases underway in Los Angeles. I said, "After all, precedent weighs on every judge. He's being asked to overturn a lot of history."

"There are watchers at this trial," Garcia said, "who aren't on anybody's side. They say we're out in front by ten lengths and going away. You should have heard F. Lee Bailey."

Bailey, a renowned trial lawyer, has argued for years in favor of polygraph evidence. I don't know what he said in court that day, but he has written: "In these troubled times when courts are backlogged . . . and lawyers and judges are forced to rely on a system where mendacity among litigants is more often the rule than the exception, the polygraph technique could precipitate dramatic . . . improvement in our law . . . Litigants and witnesses . . . not inhibited by an oath will, knowing that means of checking . . . is available, make [fewer] appearances . . . If guilty defendants are persuaded to plead guilty because of the presence of the polygraph in our column of scientific evidence, good will certainly be the product . . . Fingerprints, firearms identification, chemical tests for intoxication, blood tests for paternity, and even mechanical devices for measuring a motorist's speed, have all contributed to the accuracy and reliability of the judgment of a court. The time has clearly come for the adoption in our system of this invaluable aid to judicial accuracy."*

*The Polygraph Story, J. Kirk Barefoot, ed., American Polygraph Association, 1974.

"How soon will we know?" I asked Garcia.

"The judge wants time to study the testimony. And that has to wait until the court reporter has typed it up. 'A few weeks'—that's the way Judge Sullivan puts it. Don't sweat it, Chris. I'm sure we've won."

"I hope you're right," I said, and hung up. I very much wanted things to go Garcia's way, not just for the sake of young Digby, whom I genuinely liked, but for the sake of the polygraph. Judge Sullivan had a chance here to hand down a landmark decision. With the precedent of a federal court's acceptance of polygraph evidence to go on, it would figure that lower courts would finally unbar the door. I didn't have time to worry about it. My secretary rang through. Another attorney was on the line, wanting a polygraph examination for a doubtful client.

It wasn't weeks, it was months before Judge Sullivan gave his ruling. It had to have been a trying time for him. Appellate court decisions had excluded the polygraph both times tries had been made at gaining acceptance for it in California. When I had a moment to reflect about Digby's case, I got the sinking feeling that, however well Judge Sullivan thought of the expert testimony Garcia had brought to the stand, in the end he wasn't likely to risk a reversal in this case that would be a carbon copy of the two reversals already made by the appellate court.

Unhappily, I was right. Sullivan said that he had been impressed by the defense testimony. He felt that polygraph evidence should be admitted because of the accuracy of the instrument. But the appellate court's denials of admissability of polygraph evidence in earlier cases made it impossible for him to rule in our favor. I was in the courtroom, thoroughly depressed, on the sunlit morning when the judge gave us the news. He then asked William Digby to stand before the court and receive his sentence. At that moment, I wished I were somewhere else. I'd been the boy's main chance for acquittal on a charge of which I was positive he wasn't guilty. And I'd been unable to help him. I shut my eyes and bowed my head.

The judge's words reached me, all right. But it took me a stunned second to grasp what he'd said. He had sentenced William Digby to a term of "four years of college." He'd added a minimal fine of $750. But technically, this still meant the boy was guilty, and Garcia was upset and angry. He grimly appealed the sentence to the Ninth Circuit Court in California. I don't know how much hope he had. I didn't have any. The precedents were too heavy. They upheld Judge Sullivan's decision.

In fact, William Digby both lost and won. He wanted more than anything else to complete his college education. He was assisted by the court, and at this writing is about to receive his degree. Jim Garcia continued to do an outstanding job as public defender in San Diego and is now in charge of the Los Angeles Federal Defender's office. One of his investigators was so impressed with the polygraph during the Digby case that he asked to be trained as an examiner. He was sent to New York, where he finished among the top ten of his class. He has since left the Federal Defender's office and is now conducting polygraph examinations in the San Diego area.

I haven't heard from William Digby, but I'm sure he will ring my telephone one day, or stop in at my office—either as an attorney or a polygraphist. He is a bright young man who should go far in whatever he chooses to do.

11

Tentacles of Death

The *Columba* clunked her wooden hull against the ancient hewn stones of the jetty. Like her hundred sisters rocking on the dark bay, she was painted white. But in the murk of sky and sea surrounding her these last moments before dawn, her wallowing, broad-beamed shape looked dirty gray to Roger Fanne when he looked down at her from the top of the cobblestone street between looming warehouses. He smiled wryly to himself, this lean American boy in worn jeans, a duffel bag slung over his shoulder. Dark figures stood in a circle on the jetty. The wives and children of fishermen traditionally came down to see husbands, fathers, lovers off. But the *Columba* was no fishing boat—not anymore. No nets bulked up darkly on her splintery deck. She was not heading out after sleek schools of anchovy.

She had different business now. He didn't much like it, but beggars couldn't be choosers. He had to move on. He had no money to buy passage on any of the glossy white liners that fetched tourists here, nor even on rusty freighters. He didn't want to sign on as crewman. The freighters went too far in directions he wasn't ready for. He aimed to see the world, but in short hops. And he'd had it with this big old port city. If he'd wanted to stay in one place forever, he could have remained at home in Kansas. He went down to the jetty, boot heels waking echoes off the warehouse walls, dark rats dragging scaly tails out of sight behind broken crates to get out of his way.

He recognized the captain's filthy white cap. The man gave him a sullen nod. The black eyes of the women with shawls over their hair watched him. He didn't know why—they'd never seen him before, they'd never see him again. Maybe just because he was tall and blond, and the men here came short and swarthy. A girl smiled shyly. He didn't know what that meant. He hadn't been able to get close to any of the girls in this place. The people were old-fashioned, prudish. Not that they were unfriendly, really. They'd fed him their grape-leaf foods, poured him glasses of their turpentine wine, asked him about America, joked with him, even taught him a couple of their wild dances—only the men danced here. But he was leaving as much a stranger as he'd come.

Now, at a jerk of the captain's head, Roger went to join the four young men in sweaters and knitted caps loading cartons over the scarred gunwales of the *Columba*. The cartons were crisp and heavy and required careful handling. As he worked wordlessly, he marveled at the crazy, zigzag voyage those cartons must have traveled to end up here—from Switzerland, Germany, Japan. *Omega*, their labels read, *Seiko*. Fine watches. Contraband. Duty on them ran high along this jagged seacoast. Which meant there was profit in smuggling. In the cafés, he'd learned it was common. Easy too. Officials were poorly paid, like everyone here. It didn't take a lot of money to make them look away. So, if it wasn't the most honest job he'd ever accepted, it wasn't all that criminal. And there was small chance of getting caught. The *Columba* would skulk in and out of tiny ports under cover of darkness. Or she wouldn't dock at all but would stand out from shore, waiting for small boats to come from hidden coves to take on whatever they could afford.

Now the last of the cartons was off the jetty. Daylight edged the sea, outlining rocky islands. Gulls began to try the air above the fishing fleet, the anchored freighters. The women on the jetty murmured and kissed their men. The children clung to the sailors' legs. The men swung on board. The old engine coughed, spluttered, its noise echoing off the shut-up warehouses turning pale with the coming day. Exhaust fumes tainted the clean sea air. The rusty anchor chain rattled. The captain shouted to Roger from the bow. He ran forward to help coil a tarry hawser. The *Columba* bumped the jetty hollowly one last time and, rocking on the dark tide, nosed bluntly toward the open sea.

The crew quarters were cramped. Roger banged his head on thick low beams a few times before he learned instinctively to duck them. When the sun beat down, there oozed out of the old planks the stink of fish from the *Columba*'s honorable past. Roger's fellow crewmen had a stink of their own—tobacco, garlic, sweat. The bunks were shelves not carpentered for leggy Americans. There was no place to store your gear. The men stumbled over it, and over each other. Luckily the weather held fine. There was no need to spend time below decks. He slept under the stars. It was easy to sleep. A crummy old hulk like the *Columba* took work to keep it going. He was tired when his watch ended.

He woke sometimes in the night to see shadowy figures moving at the gunwales, to hear the muffled putter of small outboards, whispers. Moonlight showed him cartons passed overboard into waiting hands below. He turned over and went back to sleep. Except on the fifth night out. That night he was wakened by a difference he couldn't at first isolate, blinking his eyes. The darkness was closer, and something subtle had happened to the sway of the boat, the sound of the water lapping its sides. They were in port. The cartons were being handed upward to figures waiting on a dock. Buildings hulked up square-shouldered in the blackness. He slept astern. He got up to go to the rail to relieve himself. He looked down at the black water. And something white and shiny floating there caught his eye.

Up on the dock someone hissed a curse. Someone dove into the water. The splash was unmistakable. Someone swam, very awkwardly. Roger swung over the bulwark astern and let himself down hand over hand on a painter that hung there, bracing his bare feet against the scabby curved planking of the *Columba* where her painted name showed faintly in the dark. He lowered a hand into the greasy water and fished up the shiny white object. Then the swimmer's pale face was turned up to him, streaming. A dripping hand groped out. "Thanks" was spoken in the language of the place. Roger put the slippery plastic packet into the hand. He climbed back aboard but he didn't sleep any more that night.

"The next mainland port we stop at," he told the captain, "I want off." It was early morning.

The captain stared from his bunk. Roger had knocked sharply, then pushed into the small cabin. The timbers of the *Columba* creaked as she tilted through the blue water. The quavering whine of the drive shaft was noisy in here. The captain said, "You signed on for the entire voyage. Why do you want to quit? I have treated you well. I will pay you as I promised."

"You're not just moving watches," Roger said. "You're moving narcotics—heroin, morphine, I don't know. But I know I don't want any part of it."

"How did you find out?" The captain sat up, heavy belly sagging in a skivvy shirt. Black hair matted his chest and thick shoulders. "Which fool told you?"

"Nobody had to tell me. I saw it."

"You saw nothing." The captain spoke lazily, getting out of his bunk. "Whatever you think you saw—you saw nothing." He kicked into his trousers. It was done quickly, as a man learns to do at sea in a leaky old craft. And when he turned, there was a knife in his hand. It had serrated edges, the sort of blade best for slicing open the bellies of fish. The captain said. "You will continue this voyage until we reach the last port, as we agreed."

"I only want off," Roger said. "I won't say anything about the drugs to anyone. I just don't want to be associated with that kind of smuggling, all right?"

"You are an innocent American," the captain said. "You are outraged by matters you do not understand. You will go to the police." He shook his head grimly. "No. You will stay aboard. You will do your work. You will say nothing to anyone about this. And when the voyage is over, you may go your way." He stepped close to Roger. The point of the knife was a pinprick in the boy's belly. The man's breath was fetid. "But if you try to leave before the *Columba* is empty of cargo, before we have finished our business, before we have upped anchor and set out for home—well, you will not see your home again. We will take care of you right here aboard the *Columba.*" He turned away. "Now get out of here."

He bunked aft that night on the shuddering deck, as always. The captain had thrown him sharp, threatening glances all day. Another crewman, a bony youth with a scar beside his mouth, had seemed to dog his steps. But after supper they'd all gotten drunk on retsina and he'd been forgotten. He was alone now except for the man in the wheelhouse, and his back was turned. Off to port, hills outlined themselves in black humps against the stars. He slid out of his clothes, bundled them into a slicker, and crouching, heart knocking, he crept to the railing. He legged quickly over it and slipped into the smooth swells soundlessly. The water was warm. Nudging the bundle ahead of him, he swam for shore.

He arrived footsore a week later back at his room in the port city where he'd signed aboard the *Columba.* His dour, skeletal landlady had agreed to keep a box of possessions for him until he sent for them. Now he decided to take them with him—and to get out of this country for good. The captain and crew of the *Columba* were careless, drunken louts. They would be caught. And for drug smuggling, they'd be lucky if they weren't sentenced to death. It would come out that he'd been part of the crew. He wanted to be far, far away, and in a hurry. If he sold his camera, he could buy an air ticket for Italy, France, or Germany. He left for a pawnshop he'd seen near the docks.

There, he was arrested. One of the black-eyed women who had been on the jetty that morning seeing off the *Columba* came to the door. The young girl who had smiled at him that morning was with her—and so were two police officers. The woman jabbered fiercely, stabbing a finger at him. With the black shawl over her hair, she looked like some ancient sybil crying doom. He couldn't understand half her words. All he could make out was that she was accusing him of murder.

That was what he was jailed for. That was what he was tried for. The murder of the entire crew of the *Columba.* She had been found only a couple of days after he'd left her, abandoned and breaking up against a reef. Roger Fanne was formally charged with killing the entire crew, stealing and wrecking the boat, and attempting to flee the country. At the trial, the black-shawled woman, the children with voices like that knife blade the captain had pushed into Fanne's belly, kept screaming that he was a murderer, a vicious creator of widows and orphans. The lawyer the state had appointed for him hardly opened his mouth in the boy's defense. He was sentenced to die before a firing squad.

A few days later, and many thousand miles away, I crossed the lawn, still wet with dew, in front of my house to pick up the bulky Sunday edition of the Los Angeles *Times*. I liked to get a crack at it over coffee before eating breakfast, getting dressed, and going to church. In pajamas, robe, and slippers, I spread the paper on the kitchen table. On the front page was a three-column photograph of a thin young man standing in front of a public building in a Mediterranean country, surrounded by police. Under the picture was the caption: *As God knows, I am innocent of murder*. In the sunlit hush of that suburban Sunday morning, I read with growing dismay the columns of gray print that told Roger Fanne's story. When I finished the last word and reached for the mug in front of me, the coffee in it had grown cold.

I took the front section of the paper into the dim bedroom where my wife still slept. I drew back the curtains, sat on the bed's edge, and shook her shoulder. She murmured a small protest and came awake, blinking against the dazzle of the windows. "What's wrong?"

"Read this," I said. "Please. Right away."

"I don't understand," she said.

"You will," I said.

She did. After she'd read it, sitting propped against the pillows, she looked at me. "He's pleading for somebody to help him. I guess that's going to be you, isn't it?"

"That's what I wanted to hear," I said. "Now, how?"

"Phone Dave Reynolds," she said. "What you need is more information. He's with the wire service. He might be able to fill you in."

I rang Reynolds at his home, forgetting that most people aren't up at sunrise on Sundays. Luckily, he was an old friend. His voice came hoarse from sleep when he picked up the phone. But when he recognized me, he was good-tempered. "This has got to be something special," he said. "President been shot?"

"No, but some poor kid from Kansas is going to be unless I get moving. I want your help." I gave him the gist of the story. "Read it and give me your advice."

He was back to me in fifteen minutes. "I see what you mean," he said. "Let me wire our man over there. You want to polygraph the kid, right? To see if he's telling the truth?"

"I'll pay my own way over there," I said.

"I'll get back to you," he said. And he did. The American correspondent had got permission for me to examine Fanne. "But you're going to have to move fast," Reynolds told me. "He's set to be shot in a couple of weeks."

Meantime, I'd placed a call to Roger Fanne's mother, who ran a small diner in a little Kansas town. She returned my call and filled me in on Roger's background. He didn't sound to me like the kind of kid who was going to end up slaughtering crewmen on a smuggling ship. Soon after she had hung up, my phone rang again. The caller was a former high school buddy of Roger Fanne's, spearheading a movement in the town to save his friend's life.

"If you're going over there," he said, "why don't you stop off here on your way: There are a lot of people here who've known Roger all his life. You ought to talk to them."

Then came a call from a powerful Kansas newspaper. They'd started a fund to help pay for Roger Fanne's defense.

It was night before I took a chance and left the telephone. I drove to my office in Hollywood to pick up portable polygraph equipment and a tape recorder. The next morning I boarded a plane for Kansas. Fanne's friend Davis, who had telephoned me, met me with a bunch of young people at the airport. They drove me to the motel where they'd arranged for me to stay, and sat with me for hours filling me in on the kind of boy Roger Fanne was.

"He couldn't kill anybody," one of them said.

"That's crazy," said another. "He was a pacifist. He was wandering around the world, sure. What he wanted to do finally was get back to the Far East."

"See, he was in the Navy," a girl said, "after we all graduated from high school. And he loved the Far East."

With very little help, Fanne's mother ran the small café on her own, so it was late before I could talk to her. She was a plain woman, showing the weariness of years of hard work and the strain of worry about her son. But that someone had appeared out of nowhere to try to help him cheered her. She talked to me freely, and some of what I heard shocked me. She had mortgaged the diner to try to pay Roger's legal costs. "I've sent that lawyer, Mattias, more than ten thousand dollars." She smiled wanly. "I guess that's not a lot of money to most folks these days. It's an awful lot to me."

Without saying so, I thought it was ten thousand dollars too much. According to the *Times*, and according to the wire-service correspondent on the scene, the government had appointed Mattias. He was a public defender. The State was supposed to pay his costs. I had trouble getting to sleep. The more I learned about Roger Fanne and what had happened to him, the more certain I became that a thorough investigation and a polygraph test were desperately needed in this case. The next day, the newspaper presented me with their check for $1,200 from their readers to help me get there and do whatever I could for Roger Fanne. Twelve hundred dollars paid my air fare and excess baggage charges exactly. A meeting was held so I had a chance to thank the townspeople.

Then I was aboard a 707 headed for New York. We came down through thick black clouds and into heavy rain that made a mirror of the long runways at Kennedy. The rain held up my flight and everyone else's for three long hours. In the crowded terminal, I overheard people talking about that American boy doomed to face a firing squad on the far side of the Atlantic. At last the rain slacked off, and my big, wide-bodied jet lumbered down the airstrip and lifted into a clean blue sky of broken clouds. It was night when we landed at the ancient capital of the country that had condemned Roger Fanne to death.

"They're mad as hell at me," Rich Andrews said, "and at all the other American correspondents." Andrews had met my plane and was helping me lug my heavy equipment out of the terminal toward his car. "Overseas phone calls, telegrams, all kinds of pressure is coming from the States. They don't like it. It affronts their national dignity.''

"How dignified do they think it looks"—I loaded the boxy polygraph and tape recorder into the trunk of Andrews' little European car—"to shoot a twenty-year-old kid?''

"You'll find out." He dumped my suitcases into the rear seat of the car. "How much chance do you really think you've got? Even our letting the news out in the States made them sore as hell.'' He got into the car and slammed the door. I got in on the passenger side. He said, "Once they find out you're here, messing into it, they're just as likely as not to set the date forward for the execution.''

"I intend to go very quietly," I said. I shut my door and we drove off toward the lights of the city. "I don't want any publicity. I was stationed here after the Second World War. I know a few people—important people.''

"I hope they remember you," Andrews said grimly.

"For Roger Fanne's sake," I said, "so do I.''

They remembered me. As I've written earlier in this book, I worked in several countries in the late forties and early fifties, helping reorganize and retrain police departments. A few men from that time still held police posts, and one or two were intimately acquainted with the Fanne case. They gave me answers to questions I hadn't had. None of the names in the prosecutor's office were familiar to me, but I talked to a couple of attorneys there who had heard of me. Luckily I was remembered with affection and respect. I learned a little more.

I'd been given the name of a celebrated criminal attorney, Nikos Palamis. I went to see him. His offices were handsome in European period style, with dark wood paneling. But he wasn't a man whom success had made indifferent. As I outlined what I knew about Roger Fanne and my dread of what might happen to him, Palamis' face showed genuine concern. When I said that Roger's mother had mortgaged her tiny restaurant in order to pay the lawyer, Mattias, for defending him, Palamis actually rose half out of his handsome leather chair.

"What? But Mattias had no right to any fee! In this country it is

135

the law that if a defendant has no money to pay a lawyer, he is furnished one by the state.'' Palamis subsided into his chair again, darkly shaking his head. ''The man conducted a miserable defense. I do not believe he had lifted a finger to confirm the boy's story. He did not bring forward one witness who had seen the boy between where he claims he left the *Columba* and here in the city where he was arrested.''

''Then the case ought to be appealed,'' I said. ''The verdict ought to be reversed. Or at least there should be a new trial.''

''Wait until I finish with Mattias,'' Palamis said. ''Taking money for a defense when he was already being paid by the government! I will see to it he is finished.'' He looked at me. ''What an impression this must be making on a stranger from abroad.'' He leaned forward across the darkly gleaming desk. ''Look, Mr. Gugas. Let me help you in whatever way I can. There will be no charge, I assure you.''

''Thank you,'' I said. ''Now, here is what I think we ought to do . . .''

A police launch rocked beside a stone jetty—perhaps the same one from which Roger Fanne had set out on that fatal trip of his. My polygraph instrument in its tough leather case, and my tape recorder, were loaded aboard. A uniformed officer gave me a strong hand and I jumped down into the launch. The powerful engine revved, painters were slipped from their cleats and tossed aboard. We sped in a wide curve away from the grimy waterfront toward the open blue sea and far, rocky islands.

The prison rose up like a fortress, bleak against the clear Mediterranean blue of the sky. White gulls wheeled on sunlit wings around its grim towers. The captain of the prison guard met me at the landing and handed me up out of the launch. Crewmen brought my gear through the heavy prison doors, and down long cold corridors. Walking beside me, the captain praised Roger Fanne. He was a good prisoner. Everyone here, guards and inmates alike, had taken to him. He was teaching some of the prisoners English. Now we stopped at a bolt-studded door. The guard captain opened it with a key. The polygraph and tape recorder were taken inside. The guard captain withdrew and I stepped inside.

And there stood Roger Fanne. He was dressed in coarse wool

clothing. When he shook my hand, his own was cold, and it was blue from the icy air of that place. He was a tall lad, with piercing blue eyes. His face was as gaunt and drawn as had been his mother's back in Kansas. There was a crude table and two stiff chairs in the room. He sat on one, I took the other, and asked him to tell me his story from the beginning, leaving out nothing, no matter how trivial it might seem. I said I wanted to tape-record it all, and at his nod of permission, I fitted the machine with a fresh roll of tape, threaded it, and set the reels turning. What he told me makes up the opening pages of this chapter.

"Did you tell anyone," I asked, "anyone at all, that drugs were being smuggled on the *Columba*?"

"Never," he said. "No one." Those keen blue eyes of his flicked nervously toward the door. "Listen, Mr. Gugas, let's not waste any more time. I didn't kill anybody. I don't know anything about what happened to the boat or what happened to the captain or any of them. I was long gone by the time it cracked up on those rocks. I swear it. Set up your lie detector, all right? I want to be sure to get the test over with before something happens to stop it. To me it's a miracle they let you see me at all. They're trying to make some kind of bad example out of me. A lot of American kids are wandering around Europe right now, using drugs, dealing drugs, smuggling drugs. I'm not one of them, but I'm the one that's going to end up dead so the government here can scare them off."

"Not if I can help it." I took the lid off the polygraph, unwound the attachments, and made Roger move his chair closer to the table. I fitted him with the chest tube, the arm cuff, the finger stalls. I outlined quickly for him the questions I meant to ask. I tested the responses of the instrument. The tape was running. I began. I got through exactly one set of questions when the door burst open. Three panting guards crowded into the small room. "What is this?" I said.

"You must stop," one of them said. "Testing of the prisoner is not permitted."

"But I have permission," I said. "That's why I came here all the way from California."

"The permission has been revoked," the guard said. "Release the prisoner from your machine at once."

137

"Revoked by whom?" I said.

"Our immediate superior."

"On whose instructions?" The guard was reaching for Fanne. I got in his way. "Your immediate superior has no power in this matter. The government—"

He cut in, "His orders come from the government. You may talk to the prisoner as much as you wish but there will be no testing with the instrument."

They watched me detach Roger from the instrument and left. Roger was angry and disappointed. So was I. I knew from his first chart that Roger had been telling the truth. This made me more determined than ever to stay and help the boy from Kansas in every way I could. I packed up my equipment and took the police launch back to the city. In my hotel room, I didn't even take off my jacket. I sat on the edge of the bed and rang up Nikos Palamis. Voice shaking, I told him what had happened.

"Who's responsible?" I said. "What went wrong?"

"This is bad," Palamis said. "I don't know the explanation but I will find it out and ring you back." I was in the shower ten minutes later when the phone jangled. I wrapped myself in a towel and ran to pick it up. Palamis said, "I spoke with friends at the Interior Ministry. It was the minister himself who issued the order canceling your right to question Fanne. The boy has been convicted. Nothing more can be done for him."

"Except to shoot him," I said. "Can't you go higher? What about the Prime Minister?"

"We are of opposite parties," Palamis said. "My intervention would only harm Fanne's cause."

"I'll call him myself," I said.

But the Prime Minister was out of the country, and no one else had the power to intervene in the Fanne matter. I then hurried into fresh clothes, caught a taxi in front of the hotel, and headed for the American Embassy. A lean, cool, soft-spoken undersecretary told me:

"We've done what we're allowed to do under international law. We assisted Fanne in getting legal counsel."

I was outraged. "That's all you did?"

"We had an embassy man at the trial." He spread his elegantly

138

kept hands. "The crime took place on foreign soil. It was our obligation to see that he had a fair trial and he did. There's really nothing more—"

"Fair trial!" I exploded. "Look, with the help of Nikos Palamis, I've investigated that so-called trial. It was a farce. That wonderful attorney you got him never lifted a finger. No attempt was even made to establish Fanne's whereabouts when the *Columba* went on the rocks. The government introduced testimony that Fanne had thrown the boat's anchor overboard. No one alive could have seen that if it had happened, yet the defense never questioned it. Dozens of impossible allegations were made against the boy that Mattias didn't even murmur about. You want to know the truth about Mattias? He accepted ten thousand dollars from Fanne's mother back in Kansas to defend her boy. He had no right to a fee. The government was paying him. He never even prepared for the case. He spent his time in Paris with that money—on wine, women, and song!"

"That's a serious charge," the undersecretary said.

"I have documented proof," I said. "Roger Fanne deserves a whole new trial, and I mean to see that he gets it. Now, are you going to help me or not?"

He rose with a small, regretful smile. "I'm sorry. I've already told you. There's nothing we can do."

There was something I could do. I telephoned Nikos Palamis and arranged to hold a press conference at his offices. Thanks to my wire-service friend, Rich Andrews, correspondents were there from every major newspaper in the world. Better still for our purposes, the local newsmen turned out in force. Nikos Palamis told them the true story of Roger Fanne, coming down hard on the sloppy trial, the poor government case, indifferent police work, the failure of the courts to make certain justice was done. Our investigations had convinced both of us without doubt that the polygraph examination results of Roger Fanne's tests were correct. He was not guilty. Everything our men in the field turned up afterward confirmed this.

The next morning, newspapers made a dramatic stack on my hotel room bed. Every one of them reviewed in detail the shabby handling of the Fanne case and brought out the new evidence of his innocence that Palamis and I had turned up. There were even paragraphs about my anger at the failure of the U.S. Embassy to act. While I ate my croissant and drank my coffee, the radio crackled in my ear. Its news was filled with the Fanne case. And before the day was out, what I had hoped would result from the press barrage happened. The Ministry of the Interior temporarily suspended Roger Fanne's death sentence and announced that it would review the case.

When I next saw Roger Fanne in that bleak stone fortress on the island, he was able to give me a wan smile. It still depressed me to see him clad in those clumsy, coarse woolen prison clothes, to see him down to skin and bones, eyes haunted with worry. But at least, I told myself, his ordeal was probably nearing an end. He shook my hand and thanked me.

"I didn't do it alone," I said. "Nikos Palamis gave up a lot of time, a lot of cases, to work on yours for no pay. I can't even name for you all the people that helped us dig up material—reporters especially."

"What's going to happen to Mattias?" he asked.

"The Bar Association has gone after him. Conduct unbecoming an attorney. False swearing. I can't remember all the other charges. He's finished. And he deserves it."

"What's going to happen now?" he said.

"I'm going back to Los Angeles," I said. "God knows what's happened to my business." I had come here for a weekend and it had turned into a month. "But don't worry. You've got a lot of friends now. News people especially. They'll be watching. If the government tries anything off-color, it'll make headlines."

"Can you call my mother for me when you get back?"

I did so, only to learn that the crooked attorney, Mattias, had bled her for still more money. Determined to give everything she had to save her boy, she'd sold her furniture and the prized possessions of a lifetime. I doubted that she'd ever again see any of the money Mattias had extorted from her. I hated what had happened, and wondered what I could do to make life a little less grim for her. Names rolling past on the television screen that night gave me an idea. Among them had been that of a producer who was an old friend. From my office the next morning—where I'd found every- thing in perfect shape despite my thirty days' absence; I ought to

140

have known my wife would keep things going as they were supposed to—I telephoned Jed Walker. I didn't have to detail the Fanne story for him. Like most Americans, he knew about it from the close coverage U.S. newspapers and television had given it.

"I'd like to tell his mother she can go visit him," I said, "all expenses paid. She's sacrificed everything to help him. Can you help me raise the price of a round-trip air ticket?"

"What are you doing for lunch?" he said.

We met. As always with Jed Walker, the hour and a half was pleasant. When the coffee cups were empty, he pushed his aside, took out a checkbook, and wrote out a check. He tore it from the folder and passed it across to me. It was for the full amount the trip would cost Mrs. Fanne from Kansas to Europe and back. Knowing already what I'd see, I looked at the signature. *Santa Claus*, it read. That was how Jed Walker avoided the embarrassment of being thanked by the hundreds of people he aided. Only his bank and one or two close friends knew the man who stood behind that special signature. I don't have to tell you that his name is no more Jed Walker than it is Santa Claus. But he is a very real person, warmhearted and generous.

Mrs. Fanne visited her son at that craggy island prison. The newspapers made much of the story. But the news that followed wasn't what she or any of us who had worked to free Roger hoped for. He was refused a new trial. Perhaps it was the government's stubborn way of insisting that it had made no mistakes. On the other hand, the Minister of the Interior recommended that the death sentence be revoked, and the Prime Minister signed the paper that saved Roger Fanne from the firing squad. Still, he remained locked up in that cold, dank prison. If he'd been given back his life, that life was still a grim one.

Americans kept protesting, but the government stood fast. They asked why the embassy had done nothing to help Roger Fanne. They got the same answer I had received—and I want to underline it here. An American who gets into trouble—civil or criminal—in a foreign country can count on no assistance from U.S. embassies or consulates that can be construed as interference with the government of the host country, other than the recommendation of a local attorney to represent him.

Before and since the Fanne case, I have worked in a number of countries. Their systems of justice are not like that of the United States. They are slow and cold. You are guilty until proven innocent, and this can mean sitting for months and even years in rotten prisons, waiting for the courts to take your case. Yes, I love the United States, with all its faults. It's a grand place to live and work. I have no desire to live anywhere else because we still have the best system in the world when it comes to law enforcement, the courts, the penal system. I'll take my chances with our juries and appellate courts over any legal procedures of Europe or Asia.

I only wish more Americans would take the time to travel outside the United States. They'd be far better able to appreciate what we have here. Our press is free and strong. It acts on our behalf, and is not afraid to print the truth. In other nations, censorship is severe. Editors who dare challenge those in power often end up silenced and imprisoned. If it had not been for the press, Roger Fanne might have been executed for a crime he did not commit. I want to thank here the press and its dedicated reporters for their help in many of my cases over the past thirty years. Their diligence often made the difference between success and failure.

For the next two years, I received frequent letters from Roger Fanne in prison. Then abruptly they stopped coming. I tried to telephone his mother in Kansas. She had left the little town where Roger was born and grew up. No one seemed to know where she'd gone. I telephoned Rich Andrews, overseas.

"You were supposed to keep an eye on Roger Fanne," I said. "What's happened to him?"

"Nothing, as far as I know," Rich said. "Isn't he still locked up?"

"Maybe," I said. "But he's stopped writing me and I'd like to know why. Make sure he's all right, will you?"

He was all right. The government had secretly set him free. He'd been cautioned to say nothing to anyone and to leave the country at once. Evidently the authorities had made it clear to him, in that dark tower, or on the launch putt-putting at midnight toward the sleeping city, that harm would come to him if he didn't obey instructions. For I never heard from him again. I don't know where he is now, but I keep expecting him to show up at my office one day to tell me what happened after his release. I hope for his sake it's a cheerful story. He's had his share of horror.

12

Rape
of a Marine

The year was 1953. The place was Camp Lejeune in North
Carolina. I'd asked to talk to the Commanding General. I had only
two weeks and I wanted to make them count, so I was pleased not to
be kept waiting long.

"What's this about the polygraph?" the General asked.

"I think the Corps can reduce the number of criminal cases it
has to handle by giving polygraph examinations," I said. "I'm
willing to give the tests. You've seen my record. You know I'm
qualified. I think the polygraph can clear up a lot of cases where
there are doubts."

"I don't know much about it," he said.

"Let me demonstrate it for you," I said.

He did, and I ended up assigned to work with the base investigators. At the end of my two weeks, I was able to report to the

General that in 60 percent of the cases I'd handled where suspects plainly showed on their charts that they were lying, I'd gotten confessions from them. This meant a substantial saving of man-hours and money that might have been wasted in trial hearings. I was, as I always am, more pleased to be able to report that a number of Marines charged with crimes ranging from robbery to grand theft had been cleared by means of polygraph examinations.

The General looked up from the written report I'd handed him. He laid a hand on it. "Major," he said, "this is damned impressive. I'll tell you what I'm going to do. I'm going to request Headquarters in Washington to begin a program of training for qualified Marines to become polygraph operators."

Headquarters agreed. That fall, the Army's polygraph school accepted a number of Marine sergeants for training, and the polygraph program was underway. In the years that followed, the annual two-week training course I'm required to attend as a Marine Corps Reserve officer has meant for me working as a polygraph examiner with the criminal investigation section. I always look forward to this duty, and I've run into some fascinating cases over the years—none more so than that of one Marine accusing another of rape.

"This is touchy," said the warrant officer charged with reviewing the case. "This female noncom, Underwood, has gotten a career sergeant, Finley, suspended from duty."

"Career?" I said.

"He's been in the Corps fifteen years. He's got so many distinguished service medals he walks bent over. A war hero."

We sat in a sunlit office with windows that viewed a long inlet from the sea. A blue heron stood among the reeds. Somewhere in the distance gunfire rattled on a rifle range. Farther off there was the endless murmur of the surf. I leafed over the papers in a folder on my knees. "She's been in for only four years," I said, "but she's got all sorts of commendations here. No disciplinary actions of any kind. It doesn't make sense."

"They're the wrong types to get into this kind of mess," the warrant officer agreed. "That's why I want you in on this."

"Let me talk to the investigators," I said.

Both investigators were sturdy, fair-haired, blue-eyed officers, serious about their work. I asked them to go through the case for me step by step. "Before I can give any kind of meaningful test, I have to have every bit of background there is," I said.

"Well, first," the investigator named Taylor said, "her story sounds plausible. Underwood's, I mean."

"She was pretty hysterical," investigator Dunn said.

"How did it start?" I asked.

"They went to dinner in Dago together," Taylor said, "then on to a nightclub. They both drank."

"Neither one of them admits to being intoxicated, though," said Dunn. "About her, I'm not sure, but he'd taken on a pretty good load, in my estimation."

"Didn't you test him?" I asked.

"He stormed around demanding urine, breath, blood tests, anything," Taylor said. "But this was hours afterward, too late for the tests to really tell us much."

"Where did they go after they left the nightclub?"

"They parked along the beach somewhere, not far from the base. The girl says they kissed each other. The sergeant says there was more. She let him run his hand around on her breasts and her stomach, he says. Then they had intercourse. She didn't offer any resistance. She wanted it to happen. He says."

Dunn said, "She claims he got rough. He made her masturbate him. Then he knocked her around until she was forced to let him have intercourse with her. She says she kicked and screamed and tried to fight him off." He shrugged. "Nobody out there can tell us. Seals, sea gulls, and they would have been asleep anyway."

"You got the story from her?" I asked.

"She told her captain first," Taylor said. "A woman captain, Jordan. She got the story at the base hospital where they took the girl to get a medical examination."

"Sperm was found in the vagina," I said. "That's in the file folder here. She'd had sexual intercourse, all right."

"Yes, but I don't think she fought him," Dunn said. "I don't think he manhandled her like she says. The doctor didn't find any bruises or scratches. There was no evidence that force had been used."

"Torn clothing?" I asked.

146

"I don't think so," Taylor said. "It's in the property room, being held for evidence." He got out of his chair. "Let's go have a look."

Blouse, jacket, skirt, panties—none was torn or damaged in any way. I dropped them back into the box and pushed it across the counter to the Marine in charge of the property room. I looked at Taylor and Dunn. They looked at me.

"Those are the sheerest panties I ever saw," I said.

Taylor laughed. "Sure as hell not Marine issue."

Dunn said, "Anybody tried to rip those off a girl, they'd have ended up in shreds."

"Yet she says he ripped off all her clothes," I mused. "Isn't that what she told you?"

"She did, but it doesn't add up."

We pushed out of the property room through the wood and glass swinging doors. Walking down the plain wooden corridor with the two men, I asked, "What did Sergeant Finley have to say about her clothes?"

"That she let him take them off. She did it willingly, freely. He not only didn't use force or threats, he didn't even have to coax her."

"And I don't exactly believe him, either," Dunn said. "It was the first time he'd ever taken this girl out. And her record doesn't read like a tramp's—no way."

"Threats wouldn't show up," Taylor said. "Not in torn clothes, not in bruises. He's a big strong guy."

"But can you call it rape?" Dunn wondered aloud as he held open the door to the office where we'd started our meeting. I picked the file folder up off the chair where I'd left it. "Let's try to find out through the polygraph," I said. A telephone stood on the desk. I nudged it toward Taylor. "Call the attorney the Corps has appointed to defend Finley. Get his permission, get Finley's, and let's do it tomorrow morning."

Dialing, Taylor grinned at me. "Any special preparations—like for an X-ray exam?"

"As a matter of fact, yes," I said. "He shouldn't take any alcohol or any medications tonight. And he should get a lot of sleep.

Oh, and tell the lawyer he can't be present during the examination. That's standard procedure.''

A room was arranged for me in the Provost's offices. The two Marine investigators were anxious to witness the examination but I told them what went for the lawyer went for them or anyone else who wanted to be present. Anybody else in the room while a polygraph test is being given is an invitation to distraction for the subject and inconclusive results from the test. This is why the ideal polygraph examining room is soundproof, windowless, with plain walls and no pictures, the barest minimum of furniture, no patterns to curtains or carpeting.

The sergeant arrived looking fresh and confident. He was handsome, six feet tall, his uniform was crisp and sharply pressed, his shoes had a mirror finish. There were four rows of combat ribbons on his shirt. His eyes were clear and his manner professional. I asked him to sit down and tell me the story from the beginning. If he deviated in any way from what he'd told the investigators, the discrepancies could tell a lot. He reviewed the incident from the time he had picked up the girl until they'd had intercourse. In no way did he change anything he'd told the investigators.

"If that gadget works the way it's supposed to,'' he said, nodding at the polygraph instrument on the desk, "you'll see I'm telling the truth.''

It worked the way it was supposed to. And he was telling the truth. I was careful with the structure of the question patterns. I worded the key questions to avoid any possibility of double meanings or misunderstandings. I didn't stop with test number one, though I was almost certain from those charts that Finley wasn't lying or trying to lie. I went on to a second test and a third. All of them proved he'd told the truth in every detail. As I unfastened the polygraph attachments, I told him so.

"You see?'' He rose and stretched.

"But why should this young woman want to do this to you?'' I asked. "It makes no sense at all. Obviously she liked you very much. What made her turn hysterical and start screaming you'd raped her?''

He shook his head. "You've got me. She was perfectly willing.

We'd had a nice dinner, a nice evening. And, believe me, Major, she enjoyed the sex we had as much as I did." Shrugging into his jacket, he gave a wry laugh. "I understand she's even claiming she was a virgin."

"It's in the investigator's records," I said.

"I don't care where it is," Finley said. "She'd had sex before. Often. She's got a steady boyfriend. It happened all the time. Oral sex too. She told me all about him, all about what they did together. He's back East now, but he's due in California in a couple of months. Then they plan to get married."

"I hope to test her this afternoon," I said. "Meanwhile, don't say anything to anyone about how you came out."

When Corporal Underwood arrived at the Provost's offices, she wasn't alone. No more than five feet three inches tall, she had a lovely figure that was enhanced by her snappy Marine uniform. With her was her captain, a stocky woman of forty with a stubborn set to her jaw. The girl didn't have a chance to speak. The captain did all the talking. She was here to protect the girl's rights. She would sit in on my examination. She would sit in on the polygraph tests.

"I'm sorry," I said, "but that's impossible."

"Then we're going." The captain took the girl's arm.

"You can remain in this room," I said. "You'll be no worse off than Sergeant Finley's attorney. He wasn't allowed in the examining room either."

"Corporal Underwood will not take the test unless I can be with her," the captain snapped. "I am here to protect her rights."

"Her rights won't be violated," I said. "I'm an impartial examiner, Captain. I'm only interested in getting at the truth in this matter. As I'm sure you are."

Her mouth twitched. "What questions are you going to ask her?"

I didn't have to answer that, but I didn't want any unpleasantness that would upset the young woman. I asked her to step out of the room and reviewed the questions with the captain.

"Those don't sound impartial to me," she said. "Of course she was raped. Why should she say so if she hadn't been? Don't you

149

know the humiliation a girl brings on herself when she cries for help in such circumstances?'' She glanced sourly around. ''Especially in an all-male atmosphere like this?''

''The questions have to be simple and direct,'' I explained, ''clearly worded, easily understood. They all have to be answerable with a simple yes or no. This is an unpleasant matter we're looking into and there's no way to make the questions pleasant. Now, Captain Jordan, I'm not going to remind you that I am a Major and you are outranked, but I am going to advise you that by trying to block this test you're only hurting Corporal Underwood.''

She looked pale and started to blurt angry words, then thought better of it, clamped her mouth shut, and sat down hard on a stiff chair. ''Very well,'' she snapped, ''but I'll be out here with my eyes on that door every minute.''

In the examining room behind that door, Corporal Underwood was nervous. She looked tired. Strain and sleeplessness had dulled her eyes. She willingly signed a waiver permitting me to tape-record the examination. She crossed her shapely legs, making certain I saw the gesture. She smiled at me winningly, sweetly. But when she tried to light a cigarette, her hands shook. When I began asking her about what had happened that night in the car with Sergeant Finley, she rolled her eyes and sighed, as if to say she was sick to death of the subject.

''Have you seen your written complaint against the sergeant?'' I asked.

''I read it this morning in the captain's office.''

''Is it correct? Tell me what happened in your own words, please. Maybe there's something you forgot.''

''I'll never forget any of it,'' she said. But she did as I asked. Unlike Finley's, her account varied a few times from the way she'd told it earlier. I didn't call the discrepancies to her attention. But she would become aware of omissions, back up, and then repeat word for word what was in the report. The presence of the polygraph instrument seemed to worry her. She kept eyeing it. Finally she said:

''My boyfriend once took a polygraph test at a police station. They told him he failed. But he hadn't lied to them. I don't believe in lie-detector tests.''

I smiled and rose. "All right. Let's see whether I can make a believer out of you. Just let me attach these things. It won't hurt." As I went about the job, I told her, "I'd like you to think of the names of five men, including your boyfriend. When I ask you the names, you just answer no to all of them, including his. All right? And can you give me five women's names too, please. Include your oldest sister. And when I ask you those names, you just answer no to all of them. Got that?"

She was under tension. I thought I had the right answers on the first chart but I double-checked with a second test. I'd been right the first time. I gave her her boyfriend's name, Hal, and her sister's name, Mildred. Those lovely eyes of hers opened wide. She said something with a shaky little laugh. I didn't catch the words but it was easy to see that having become convinced that the polygraph worked, she was more nervous than before.

"I have to go to the rest room," she said.

"All right," I said, "but come straight back, please."

She went out quickly and shut the door. But it wasn't a sound-proof door. The walls of the barrackslike Provost office building were thin, and I heard her talking excitedly. I stepped to the door and asked her to return. The captain glared at me. She had a grip on the young woman's arm again. It looked as if she was trying to lead her away. If I hadn't stepped out of the examining room when I did, I might have found an empty outer office. Wordlessly, Corporal Underwood came back inside with me and I shut the door. The tests took very little time. She delivered her answers, "Yes" and "No," in a very quiet voice. Her readings on the chart showed strong emotional tension. After the second test I was sure she'd lied.

"All right," I said, "let's try one more time."

"No," she said, "I can't. I feel sick."

"Relax," I said. "Just sit back and let your stomach settle down. You'll be all right."

"No, I won't," she said, "I'll never be all right again." And she burst into tears. I handed her a box of tissues. She groped out blindly for them. It was minutes before she could stop sobbing. She dried her face, blew her nose. Sniffling, hiccuping, she said to me in a wobbly voice, "You don't have to waste your time, Major."

"I guess not," I said. "Why did you put Sergeant Finley

through all this? Don't you realize you very nearly destroyed him?''

She nodded mutely, unable to look at me. She said in a soft, choking voice, ''I was afraid I'd get pregnant. I'm not a virgin the way I said. I had sex with my boyfriend—with Hal. But we always used something—for birth control, you know? And with the sergeant, it didn't happen like that.'' She blinked helpless, scared eyes at me. ''I was in my fertile time. I was sure I'd get pregnant. If Hal found out, he'd kill me. So what I thought I had to do was claim I was raped, don't you see? Then if I was pregnant, I could get a legal abortion or terminate the pregnancy or something—because it was rape. Hal and I are supposed to get married in a few months.''

''Then Sergeant Finley didn't rip your clothes off?''

''No,'' she whispered shakily, looking away.

''He didn't use any kind of threats or force?''

She mutely shook her head. She looked at me. ''I'm sorry. I didn't want to hurt him. I was just trying to save myself. Will everything be all right now?''

I said gently, ''You'll have to repeat what you've told me now to the investigators who questioned you before—and to your captain.''

She stood up, hands to her mouth. ''Oh, no,'' she said, shaking her head. ''I can't tell the captain. I can't.''

''We'll save it,'' I said, ''until after we have your written statement. She can read that.'' I rang for the investigators, Taylor and Dunn. ''Come straight in to me,'' I said. ''Don't talk to the captain in my outer office.''

But when they arrived, the captain asked to come inside with them. I told her she'd have to wait. It surprised me that she didn't kick up a fuss. She was well known for making trouble with the criminal investigation section when any of the young women in her charge were in trouble. Maybe she had suspected from the first that Corporal Underwood hadn't told the whole truth in this case. She'd stood up to me as best she could. Now she must have sensed that no action on her part could turn things around. That was what I thought. How wrong I was.

After Taylor and Dunn had advised Underwood of her rights, had listened to her revised account of what had happened that night with Sergeant Finley, and after she had written out the statement in her own hand, I stepped to the door and invited the captain in.

"Corporal Underwood was lying," I said. "She's admitted it."

"What! Let me see that paper." She snatched it from me, ran her angry eyes over it, then flung it down on the desk. "How did you get that? What kind of browbeating methods did you use on this poor girl?" Her arm went protectively around the corporal's shoulders. "Men!" she blazed. "You make me sick. A girl can be beaten and raped and you only shrug. But let one of your own sex be accused of rape, and it turns into gentle lovemaking." She laughed contemptuously. "And why not? What's easier than confusing and upsetting a girl who's already on the verge of a nervous breakdown after what happened to her? Of course she said what you asked her to say. Anything to get away from your kind."

"Now, just one darn minute," Taylor objected.

"Captain," I said, "calm down. You're way out of line."

"This doesn't say so!" She snatched up the confession again and waved it under my nose. "She told me she'd been raped. She was in tears, she was hysterical." The captain whirled on Taylor and Dunn. "She told you she'd been raped. And now, suddenly, she wasn't raped. Am I supposed to believe that? Really? Would any thinking person believe it?"

I said to Taylor and Dunn, "Take the corporal out of here, will you? Give me a few minutes?" They led the young woman out and shut the door. The captain lunged after them. I stood against the door, holding up my hands. "Not you," I said. "Not yet. You're going to sit down right here and listen to me. That's an order, Captain."

Furious, face flushed, mouth working tightly, she stood for a moment, glaring at me. Then she turned sharply and took a chair. I went to the desk and rewound the tape on the machine that stood there. She stared:

"Do you mean to say you recorded that girl without my permission?"

"I didn't need yours," I said. "I had hers. She signed a waiver." I held out the slip. "Here it is."

"I don't want to see it," she said. "It doesn't mean anything.

You probably threatened her with God know what unless she did sign it."

"Be quiet, Captain," I said. "Not another word from you. You're out of control. You don't know what you're saying. You are wide open at this moment for a charge of conduct unbecoming an officer, and if you don't think I'll press that charge if I have to, you have another think coming. It is also clear to me, and I think officers Taylor and Dunn will bear me out in this, that you have made every effort to interfere with and impede an investigation. We can and will press that charge, too, if you insist."

White-faced, she said nothing. Her eyes on the tape recorder, she listened to the pre-test interview, she listened to the test questions and the answers Corporal Underwood had given. She listened to the tearful breakdown that followed, and Underwood's remorseful outburst. When the tape began to produce nothing but a soft hiss, she raised her eyes to mine.

"I'm sorry," she said stiffly.

"Did you hear any browbeating?" I asked. "Was your corporal abused or mishandled or threatened in any way?"

"No." She stood up. "I'm sorry, Major. If we had more investigators like you, I wouldn't worry all the time about my girls being taken advantage of. You're thorough and honest. But there are other investigators here who—"

"They have to follow regulations," I said. "And the regulations are strict. You know that. You know what they are. And you know that any time any investigator gets out of line, you can file charges."

She didn't comment on that but she thanked me again for clearing up the matter. So did the sergeant's lawyer. And when the Commanding General heard how the case had come out, he called me to his office. After I'd run through the whole story for him, he smiled delightedly. Better even than his smile and his warm handshake was his promise to set up soundproof, air-conditioned examining rooms with the newest polygraph and recording equipment for the criminal investigation section.

Corporal Underwood was discharged from the Marine Corps "for the good of the service." Sergeant Finley now holds the rank of Lieutenant Colonel. Investigators Taylor and Dunn have solved hundreds of cases and cleared many Marines of charges through use of the polygraph. Their results tally with those at other bases throughout the armed services. Unhappily, new restrictions have been clamped on the use of the polygraph by the military, following recent congressional hearings. And while I welcome standardization of procedures to end abuses and assure uniform fairness, still the restriction that demands that every examination must have prior approval by a higher-echelon officer has resulted in a tangle of red tape which has deprived many accused servicemen of a reliable aid in clearing them of suspicion.

13
The Professional Five

Los Alisos was a suburb of curving avenues under handsome old trees. Fronted by well-tended lawns and flower beds, the houses sprawled, comfortable, expensive. The building style was mostly Spanish California—thick white walls, iron grillwork, red tile roofs. The morning was sunny and quiet. It wasn't yet nine o'clock. Glossy estate wagons, driven by beautifully groomed young matrons, rear seats loaded with bright-eyed, shiny-faced children on their way to school, purred past me as I checked addresses. A mockingbird sang overhead as I went up the walk to Bernard Maxwell's door.

"Gugas?" The man who opened the door was a successful corporation lawyer. He was lean, with clear dark eyes and prematurely white hair. "I'm glad to see you. Come in." I stepped inside and he closed the door. He turned the bolt. Too late. He'd been robbed the night before—jewelry, sterling tableware, a valuable coin collection. This meant he'd joined more than twenty of his Los Alisos neighbors whose homes had been plundered over the past two months. He led me through a long living room with low arched windows into a study. He spoke as we went. "This thing has got to stop. I've attended neighborhood meetings. It's nothing but talk, talk, talk. I've written the papers—so have we all. The police put on more patrols. But do they ever catch anyone? No."

"You've had your own citizens' patrols too," I said. "Armed with CB radios—right?"

"They see no evil, they hear no evil," Maxwell said. "Sit down." He gave me a crooked smile as he took a high-backed leather executive chair behind a glossy desk. "It's pleasant to welcome somebody besides a burglar alarm salesman."

"It looks as if you should have bought," I said.

He barked a laugh that had no humor in it. "Waste of money. Someone lets the burglars in. They know exactly where to find what they're after. It's servants. It has to be."

"A lot of people have hired private detectives," I said. "They haven't traced anything to any servants."

"Yes, well—they've given them lie-detector tests, too, haven't they?" Maxwell smiled. "But the people they've had in to investigate, the people they've hired to give the tests, haven't known their jobs." He snorted. "Any more than servants do these days. But they ask the moon when it comes to wages. And make one misstep in how you talk to them—for instance, asking them actually to do some work—and they're off to another employer."

"It's your own people you want me to give polygraph examinations to," I said. "How long have they been with you? You don't trust any of them?"

"In my father's time, they were with you when you were born, and they were still there when you died," Maxwell said. "Nobody's been with me more than a year or two."

There were a housekeeper, nanny, maid, a cook and her helper, a houseman-chauffeur, and a gardener. The study was quiet but still not the ideal place for polygraph examinations. Yet none of the servants was disturbed. The raw nerves belonged to their employer, not to them. They had clear consciences and not one of them was put off by the polygraph or by the direct questions I asked them about the missing jewelry, silver, and coin collection. I had reported the negative results to Maxwell and was packing up my gear when the police detectives working the case came in.

"They're smart professionals, Mr. Maxwell," one of them said. "They don't need inside help. Just layouts—the sort of knowledge anyone familiar with the place might have."

"Who?" Maxwell snapped.

The detective shrugged. "If we knew that, we'd have the case solved. We'd have them all solved."

"You said it yourself," I pointed out. "Servants don't stay, they keep shifting jobs. Homeowners here don't change. It could be someone who worked here years ago."

"I feel helpless," Maxwell said, "and I don't like that." He eyed the detectives. "You say the thieves are professionals. What about you, aren't you professionals?"

The detectives shifted their feet uneasily. They were well set up, well groomed. They weren't used to taking criticism and they didn't like it. Their jaws set. "We are, and we'll catch them. It's only a matter of time."

"Meanwhile, they're smarter than you are," Maxwell said. "Meanwhile, they're someplace in these twenty square blocks right now, rifling someone else's home, while you stand around here."

The detectives left, stiff-faced, not showing their anger. When I went down the path to my car to load in the polygraph equipment, they were still parked on the street. I shut the lid of my trunk and walked over to them.

"What does your spot map suggest?" I asked.

"That son of a bitch," one of them said.

"What spot map are you talking about?" the other asked.

"Haven't you got a map on the wall at your office?" I asked, astonished. "Of Los Alisos? With pins stuck in it to show which houses have been hit?"

"What for? We all know which houses have been hit."

"You might be able to see a pattern," I said. "You might be able to predict where they'll break in next."

The detective at the steering wheel looked at the other. He

jerked a thumb at me. "Look who's telling us how to do our job."

They didn't seem to me to be doing it. I'd thought Maxwell was only showing bad temper. Now I wondered if perhaps he hadn't been right. What I'd suggested was basic to any investigation of crimes that follow a pattern, like the Los Alisos robberies. There was another procedure I couldn't believe they'd have overlooked.

"What do your informers tell you?"

The driver turned the ignition key. The unmarked car's engine started. He kicked free the parking brake. "We don't need informers," he said, "any more than we need Maxwell, or you." The car slid away.

I wasn't that surprised. In real life, things aren't quite the way they show up on the television private-eye shows. Most police detectives and their superiors take a dim view of outsiders trying to help them. When Barnaby Jones or Jim Rockford are depicted working hand in hand with the police on an investigation, you had better believe that's fiction through and through. It makes no difference how experienced the private investigator might be, the police simply do not want anyone getting in their way. The same goes for television and newspaper people, who can break a story prematurely and scare off suspects the police have been hoping to surprise. On the other hand, newsmen and women have solved many cases where poor or halfhearted detective work has produced nothing. And sometimes the time and attention a good insurance investigator, for example, can give to a case, can bring about a solution where the police, with too many crimes to solve, can't manage it. Unpleasant as these detectives were, I didn't want to get in their way. At the same time, I was with Bernard Maxwell and the other citizens of Los Alisos in wanting to bring the burglaries to a halt. Maybe there was something I could do about it . . .

Ted Wheeler grinned a welcome to me across the counter of his small TV and stereo repair shop. He'd done time in Chino—and put it to use, learning the skills that let him set up for himself in an honest business once his sentence had been served. I'd tried to be of some help to him, and he hadn't forgotten. The day was warm. He stepped next door to a hamburger stand and brought back a couple of soft drinks dense with ice in paper cups. Then he opened the counter flap for me and we sat in his workroom, drinking the Cokes, talking, surrounded by the blank gray faces of dismantled television sets.

"Who's doing the Los Alisos jobs?" I asked him. "Who's back of them? It's got to be a gang. It's got to be professional. They're making the police look like idiots. It's getting to be a joke."

"A half-million-dollar joke," Ted Wheeler agreed.

"They don't break in," I said. "Not any way anybody can trace."

"Open windows. Think about those house-cleaning outfits that come in once a week to polish floors and do things like that. Can't they forget to lock a window after they wash it?" He smiled faintly. "But who needs them? Most of those places have dumb back-door locks, the kind you can slip a credit card between the frame and the door."

"What do they do—dress up like plumbers?"

"Sometimes. One of 'em always carries a toolbox."

"You know them," I said. There was, in fact, not much Ted Wheeler didn't know—and if you gave him time, he'd even find that out for you. He'd often been useful to me. He knew every kind of professional thief—in prison, out of prison. "You recognize their *modus operandi*."

"Coveralls only sometimes," he said. "Mostly business suits, neat but not gaudy, right? Haircuts, new shoes. And no repair trucks—they're a pain, you know? Old cars, models nobody would look at twice."

"Pillowcases to drop the lot into," I said.

"Not white ones," he said. "Dyed so they don't show."

"The police aren't getting anywhere," I said. "You better talk to them."

He stared at me. "After what they did to me on that Galindez job? After the way they worked me over? Chris, they damn near framed me."

"There's a team of insurance investigators." I stood up. "With what you know, they could crack this. Will you talk to them?"

"I don't know who it is." He took the paper cup from me, only ice left in it now. He went into a little washroom and I heard the ice go into a handbasin, the cups go into a wastebasket. He came out. "I only know who it could be."

"All they need is names to check out," I said.

"Who they need is the fence," he said.

"And who would that be?" I asked.

He moved his shoulders. "There's four, five, six."

"Will you give the insurance people the possibilities?"

He did. They put six shops under surveillance—antique jewelry, used furniture, paintings, unremarkable side-street operations, legitimate if not very profitable businesses, by the look of them. Patiently they jotted down the license numbers of cars that swung often into the cramped parking spaces back of the shops. When these cars turned out to be registered to known former prison inmates and parolees with convictions for the kind of burglaries now plaguing Los Alisos, the police walked into the dusty hush of R. SHAFER, ANTIQUES, and took the trim, gray-haired owner off to headquarters. He was mannerly, but he wasn't about to assist the police in any way. Since they had nothing on him but the fact that some of his customers were ex-convicts, they couldn't hold him.

"He's a former convict himself," Sherm Richards, head of the insurance investigating team, told me on the phone. "The names of the men that keep turning up at his shop are all on the list of possibles your Ted Wheeler gave us. Shafer is in on those robberies."

"And you want me to give him a polygraph test?" I asked. "Why should he cooperate?"

"He's got a big ego," Richards said. "The police gave him polygraph tests and he beat them. He's smooth and smart—for a lawbreaker. He's already agreed to let you test him."

Shafer looked like the typical dealer in square pianos and murky second-rate oil paintings. He wore tweeds. He smoked a pipe. His manner was quiet and his speech educated. I wondered to myself what kind of figure he had cut at San Quentin. He had known a number of housebreakers there. I had their names. Most of them tallied with the Ted Wheeler list. I explained that these names would be part of my test questions, along with inquiries about the Los Alisos burglaries.

"That's fine with me, Mr. Gugas," he said. "I'd like to have this over with, now. I'm getting just a shade weary of police harassment. So are my family. I'm not in the crime business anymore. It seems to me time I was left alone."

"You don't know anything about those thefts of jewelry, coin collections, and silver?"

"Only what I've read and seen on the TV news."

"You haven't heard anything about who might be responsible for the thefts?"

He looked at me with amused blue eyes. "Not a word."

"Sit over here, please," I said. "Now what I'm going to do is—"

He gave a quiet laugh as he sat in the chair beside the polygraph instrument. "You don't have to explain to me how it works. I've been tested before. It's never helped anyone but me."

"Fine," I said. "But I'll need to check out your responses to the instrument. Here's a box of coins. I'll step out of the room. You 'steal' a few of them, write down what you've taken on this slip of paper, then total up the amount." I gave him a minute, then came back and switched on the instrument. "All right," I said. "Now answer 'no' to all the questions I ask you. That way you'll have to be lying sometimes and telling the truth others."

"I never had this kind of test before," he said, a little uneasily. "What's it got to do with anything?"

"Everybody isn't a satisfactory subject," I said. "I need to see whether you react normally."

The test worked perfectly. When we checked my readings of his chart against the list of coins he'd taken and his tally of their value, I came out 100 percent. He gave a grudging show of amusement at the test but I thought he looked a little flushed. Was his self-confidence slipping? Had he sensed that instead of smart he'd been merely lucky with the police polygraphers? There was no question that he was impressed with the instrument's accuracy. I thought he was also beginning to be scared.

My list of housebreakers numbered fifteen names. I told him I was going to read them off slowly. The overall question to which he had to answer yes or no was simply: Were any of these persons involved in the Los Alisos burglaries? I told him that I would then ask him whether he himself was in any way involved in the burglaries, or had any knowledge of them whatsoever. He agreed with a murmur and a nod and sat quietly through the test. But before it was over, his face glistened with sweat. I ran him through the list and through the questions a second time, changing the order particularly of the control questions—those that meant nothing to the thrust of the test but allowed me to check out Shafer's physical condition, breathing, blood pressure, when for an instant tension was broken. I ran still another test. I detached him from the instrument and showed him the charts.

"This is where I mentioned Ron Houston," I said. The pens had moved sharply. "This was Norm Glazer. This was Ken Stewart." I saved the best for last. Every time I'd read aloud to Shafer the name Hector Rodriguez, the reaction indicators had peaked. Shafer was staring now at the jagged lines. "That one?" I said. "Oh, that's Rodriguez. He was the leader of the Los Alisos gang—right?"

Shafer almost coughed himself into a fit. Finally, gulping, gasping for breath, he nodded. He wiped his eyes with a handkerchief. "Okay, okay," he said hoarsely. "Rodriguez is right. But, look, I can't tell you anything else. Don't ask me."

"I've got four names," I said. "You told me without being able to help it. You can't change it back."

"That's all right," he said stubbornly. "I'm not saying another word. I never told you anything. Those guys are killers. It would be worth my life." He hurried into his jacket. "I'm getting out of here."

"Did you think you could really beat my tests?"

"Not after that stunt with the coins," he said. "I ought to have cut and run right then."

"You have to talk to the insurance people," I pointed out. "They paid for this test. You agreed to it. They're waiting outside, remember?"

"Too bad," he said, "but I'm not talking. All I'd get for it would be a shallow grave in the desert." His smile was wry. "And that's not my idea of death with dignity."

But he was in too deep. The insurance investigators convinced him that after the polygraph test, there was no point in his standing mute. The damage had already been done. Within five days, the police had picked up and jailed Houston, Glazer, Stewart, and, most importantly, Rodriguez. The Los Alisos burglaries stopped. From the shops the insurance investigators had kept watch on, much of the jewelry and other stolen valuables were recovered and returned to Bernard Maxwell and his neighbors. Some of the stones from rings, necklaces, and bracelets had been pried loose and the settings melted down, but there hadn't been a lot of time for that.

The housebreakers, all of them men with long criminal records, were sent to prison. So was the fake-antique dealer whose failure to fool the polygraph machine had resulted in the breaking of the case. He hadn't been behind bars for long before he was savagely beaten. It wasn't quite a shallow grave in the desert, but it was the next worst thing. Who attacked him? Prison officials never learned that. But criminals don't forget those who inform against them. Shafer had been right to be afraid.

14

The Greedy Minister

Galilee Church formed a handsome new complex on donated land in an old section of Los Angeles. The trim tan stucco buildings framed a courtyard—steepled church on one side, Bible college at the rear, evangelical mail-order publishing plant and bookstore in the other wing. Two morning services were not enough to accommodate the eager crowds who came flocking every Sunday to heap the collection plates with money, and to listen spellbound to the sermons of the sleek, white-haired, honey-voiced man in flowing purple robes who called himself the Reverend James Bishop.

Students at Galilee College crammed the classrooms. The list of prayerful high schoolers waiting to get in was long—it didn't matter that the fees were steep. Mail trucks backed up to the loading bay door of the publishing firm daily to pick up bundles of books for every corner of the globe, while into the front door flowed an endless stream of orders accompanied by fat checks. Rev. Bishop had advice, counsel, and comfort to spare—even for the lonely and unhappy, the old and the sick, who sought him out in person. Admission to the hushed church parlors and his own ineffable presence for a spiritually soothing hour cost only ten dollars a time.

No wonder James Bishop always wore a tranquil smile. He had it made. But time flies when you're having fun, all good things must come to an end, and one morning the Reverend James Bishop woke up in deep trouble. I'd glimpsed the stories in the *Times*. A couple of old women from the congregation at Galilee Church had handed over to James Bishop their life savings, their houses, and the contents of their safety-deposit boxes, on the minister's firm assurance that in this way they were securing for themselves a special place in Heaven. For some reason, they'd now changed their minds.

"They claim he hypnotized them," James Bishop's attorney told me on the telephone. "The Reverend wants to take a lie-detector test to prove to them and to the world that that charge is absolutely false."

"But did he take their money?" I said.

"And property deeds, stocks and bonds, jewelry," the attorney said. "Absolutely. As offerings to the Lord. They were gladly and freely given. It happens all the time. People love the Reverend Bishop. They can't think of enough ways to praise and thank him for his ministry."

"Why is this happening, then?" I asked.

"Jealousy," the lawyer snapped. "The other churches in the area are furious. Their sanctuaries stand empty because they have nothing to offer. They see their congregations swarming into Galilee Church. They're trying to destroy it by smearing Rev. Bishop."

"You mean the old ladies were plants," I said, "put there by the other churches to frame him?"

"That's exactly what I mean," the lawyer said. He gave a scornful laugh. "Hypnotized them, hell. They fell all over themselves to dump everything they owned in his lap. I've seen it happen."

"There are other problems, too, aren't there?" I asked. "I seem to remember the Internal Revenue boys are upset because your Reverend isn't paying enough income tax. The police bunco squad

166

is in on it, too, am I right? Some of the parishioners think he's fleecing them.''

"I'll send you the documents," he said. "It's all a conspiracy to bring down a wonderful spiritual leader. You'll see that when you read what's happening."

The stack of complaints and depositions was a thick one. The lawyer hadn't given me any idea of the number and variety of charges being leveled at his precious Reverend. There was no end to it. There was also no way I could examine him on everything in the files the attorney had given me, and I rang him up and told him so.

"There are twenty charges here," I said. "What do you want me to examine him on?"

"All of them, of course," he said.

"A polygraph examination doesn't work that way," I said. "It can handle only one or two subject areas. Give me specifics. Tell me what you regard as most important."

"They're all vicious lies," he said. "They're all important. You pick out whatever you want to."

"That wouldn't be right," I said. "This is your case. Surely you've got some idea what you need in order to defend him in court. Talk to him and call me back."

The next day the attorney walked into my office with a list of more than a hundred questions he wanted me to ask James Bishop on the polygraph. This man had plainly never made use of a polygrapher before. I was appalled. I didn't know whether to laugh or cry.

"A polygraph examination is limited to only four key questions," I said, "and they all have to be on one specific issue." I handed back the list. "You check off the important ones, and we'll go from there."

He stared. "But—but you're the best polygrapher in the state. I've checked your references. Surely you're joking. Four questions? How can you find out anything that way? This is a complicated case."

"I'll talk to him about all the matters you've brought up," I said. "A test takes only a few minutes, but I'll spend hours with your Rev. Bishop, examining him on every aspect of the case, and his life and background before—"

"Life and background?" the attorney gasped.

I tapped the stack of papers he'd sent. "You didn't include a biography and career summary here," I said. "If you've got it, that will save us time. From all I gather, Rev. Bishop is a busy man. You did check up on his background, didn't you?"

"What for? He's been a minister of the Gospel for twenty years. What are you implying?"

"Only that the prosecution is going to check up on every move he's ever made," I said. "You can count on that. It would pay you to know everything they know."

"I couldn't go checking up on Rev. Bishop," the attorney protested. "That would be an insult. It would be worse than that. It would be sacrilege."

"You're going into a courtroom, not a church," I said. "Just how many criminal trials have you prepared for?"

He grew red in the face. "I know my business."

I doubted it, and for a minute I considered placing that stack of information against the Reverend James Bishop back in the attorney's chubby hands and showing him the door. I'd run into lawyers before who knew nothing about criminal law. They not only botched up their client's cases, but they fought me over the results of polygraph examinations I gave that didn't come out the way they wanted. Now the attorney was telling me:

"What more defense do I need than what everybody knows—that a person can't be hypnotized against his will, and even if he is hypnotized, he can't be made to do something he wouldn't do normally."

"I'll go into the hypnotism matter in my pre-test interview," I said. "But I want you to take this pen and paper, here and now, and write me out a short list of the questions you want me to ask on the polygraph itself." He started to argue but I cut him off. "Otherwise, I'm afraid I can't accept the case."

With a shrug and a sigh, he did as I asked. When he'd left, I made notes of our interview. I didn't want a backlash from the inexperienced counselor when and if things didn't go his way. If he believed wholeheartedly in the sainthood of the Reverend James Bishop, I had my doubts. There was an awful lot of smoke for there to be no fire. Still, I kept an open mind, and when Bishop himself

168

walked into my office for his appointment a few days later, I found it hard not to like him on sight. His handshake was firm, his smile warm and affable. He carried a Bible. In the interview room, I asked him to lay it on another chair. He didn't object.

"May I smoke a cigar?" he asked genially.

"I'm afraid not in here," I apologized. "What about a cigarette?" I pushed a pack toward him. He waved it aside, reached into a pocket of his sleek black suit, and produced a diamond-studded cigarette case. It held an expensive, fashionable European brand. When he slipped the case back into its pocket, it clicked against the large, showy gold cross he wore on a chain around his neck. His cigarette lighter was also large, showy, and gold. He flicked it, blew smoke, and dropped the lighter back into his pocket. He glanced at a gold wristwatch.

"This won't take long, I trust?"

"My job is to get at the truth," I said. "How long do you think that should take?"

He didn't have an answer for that. He only raised his carefully trimmed white eyebrows at me for a moment. Then he said, "I have a luncheon appointment. An important one. With an important person."

"You'd better cancel it," I said. "We'll be here a lot longer than two hours."

"Seriously?" He flicked a glance at the polygraph instrument. "I can't think why."

"Because before I can ask you anything, I've got to know something about you. I need to know from you, yourself, the story behind what's happening. There's no other way I can frame intelligent questions and expect results from the instrument that will satisfy you, me, and your attorneys."

He cleared his throat. He moistened his lips. He twitched a sick little smile. "It's—it's all a bit more complicated than I'd been led to expect."

"Not really," I said. "Time-consuming, but pretty direct and easy. Why don't we start at the beginning. Where were you born?"

He stood up. "I'd like to go to the men's room."

"I'll go with you," I said.

He didn't much like that, plainly, but I went along anyway. As he finished washing his hands, he took a small metal container from a pocket.

"Hold it, please," I said. "What's in that?"

He shook pills into his palm and held them out to me. "Valium," he said. "My doctor suggested I ought to take them before your examination. He felt I was under stress from all this nastiness I'm being put through. He thought I'd do better on your test if I were relaxed."

I took the pills and the container. I put the pills back into it, capped it, and handed it back to him. He hesitated, then with a sheepish shake of the head, dropped the cylinder back into his pocket. I didn't care if he took Valium. Clients often take it before coming to me for polygraph examinations and I haven't found it affects the results one way or another. But I didn't want him to take them believing they would help him relax. I wanted him under stress. Besides, I'm no pharmacist. Those pills might have been Valium. They might also have been something stronger—or weirder.

He walked a little more heavily as we returned to the examination room. There was a tic at the corner of his mouth. He ground out the cigarette in the ashtray on my desk and promptly lit another. He'd wanted those pills to quiet his nerves. Now that he hadn't been allowed to take them, his negative reaction to being here and having to face questioning was cracking through the surface. He forgot to use that dazzling, kindly smile of his. He only grunted in response to my comments on the weather and a couple of news events that were causing talk at the time. He was withdrawing, and that wasn't going to get us anywhere.

"You've done a remarkable thing," I said, "starting that church and making it grow the way you have. How did it happen? You're a phenomenon. How did it start? You were going to tell me where you were born."

"Alabama," he said. "My father died before I was twelve. My mother left my brother and me to run off with some man. An aunt did her best to raise us. We were very poor. No chance at anything, least of all education."

"That's remarkable," I said. "You've come a long way."

He smiled. He didn't need pills to relax him. All he needed was

170

flattery. "Religion interested me from the start. When World War II came along I served as a chaplain's aide for four years. Then I went to work for Orrin Swett, a Southern evangelist. You've probably never heard of him, but he was very successful. I found a niche there as public relations man. It seems I have a gift for public relations."

"It certainly does," I said.

"But, of course, that wasn't fulfilling. I wanted to preach. I'd felt the call for a long time. Finally I had enough saved to pay my tuition at a little Bible college." He grimaced. "They couldn't teach me anything. My knowledge of the Bible was miles ahead of theirs. I'd wasted my money. I wasn't going to waste my time. I began traveling, putting up posters, paying for little announcements on country radio stations. I held revival meetings wherever and whenever I could. Making my way west."

"To found Galilee Church?" I wondered.

"That was later. There were other small churches before that. Storefronts, mostly. In one of them I met a fascinating man, a hypnotist. I asked him to speak to my congregation. He impressed them deeply, but I was the one his message struck home to. I've never seen a collection plate fill up the way the ones in that little building did that night. I begged the man to teach me hypnotism. He had engagements elsewhere, but he sold me a couple of books on the art, which he carried with him. Later I attended seminars whenever I got the chance."

"And became an expert yourself," I said.

He gave me a thin smile. "I passed an examination and got my certificate."

"You use the technique a lot?" I asked.

"Never. I had to hypnotize ten subjects in order to qualify. But it's been years since I've done anything with that skill."

"What about at Galilee Church? You know, some of the claims against you are—"

He held up a hand. "Never," he said solemnly. "I have never used hypnotism on any of those people. That's a false and malicious charge."

"You're an expert at faith healing," I said.

"I take no credit for that. It's true, the Lord has chosen to heal through me—and through the faith of those who come to me for the laying on of hands.''

"You've not only built an impressive plant," I said, "but you've managed to collect a lot of money besides. You pay yourself a big salary. And the IRS says you're not reporting half the income you really get.''

His smile this time was martyred. "You know the government's attitude toward churches. It's the sad old warfare over the things which are Caesar's and the things which are God's.''

"I know the quotation," I said. "But what about all those special spiritual enlightenment classes you give? They say you don't deliver. People spend hundreds of dollars to learn how to get results from prayer, and nothing happens for them.''

"It's a highly subjective matter," he said. "I can show you files bulging with letters from men, women, and children who have read my books and give glorious testimony to the truth of what I've taught them.''

"You charge for your books, of course," I said.

"The laborer is worthy of his hire," he said. "The people who claim my counseling has not helped them and their families are troublemakers, trying to destroy me. As to their losing their money—well, somebody paid them to come in and disrupt those classes and try to cast doubt on me. They haven't lost anything. It pains me''—and he looked pained to try to convince me he meant it—''to think of those poor twisted souls being used by jealous and spiteful men who call themselves preachers.''

"You're emptying out their churches," I said.

"By doing God's work," he answered. "The doors of Galilee Church are open to all, regardless of race, creed, or color. Be you high or low, rich or poor, you are welcome. Do you know how many thousands my ministry has helped during floods, tornadoes, earthquakes, both here and abroad—with clothes, blankets, food, medicine, money? And not one cent asked in return. Do you remember that dam that burst in—''

"That's all right," I said. "Let's don't get sidetracked on details. I've had you talking a lot. I don't want you to tire yourself.'' The fact was, I was the one getting tired. James Bishop's words flowed smoothly and without effort. I gave him a list of test questions, got his tense nod of approval, sat him in the chair beside the polygraph instrument, and adjusted the attachments. He folded his hands and murmured a quiet prayer.

But his eyes opened as I took the chair at the polygraph and switched it on. Nervousness showed in the quick movements of his eyes, following my every action. His well-kept hands quivered as he sealed the test coin into its envelope. After running the coin test, and telling him which bit of silver he'd chosen, I saw him moisten dry lips with the tip of his tongue. He had nothing to say, but it was clear I'd convinced him that the polygraph could detect falsehood—and that fact didn't make him happy.

The key questions in the real test concerned his supposed use of hypnotism to coax gifts from church members, and his alleged failure to report accurately on his income to the IRS. He sat motionless, eyes shut, as if in some sort of trance. He wasn't the only hypnotism expert in that small room, and I judged he was working at self-hypnosis. If so, he wasn't very good at it. To even innocuous questions such as, "Is your name James Bishop?" and "Were you born in Alabama?" his physical reactions were strong. After test number one, I asked curiously:

"What upsets you about your name?"

He narrowed his eyes at me. "What? Nothing. Why should it?" I didn't answer and he gave a small bewildered laugh. "As a matter of fact, James Bishop isn't the name I was given at birth. I changed it."

"Did you? And what about Alabama? Where were you really born?"

"I don't even know. My aunt didn't like to talk about my mother—so she never told us boys where it was she'd rescued us from after our mother abandoned us. Some southern state. I don't know which one." He eyed the polygraph, shaking his head in amazement. "You mean that machine can identify something like a changed name and—"

"Any emotional concern you have," I told him, "is going to show up plainly on the graph. Now, suppose we run through the test again, just to make sure of the readings?"

We completed three tests. By that time it was unmistakable to me that he'd lied about the hypnotism and about his income. I undid the attachments. He sighed in relief, and wiped sweat from his face with a fine linen handkerchief.

"Well, how did I make out?"

"Badly, I'm afraid." There was no point in not being direct with him. "You responded strongly to every critical question I asked you. Which is just another way of saying, you weren't telling the truth."

The Reverend James Bishop gave me his softest and most winning smile. His eyes twinkled like two stars on a clear night. "You're a bright young man," he said. He watched me pull the chart off the polygraph instrument and lay it on my desk. "How would you like to join the Galilee organization? You'll have complete freedom to do whatever you like, and I give you my word, you'll make a great deal of money. I've read a bit about lie-detector experts. A good many of them move on to counseling." He chuckled. "Obviously, learning this science teaches them a lot about human nature. Some of them give advice in marital affairs, family problems. I'd like to set up something like that in our organization. How would you like to head up that division?"

"Thanks," I said, "but I don't have the credentials."

"Ah!" He waved a hand. "To hell with credentials. You forget, I have a school. I can grant any degrees I like. Just name it, Mr. Gugas. I'll make you the best-looking diploma you ever saw."

"I think I'd rather earn it," I said. "Anyway, I'm not interested. I'm doing what I want. I'm my own boss. And you're in trouble." I pointed at the charts. "Look here." And I went over his responses with him.

He cocked an eyebrow. "It's a good thing I didn't take a police test, isn't it?"

"Will you tell your attorney, or shall I?"

Bishop's smile was gently chiding. "He won't believe you, you know. He has all the faith in the world in me. You go right ahead and tell him, though. I suppose that's part of your agreement. I'll deny whatever you say, so it can't make any difference to me, now, can it?"

"When he gets into court it can," I said. "He can't defend you if he doesn't know the truth. It won't hurt him, win or lose. But it will hurt you."

174

"Faith can move mountains," he said stubbornly, and bent to pick up his Bible off the chair. "This has been an interesting experience." The smile he gave me now had no charm. It was a cover for anger. "But it won't affect the outcome of this matter. God will vindicate me. I've served Him faithfully. The forces of darkness have hounded me for years. I'm sorry to have to number you among them."

He was getting overexcited. It wouldn't help to try talking sense to him. But I did have a question:

"You tried to hypnotize yourself during the tests, didn't you?"

His laugh was sour. "I never was very good at that." He pulled open the examination room door, then turned back with the old coaxing grin. "Sure you won't consider my offer to come work for me?"

"Afraid not," I said.

With a regretful shake of his head, he gave me that fine, firm handshake of his that said he was the most trustworthy man in the world, and headed off across the reception room, smiling warmly at the receptionist and at a young couple who'd come for an appointment. As he went out the door into the hall, I couldn't help grinning. I liked the old fraud, however disgusting his philosophy. He had a knack for putting people at ease that was the hallmark of every first-rate con man. While he set you up for the kill, he made you feel warm and wonderful.

The next day I had lunch at the Brown Derby with his attorney. "The Reverend Bishop did use hypnotism on those old ladies," I told him. "Not once but three times; the polygraph charts show that. His reactions were plain. And the bunco squad people are going to make a strong case against him. Now, you'd better sit down with him and find out exactly who he's been fleecing and what he's been doing with the money that church is making."

"You can't hypnotize people and get them to do what they wouldn't do otherwise," he said.

"I'm not going to ruin your lunch by arguing with you about it," I said. "But I know hypnotism and how it can be used in exactly the way you say it can't. That's not the point right now. You've got to get him to level with you about what he's been up to, so you can defend him. You mustn't make a God out of the man."

175

"I haven't done that," he said stiffly.

"He warned me you'd believe in him, no matter what I told you." I sighed. "It looks like he was right."

The attorney gave me a pitying smile. "He's always right," he said.

But he wasn't. Not this time. The Reverend James Bishop went off to the penitentiary. Galilee Church closed its doors forever. So did the college and the publishing house. I don't know whether or not the IRS ever collected the tens of thousands in back taxes they had coming. But I do know that the two old women who'd brought the first charges against the sainted evangelist never got back their homes, their jewelry, their stocks and bonds. Nor did anyone else in the congregation who'd ever given him anything. James Bishop may have been only a second-rate hypnotist, but he was an expert magician, whose best trick was making other people's valuables vanish into thin air.

15

Talking with the Dead

Bishop wasn't the only sharp operator I've run across in my years as a polygraph examiner. Southern California, where I have my offices, is a Mecca for confidence games of all kinds, many of them masquerading as religions. Los Angeles probably has more laws on its books to protect its citizens than any other place in the world. It needs them because there are so many smooth, fast-talking sharpies in Hollywoodland that local and state agencies can hardly keep up with the hundreds of rip-offs that yearly cost a gullible public millions of dollars.

Everyone knows that P. T. Barnum said, "There's a sucker born every minute." What is forgotten is the second part of that cynical quote: "—and two to take him." In my experience, Barnum was a master of understatement. A sucker is born every second and, in California, there are a dozen to take him. Hardly a day passes that the police bunco squad isn't called to probe some get-rich-quick scheme in which oil stocks, gold mines, silver mines, and other nonexistent bonanzas have been peddled to investors whose greed outmatches their common sense.

Even more numerous than the phony salesmen are the fortune-tellers, palmists, tea-leaf readers, crystal gazers, Tarot-card charlatans, mind readers, mystics, and spiritualist mediums. It's too easy to pass these off as penny-ante operations. In fact, as long as there are people foolish or desperate enough to believe that some confidence trickster in a dime-store turban can tell them what's going to happen tomorrow, or let them converse with dead relations, or give them the secret to winning at the races, this racket is going to go on making a comfortable living for the crooks who practice it. In big cities, laws against it multiply, but these phonies move fast, and seldom do their victims complain—they tend to keep believing no matter how often they're taken.

The gypsies have told fortunes for centuries all over the world. They still work Los Angeles under cover. My wife and I once lived in an apartment owned by gypsies. The head of the clan was a wealthy woman. She owned real estate all over the city. Anne asked her for a reading to learn what the future held for the Gugas family. The tiny, dark woman fastened Anne with her piercing eyes. She hadn't made a move to lay out the greasy playing cards.

"Honey," she said, "do you ever go to church?"

"Why, yes, of course," Anne said. "I'm Catholic. I hardly ever miss mass."

"Then pray to God for guidance and help," the gypsy woman said. "Your future cannot be told by anyone but God."

I've never forgotten those words, and Anne has never again asked for a reading of the future from anyone.

But my interest in the fortune-telling racket and its thousand variations didn't die. I had a friend in the police bunco squad. His stories about confidence games were always good for a few amazed laughs at the bar we used to go to after finishing our night college classes. One evening, as the jukebox played and young men laughed and chatted around us, he told me of a man I'll call Clyde Vernon, an investigator who made a circuit of the major cities of the U.S. exposing mystics, fortune-tellers, and mediums who claimed they could talk with the dead. Vernon got paid for his work and evidently was good at it.

"You know, he sounds fascinating", I said. "I'd like to write him up for a national magazine."

"I'll get through to him," my friend promised, "and put him in touch with you, if he's interested."

He was interested, and rang me up a few days later. We met that night in a restaurant in downtown Los Angeles that was a hangout for law and police-science students—which I then was. We got a big table, and he held several of us spellbound with his stories of how he'd exposed fraudulent seers and shamans in dozens of cities over the past ten years. Over the remains of our meal and after-dinner coffee, we kept asking for more. He waved a hand.

"They're all alike," he said. "You know the drill. The phony rents a big house, checks out the local society news, zeros in on as many wealthy widows and bereaved husbands with big bank accounts as she can, holds their hands, grieves with them, consoles them. A few at a time, she lures them to the place at night, darkens the room, sits them all around a table, moans a little, has a hired hand in another room work wires and levers that lift the table, float trumpets tooting around in the shadows, and twang guitars mysteriously from overhead."

He paused to drink what cold coffee was left in his cup, grinning and shaking his head.

"It never fails. The medium sits there slumped down in a big, carved chair, eyes shut, chin on her chest, and out of her mouth comes the voice of some little dead child or some mourned-over grandfather. 'It's beautiful over here. Do not grieve. I'm happy and serene. We'll meet again. I love you.' And then the voice begins to fade out. But not before it says something like: 'Don't forget to give Madame Psycho a big fat check.' "

We laughed. He looked at me:

"Did you ever polygraph any of these fakers?"

"A few," I said. "And I've caught most of them lying." I gave him a quick rundown of these cases. "And one thing you're absolutely right about—those big fat checks."

"How'd you like to work with me?" Vernon asked. "If I can get some of these beauties to take a lie-detector test."

"That's a big if," I said. "But yes, I'd love it."

It took him a while. I'd thought it would. Working under cover to expose confidence tricksters is one thing; getting them to expose themselves is another. After all, they know they're running a crooked game. If they have any suspicion at all that there is a means, like the polygraph instrument, by which they can be nailed for the frauds they really are, it stands to reason they'll make wide circles to keep away from it. A crafty little group of plausible ladies and gentlemen was running séances on the West Side of Los Angeles. Vernon approached them. They refused even to talk to him. He'd gotten complaints about them from men and women they'd fleeced.

"But they hadn't made any waves with the medium herself or anybody in her shop," he told me over lunch. "So I persuaded them to set up a date for another séance, and to ask permission to bring a friend—a man who'd just lost his wife in an automobile accident and was terribly upset."

"You?" I said.

"You've got it—glasses, a mustache, gray in the hair. But that's getting ahead of the story. I watched the house—excuse me, the Chapel of Transcendence—all day. They got some interesting deliveries. Some of the equipment I recognized. Sound stuff, black light, you know—you and I could buy it anyplace. But there was a lot of very odd stuff that your local friendly dealer just doesn't have."

"You have to spend money to make money," I said.

"Right. So I knew we were in for a show that night. I warned everybody. But we all kept straight faces. You get that clammy handshake at the door. There's the overpowering smell of fresh-cut flowers. There's the muted organ music out of those loudspeakers they'd moved in that afternoon. There are the tears and sniffles of the bereaved. There are the tender smiles of the spiders about to eat you. Everyone talks in murmurs and whispers."

"You ought to write a book," I said.

"Then you get ushered down the carpeted, paneled hallway and into the presence of the great lady herself."

"About two hundred pounds?" I asked.

"Not this one. This one's more the Vampyra type—young, big

180

eyes, hollow cheeks. She's pale. She's got these long curtains of straight black hair. She's got a band around her head with a silver crescent-moon amulet at the front. You touch her hand, it's like a frozen fish. Sure enough, there's the table with the velvet cloth and the big carved chair for her and the chairs for us.''

"Trumpets and guitars again?'' I said.

"Wait a minute,'' he said. "We sit down. Somebody silent and shadowy pulls out the chair for you and puts it carefully under you and you look around to say thank you and they've vanished. She tells you in this deep, mournful voice to lay your hands on the table and be sure all the hands are touching. The lights go down another forty watts. It's damn near pitch black. She moans. A cold wind blows over you from someplace, smelling of perfume.''

"Shaving lotion in the air conditioning,'' I said.

"A good brand, though,'' he said. "And the sound was quadraphonic; I mean, you could have sworn those trumpets drifting around were really making the music. I didn't tell you, the room was all draped in black velvet, even the ceiling. The pulleys and little wheels running on tracks, the wires—man, you never saw such a setup. The baby spotlights for picking out the masks, and cheesecloth drifting around supposedly being the spirits of the dead—it was some layout. I felt almost sad, diving for the light switch and breaking it up.''

"I still bet you felt a lot better than Vampyra did,'' I laughed.

"Believe it,'' he said. "There were eight of them in on the thing. The Business and Professional Code doesn't like their type. They've got about a dozen charges against them. I don't know whether they'll go to jail or not. But one thing I feel good about.''

"What's that?'' I said.

"Every other fake medium has left town.'' He grinned.

Years after my encounter with Clyde Vernon, I picked up the telephone in my office to hear the famous voice of television talk-show host, Biff Larkin.

"Have you ever heard of Peggy Smith?'' he asked me.

"The name sounds vaguely familiar,'' I said. "Is she going to be a guest on your show?''

"She's a medium, communicates with the dead. A lot of famous people have gone to her."

"I remember," I said. "What do you want me to do?"

"The producers want her on the show," Larkin said, "but I don't know. Sure, she's newsy right now, and that's a plus. But I don't like it. I think she's a fake."

"There are a lot of those in her line of work," I said. "But nobody's proved anything against her."

"Right. We tested her ourselves," he said. "I've put investigators on her. My whole staff went with me to one of her sittings. I didn't tell her I had operatives with cameras snapping every minute of the proceedings—"

"In the dark?" I said.

"On infrared film," he said. "Everything was on the level. The pictures didn't show us anything out of line. But she's not stupid. Maybe she'd found out we were checking on her. She wants the show, so she wasn't about to get caught faking something."

"And you still don't trust her?"

"I'd like you to give her a lie-detector test. I already proposed it to her, and she's agreeable."

"Can you have her at my offices tomorrow morning?"

"You come here to the studio," he said. "I'll fix up a room for you any way you want it."

I gave him the specifications and he met them. The room was soundproof, air-conditioned, ideal. I set up my polygraph, my tape recorder, and then I met Mrs. Peggy Smith. She was in her forties, handsomely dressed and groomed. Her handshake was firm, her smile charming. She chatted easily with me about books, music, countries overseas where we'd both traveled. She enjoyed dropping names, and I heard a bewildering assortment in the quarter hour we spent getting acquainted before the pre-examination interview. Cabinet ministers and their wives, international film stars, opera singers, rock musicians—the list of her clients glittered.

It seemed to me that, with all the exposure in the media she'd enjoyed thanks to her famous associates, if she weren't sincere, the news would have broken before now. On the other hand, it soon became obvious that her endless stream of talk, however graciously delivered, was prompted by nerves. She kept rubbing at an eyebrow, and I began to get the impression that she was simply giving a recitation, just as fast and hard as she could give it, without even noticing who was listening. She didn't look at me. She looked past my shoulder at the wall of the little studio. Then, suddenly, she was peering into my eyes. Something had warned her that I was puzzled by her behavior and was beginning to add it up to fear.

"Excuse me a moment," she said. "There's a ladies' room down the hall, I believe."

In a few minutes she was back. It wasn't warm in the corridors of the television studios, but now she was sweating. Big drops of perspiration were on her forehead. Without comment, I handed her a box of Kleenex. She looked at it a moment before accepting it. She looked at me. It was obvious she was embarrassed.

"I've no reason to be nervous," she said, dabbing at her face with the tissues. "It really doesn't mean I'm guilty of anything." She gave me her most charming smile.

"I'm used to it," I said. "There's really nothing to be nervous about. The whole thing takes only a couple of minutes. Now, here's what I'm going to ask you." I ran over the key questions—about the possibility of fakery in her séances, about whether or not she could speak with the spirits of the dead. She didn't demur. I attached her to the polygraph. "Now, just relax completely," I said. "The only answers that will work are 'yes' and 'no.' Take plenty of time. All right? Here we go."

She sat quietly and made no effort to distort the reactions of the pens on the chart. The first test showed concern over the key questions. I asked her about two episodes in her life where I was certain she would lie. She did beautifully—she was an excellent reactor. Now I had something against which to measure any reactions that would occur on the main questions. Her first chart was a classic. She responded to every major question with a 'no' answer and it was obvious from the heart, breathing, blood-pressure, and skin tension reactions that she was not being truthful. At the end of the third test, I unfastened the attachments.

"Well—and how did I do?" she asked brightly.

"You failed," I said. "I'm sorry." She surely must have known she wouldn't pass. I couldn't understand her having agreed to take the examination. "I don't like it," I said, "but I'm going to have to tell that to Mr. Larkin. He's the one who engaged me to give you the tests. What are you going to say to him? You can no more talk with the dead than I can, Mrs. Smith.''

With a faint half-smile, she rose from the chair. She seemed perfectly self-possessed now. There was no sign of the nerves that had shaken her before the examination. No sign, that is, except that she didn't answer me. She'd brought a light coat. She picked it up from where it lay across a chair back. I reached to help her put it on, and she stepped back. The gesture might have been one of avoidance or it might not, so very casually was it done.

''These tests are accurate,'' I said. ''You know that.''

She checked her appearance in a small mirror.

''You think I'm mistaken?''

She dropped the mirror back into her handbag and reached for the doorknob. I offered her my hand. She walked by me without so much as noticing it. She went off down the hall, not hurriedly, with her usual graceful stride, but looking neither to left nor to right, nor acknowledging that anyone else existed. The producer of the Biff Larkin show had been waiting outside the room where I'd given the tests. He watched her breeze past with raised eyebrows.

''What turned her to ice?'' he asked me.

''She failed the tests,'' I said. ''She's just as big a fraud as everyone else in her racket.''

''That's going to make a sensational show,'' he said.

''What? Oh, now, wait a minute!'' I said. ''You're not going to humiliate her publicly.''

''It's part of the agreement,'' he said. ''We were free to take any measures we chose to expose her. She understood that. She even asked for it.''

Biff Larkin walked up to us. ''She didn't make it, did she? I can tell from the look on your faces.''

''She's upset,'' I said.

''Not half as upset as she's going to be,'' Larkin said, ''When you read the results of the test on the air.''

''I? Look, I'm not a performer. I'm not a celebrity. I don't belong on television. If I'd known you expected me to get up in front of cameras I'd never have taken on the assignment. Can't the announcer read my findings?''

Larkin shook his head. "You're the expert," he said. "It's got to come from you. The audience needs to hear it in your own words."

"It sounds like a vendetta," I said. "Hell, I don't have anything against Peggy Smith. I've embarrassed her enough already."

The producer said, "I'm sorry. We can't change the format now. We've only got a couple of hours before air time. It's all set up."

"She failed the test," I said. "But she didn't admit to me that she'd failed it. It's not going to go over well with your audience."

"She's got a little while to think it over," Biff Larkin said. "Maybe she'll own up when she's on the air."

I thought she was made of stronger stuff than that, and I was right. The first part of the broadcast interview went off politely, without a hitch. There was interesting film footage of a séance with Peggy Smith presiding. Infrared photographs were shown. The voice-over commentary underlined the dramatic rising and drifting of the table as those at the séance sat around it with their hands on it. The script pointed out that there was no evidence of trickery. Then it was my turn. I reported as simply and directly as I could on exactly what the polygraph charts showed—that Peggy Smith had not been truthful either about her table-tipping tricks or about her ability to talk with the dead. The director kept cutting away from me for close-up studies of Peggy Smith's face. It remained expressionless. She was quietly but determinedly noncommittal during the remainder of her segment on the show, she left without uttering a word to anyone.

She had played her hand like the expert confidence woman she was. She'd outfaced Biff Larkin's open skepticism and my scientific evidence. Simply by refusing to admit that she was wrong, she got the viewing audience on her side. The switchboard at the broadcasting complex buzzed and flashed with hundreds of angry calls. There was no way for the Biff Larkin staff to keep up with the protests. In the following week, sack after bulging sack of mail was dumped in Larkin's offices. Every letter was an enraged outcry against Larkin for his demeaning treatment of Peggy Smith. And there were no kind words for Chris Gugas, either. My own office got its share of furious phone calls and letters.

I'd expected the backlash. Larkin and his producer hadn't. They regretted the episode—not because they weren't convinced Peggy Smith was a fake, but because the persons who watched their show hadn't wanted to look at the truth: They preferred their illusions, which is what makes it possible for phony psychics, card readers, spiritualists, and all the rest to go on raking in money. I'm convinced that if, as a lot of other con-artist mystics have done when confronted by their polygraph charts, Peggy Smith had confessed she was running an elaborate game for profit, the viewing audience would have reacted differently. That segment of the Biff Larkin show would have been a public service. Those who'd watched would have gone on in life wiser and safer from exploitation.

But without her confession, the polygraph evidence did nothing to educate the public, and the experience put me off the exploitation of the polygraph by television for some time. I had helped no one. And I still cannot see any way the thing could have come out differently. After all, whether or not Peggy Smith believed the polygraph could prove deception, she couldn't refuse a test once Larkin proposed it. She claimed to be able to talk with the dead, and if the polygraph worked as Larkin said it did, it could only prove her claim—wasn't that right?

She was a sharp judge of the ageless human hunger to be hoodwinked. Experience had taught her that by standing pat and admitting nothing, no lasting harm could result for her from the Biff Larkin show. Yet I know I put her through a lot of pain and humiliation, and I can't help regretting it. Ironically, the sympathy the show gained her must have drawn to her a lot of new clients. So perhaps I ought to chalk the matter up to experience and forget it. But in all my years as a polygraph examiner, I've never been able to shake off sympathy for men and women who have gotten themselves into trouble—often trouble far more lethal than Peggy Smith's.

16
The Gangster's Moll

She wasn't flashy. She wasn't loud. To look at, Betsy Filler was a woman of wealth, taste, and refinement. She had to be past fifty, but her face was smooth. Her makeup was simple, her clothes elegant and expensive without calling attention to their cost. She took my hand and shook it warmly. Her perfume was understated, pleasant. Her eyes sparkled as she talked. She'd come in on the arm of her lawyer, a counselor with a nationwide reputation, a capable and careful man, who had phoned me a few days earlier for an appointment. Betsy Filler had a long list of bedmates, all of them in organized crime. Now a governmental committee wanted to learn all she knew about their rackets, their shakedowns, their murders.

"Where would you like me to start?" she asked softly, as she sat down alongside her attorney.

"What about a general review of your past?"

"That would take all day." She laughed. Then her face straightened, her eyes hardened. "I'll tell you this, though. I have never known what any of my boyfriends were into. And I sure as hell never got into any of it myself."

"You mean you didn't know they were racketeers?"

"I hate that word," she said. "Sure—hell, yes, I knew they were doing illegal things. But that wasn't any of my business. And I knew a lot better than to ask questions. What would that get me, anyway?"

"Why do you think they want to talk to you?" I asked. "They must think you know something."

"They only want to put on a circus," she said. "I can't tell them anything important. They want to know about Eddie Moreno's murder in that restaurant. They want to know about Al Pastore's disappearance. I can't tell them anything about that, or any of the rest of it—money, territories. What do I know? I'm a kept woman, that's all I am."

"You didn't attend any meetings? At that place in the Maine woods? Down in the Florida Keys?"

"Never. Why would I? Do you think they wanted my advice? You think they kept me around for my brains?"

"Even men like that let down, once in a while," I said. "Relax. Have a few drinks too many. Surely they talked to you sometimes, told you what was going on."

"What happened between me and my boyfriends is strictly my business," she snapped. "I'm not going to get up in front of the committee and the whole country and talk about my sex life. I don't care what Mr. Peter Whitmore here"—she glared at the lawyer—"told you on the telephone. I'm not talking about my intimate life."

"We agreed," I told her with a smile, "that that is off limits. It's not what the committee wants, so it doesn't need to concern us here."

She looked relieved and lit a long European cigarette. She set it in a jeweled holder, then she smiled back at me through the smoke. "I've checked on you, Mr. Gugas," she said, "and I know I'll get a fair shake. That's why I agreed to see you." She glanced wryly at the lawyer. "It's Petey, here, I'm a little worried about. He doesn't trust me."

"Of course I trust you, Miss Filler," he said.

"If you trusted me," she said coldly, "you wouldn't need a lie-detector test to convince you I don't know nothing—anything about Joey Garino's business, or Nick Caplan's, or anybody else's. What if I did sleep with them? I was in love with them. Is that unconstitutional?"

"What the committee investigators claim is that you're privy to many mob secrets," I said.

"And that is bullshit," she said flatly. "If I had any secrets of any kind, you'd be talking to me right now through six feet of grassy ground at Forest Lawn. I'd have been a dead woman long before this silly committee was ever convened. Look"—she leaned forward earnestly—"I don't know one damn thing about anybody in the syndicate. And even if I did, do you think I could squeal on men I love, men who have been very, very good to me?"

"That's a different question," I said. "Do you or don't you know what the committee thinks you know?"

"Absolutely not. My God, you're worse than he is." Again she meant Whitmore, her attorney. "I don't know a thing about the rackets or how they work. Can't you understand? It doesn't pay to know too much. Power changes hands. People double-cross other people. Information leaks. You could be held responsible and end up with a couple of bullets in your head. The desert and the rivers and the ocean are full of people who stuck their noses in where they shouldn't. I'm too smart for that. That's not bragging. I've got proof." She smiled thinly. "I'm still alive and well."

I read to her from the committee charges.

"Meetings!" She cut me off. "If they believe that, they'll believe anything. They don't know this type of man. They wouldn't allow a woman, any woman, to listen in on their business affairs." Her laugh was ironical and without gaiety. "Organized crime figures—they're not the monsters the media make them out to be. They love and respect their women and their families too much to allow them to be mixed up in any kind of illegal conduct. That's Old Country, old-fashioned, but, by God, it's decent and they mean it."

Whitmore interrupted. "How much do you know," he asked me, "about how the Mafia operates?"

"I'm what you'd call an avid reader of books and articles about

189

the Mafia," I said. "But I'm no expert. And I don't have any personal knowledge."

"Right," he said, and looked at his client. "Betsy, you better fill him in on how they work."

"What!" She sprang to her feet. "Why, you lousy shyster! What in Christ's name do you think I've been telling you all this time? What have I just been saying to this nice man?" She bent and shouted into his face while he shrank lower and lower into his chair. "I don't know nothing—anything about the Mafia or what they do. He gets it out of books, right?" She waved a kid-gloved hand at me. "Well, so do I. And you know what it is? Fairy tales made up by professional writers trying to scare the public with how hideous and sinister the mob is." She plumped down in her chair again. "Look, my relationship has always been very sweet and loving and rewarding with these men." She shot Whitmore a poisoned look. "And if you don't believe me, then I'll get me a mouthpiece who does."

"Betsy," Whitmore gestured, "I didn't mean—"

"Oh, shut up," she told him. She spoke to me. "Sure, there are bastards and butchers in every group. But I never heard of any of my men being in anything. We made love—that's all. I never had anything to do with anything else. So they're supposed to be killers? Who says so? Does this committee actually think I went around asking Nick or Joey or Johnny or any of the rest of them who they killed, for Christ's sake? That's really stupid. No wonder the country's in a mess with those fatheads running it. I don't ask my boyfriends where they get their money, either. Or how much they get. There's always plenty for me."

"Joey is the lucky man right now," I said. "How does he feel about your testifying to the committee?"

"He's not worried. He knows I can hold my own with anybody. You know what I can tell them? Where to buy the best clothes—England, France, Italy, Hong Kong, Singapore—the names of the best restaurants, *and* the names of the maître d's. I can tell them how much it costs to live the way I live, jets, the *QE II*, Claridge's, the Côte d'Azur, Rio, you name it. The going rate for a new ninety-foot yacht in the Mediterranean, or a Rolls in Beverly Hills, diamonds in Amsterdam, rubies at Tiffany's, truffles in five different Paris restaurants."

190

"They're not going to ask you any of that," I said.

"What they're going to ask me, I'm not going to answer," she said. "Because I can't. I don't know." She stubbed out her cigarette in the ashtray on my desk. She looked at me levelly. "And your machine will prove I don't know it. And that's what we're here for, so let's get going. Ask me anything you want and you'll get the truth."

"You honestly mean," I said, "that you know nothing about any Mafia operations? The men your name is linked with make that hard to accept."

She narrowed those glittering eyes at me. "Hard for you to believe?"

"What I believe is neither here nor there," I said. "Hard for the committee and their investigators to believe. Aren't you just a little bit scared of facing them with this story? You know, they're not going to take you for stupid. You're an intelligent woman and you show it."

"And I use my intelligence to keep out of trouble. I don't pry into what's none of my business."

"But you do admit some of your friends have been indicted for serious crimes."

She smiled. "And never convicted." She crossed her legs, smoothed her skirt. "Look, have you ever heard of a woman, any woman, ever being arrested and tried for mob connections? No. And you never will."

"There has to be a first time," I warned her.

Peter gave a low moan.

She looked him up and down contemptuously. She turned back to me. "I've only been subpoenaed—and that only happened because my name's always getting in the papers. But I have news for the government. They won't get shit from me. And you know why? Because there is nothing to the so-called evidence they say they've got against me. Sure—they'll get their kicks shoving around a real live gangster's moll. That's a hell of a way to treat a woman, but I can take it." A corner of her mouth tightened in a wry, tough smile. "It's the only thing they can pin on me."

Whitmore sighed and sat up. He spoke for the first time since Betsy had threatened to fire him. "It's not going to be that simple.

191

They've got reason to believe you know things they need to know.''

"Such as?" she said.

"If I knew that," Whitmore said, "we wouldn't be here. I want you examined by Mr. Gugas so I don't get caught with my pants down, trying to defend you. You have to remember, Betsy, if they catch you lying, they can slap you with a perjury charge. And lying to the government is not a light rap." It was his turn to smile ironically. "And I don't care how nice the prison they send you to is, it won't be Claridge's."

"Prison!" she yelped. "Will you listen to him? He's supposed to be on my side. Already he's got me locked up in a cell! You asshole! I am not going to lie. I've got nothing to lie about. Can't you get that straight?"

It looked to me as if she was getting ready to bash him with her snake-skin handbag and I quickly changed the subject. "In all these years, hasn't one of these men ever slipped up and told you about anything—anything at all—illegal?"

"Well, for God's sake," she said, "I suppose so. I have to admit it's possible. I mean, it's human nature, isn't it? Those guys are human, just like you." She shrugged "Maybe they did. But if they did, I forgot about it. It's twenty-five years. Who remembers? I wasn't interested. I knew they were into stuff that wasn't kosher. I'm not deaf and blind, am I?"

"How did you know?" I asked.

She stared at me as if I were a retarded six-year-old. "For Christ's sake!" she said exasperatedly. "You can't live with a man and not know at least something about what he does. He doesn't have to come right out and tell you he's a gangster." She grimaced. "Boy, how I hate that word. Look, you just know. I mean, what nine-to-five businessman meets at his own apartment all hours of the day and night? Why would they sit around whispering to each other? What car salesman or bank vice-president or advertising agency jerk carries rolls of fifties and hundreds? And you know that's all anybody with half a brain has to see—guys that pay cash for everything. You know what they're into has got to be crooked."

"That's exactly what the committee is going to be asking you," I said. "And they'll hammer at you. They won't take vague gener-

192

alities. They'll examine and cross-examine. They'll turn every word you say over to see what's under it.''

Whitmore nodded glumly.

"They won't find anything under it,'' Betsy Filler said. "Because there isn't anything. What I suspected isn't evidence, damn it. Even I know that much about the law. And there's no way I could swear on a Bible any of these friends of mine ever did a dishonest thing because I don't know they did. I don't have any proof. And the committee isn't going to get any proof out of me.''

Whitmore rose and left to use the men's room.

"Look,'' Betsy whispered to me as the door closed behind him, "I don't trust that dude. He used to work for the government. How do I know he still doesn't? Maybe he's setting me up.''

"Nobody can set you up if you tell the truth. He's not working against you. He's acting like a first-rate attorney, and that's his reputation. He's being cautious. Having you take a polygraph examination is an excellent move. That way he'll be certain you don't withhold information that, if it came out at the committee hearings, could get you cited for perjury or contempt.''

She sulked. "I don't like the way he keeps asking me the same stuff over and over again. What's he trying to trip me up for? Why won't he believe me when I tell him I don't know anything about my lovers' business?''

"He's acting like the counsel for the committee will act,'' I said, "to try to be as sure as possible you won't be surprised when you're under oath.''

"It can't happen,'' she said. "I don't know anything.''

Whitmore came back. "Look, I've got to run. I have to be in court at two o'clock. There's only just time for me to drive there if I start now.''

"I don't know how we're going to get along without you,'' Betsy Filler said. "But let's try it on for size.''

Whitmore left and she relaxed. For a while, I asked her about her travels. We'd visited some of the same countries and we compared notes. She was easy and amiable and talked, for that brief period, at least, with the grace of a Vassar graduate. The rough edge left her voice. She dropped her trooper's vocabulary. I hadn't planned to polygraph her today but I wanted to try, now that we were alone, to get some ground under my feet in order to make the most of the testing when it did take place.

"When they gunned down Ed in that restaurant," I said, "everybody was talking about it. You mean that Nick never said a word to you about it? You'd both been there till a half-hour before it happened."

"Ed was no friend of Nick's," she said. "He didn't talk about him alive, why should he talk about him dead?" Her voice was a saw blade again.

"When Al disappeared," I said, "half a million dollars in union pension funds disappeared with him. You never heard about any of that money? You never saw anybody at one of those quiet evenings at home you talked about flash open a briefcase stuffed with that kind of green?"

"I said they had the meetings," she snapped. "They—the men. I never went in there."

"Then how did you know they sat around whispering?"

"Get off my back," she said, and stood up.

"You didn't take them in late-night coffee or drinks?"

"What they wanted they got for themselves," she said. "I kept out of their way, believe me. If any of them ever so much as thought I'd heard anything, my life wouldn't have been worth a dime. Those guys don't trust anybody—including me. And they play very, very rough."

I didn't ask her how she knew that. But I was certain she did know it. I was certain she knew more than enough to justify the committee's sending for her. I didn't press her any further, though. It wasn't getting me any further than it had gotten Whitmore. I asked her to return the following morning for the polygraph tests and she agreed. She held my hand in parting. Her smile, her voice, were warm.

"Look," she said, "don't get me wrong. I'm not pissed at you. You've been fair. You're only doing your job, asking this stuff. But, believe me, Mr. Gugas, sweetheart, I don't know anything, and your machine is going to prove it."

She wasn't warm and bright when she came back with Whitmore the next day. Her eyes were cloudy. Her mouth pouted. And she was brusque. She pointed at an inner office door. "Is that where we do it?"

"That's it," I said, "but there's no rush."

"I've got another appointment," she said. "Let's get going." She glanced at a diamond-studded wristwatch. "I've only got an hour."

"Then we'd better not try to do the tests today," I said. I looked at my secretary. "Will you set up another appointment for Miss Filler?"

"I don't want another appointment," she said. "I'm here. I want to get it over with now."

"It can't be hurried," I said. "You'll miss your other appointment." I touched the telephone. "Maybe you'd like to call and cancel it."

"The hell with it," she said. "Let 'em wait." She marched toward the examining room door. Whitmore started after her. I asked him to wait. I followed Betsy Filler into the examining room. She was standing, looking around at the plain walls, plain furnishings, with a cocked eyebrow. "You sure don't go for luxury, do you?"

"No distractions," I said. "It helps you concentrate."

"I don't need to concentrate." She sat down in the visitor's chair and unbuttoned her coat. I sat at the desk. She rummaged in her handbag for one of those fancy cigarettes. She didn't bother this time with the holder. As she bent across the desk, her eyes were attracted to the built-in polygraph instrument. Her gloved hand shook, holding the cigarette for me to light. She settled back looking pale.

"Are you all right?" I said. "You look ill."

"I didn't have a good night," she said. "I got to thinking about some of the questions you asked me yesterday. And, well, there are some—what should I call them—gray areas that maybe I ought to try to explain."

"We're going to need an accurate record of all this," I said. "No third person can be in the room when a polygraph examination is being taken. It simply won't work. So, with your permission, I'll turn on a tape recorder."

"Who gets the tape?" she asked sharply.

"No one but you and Pete Whitmore," I said.

"Okay," she said, and watched me touch a switch. "What I want to know is about this gadget—what did you call it? Polygraph? How does it react when somebody's not sure of the answer to a question? Is it going to jump all over?"

"You could put it that way," I said. "It's designed to measure how your breathing and blood pressure react when questions bother you. Just what gray areas did you mean?"

"Well, about those meetings—Maine? Florida? And a couple of other places, besides. I didn't, like, sit in on them, understand? But I was—I was there. I mean, Johnny, when I was going with him— he'd take me. And in the hotel, you know—I saw him shake hands with this person and that person. And—"

"And those persons are Mafia and syndicate figures the committee is going to ask you about?" I said.

"You've got it," she said unhappily. "And he told me he was meeting with this one and that one, right? I mean, not what the meetings were about, understand? But he said who'd be there. So I know that, don't I?"

"I'm afraid you do," I said. "What else?"

"Well, after a couple of meetings, Johnny was really pissed off when he got back to the hotel. I mean, there was blood in his eye. He was raving."

"To you," I said. It wasn't a question.

"Right." She twisted out her cigarette and right away was scrabbling for another in her bag. "He said he was being screwed out of his territory. I didn't know what he meant. I mean, not in particular. I didn't ask. He'd been under a lot of pressure lately, I knew that. And he'd been spending all this time in Florida where his bosses were. He was uptight, not himself at all."

"You're sure you don't know what this so-called territory was, where it was, what he did with it before he got screwed out of it?"

"I swear it. But I'm scared of being asked."

"I don't blame you," I said. I came around the desk and gently took away the cigarette, the handbag. I asked her for her gloves. Then I fitted on the polygraph attachments. "Relax. This isn't going to hurt. And I'm not going to ask you anything in any gray areas where you can't make up your mind how you feel. That wouldn't

196

get us anyplace. Now here are the questions I think we'd better test you on. You tell me whether they're all right with you.''

"Those are all right," she said when she'd heard them. "Only five? Is that all you're going to ask?''

"I'll intersperse unimportant questions," I explained. "Like 'Is your name Betsy Filler?' and 'Have you ever been in St. Tropez?' Just to check on how you react to ordinary, nonstressful questions."

"I guess you know what you're doing," she said.

I laughed. "I think so. I've been at it quite a while." I sat down at the instrument and switched it on. The first chart was hard to go by. She kept fidgeting in the examining chair. "We're going to do it again. This time, try not to move around, please. It adds components to the chart that aren't any help." She agreed to sit still but she was nervous and forgot. Still, by the time I'd run four charts, I was positive that on three of the five key questions she was lying. I switched off the machine and detached her from it.

"I blew it, didn't I?" she asked. "I told you I wasn't sure about those questions. They made me twitchy every time."

"No," I said. "You agreed on the questions. We took out the ones you were undecided about, remember?"

"Okay, okay." She went to her handbag for another cigarette. She lit it for herself this time. She paced. "We agreed, right. I was sure I could pass those five. But then I got to thinking while it was going on and my mind just wouldn't stop spinning. Last night in bed I got worried sick I wouldn't pass the tests one hundred percent and then what was Whitmore going to say."

"You should have been honest with him from the start," I told her. "Why not start now? Be honest with me. It's no good trying to get away with lies or half-truths—not with the polygraph. That's what it was invented to uncover. If you come out honestly with the way things really were with you, Joey, and the others—what they did, where they went, why they went there, who they saw—then you've got a chance. If you don't, I'm really afraid you're in for a bad time."

"Maybe." Grimly she tugged on her gloves. "But at least I'll stay alive. Look, Mr. Gugas, honey—let's forget it, shall we? You want to know the truth? I remember too much. Twenty-five years with these men? How could I not remember too much. I don't mean

197

racket secrets, any of that. Yeah, I suppose the government would like to know the minor stuff I heard and saw. How could I help but see and hear it? How could I help but remember it?''

"Joey isn't cool about this," I said. "That's one untruth you told me. You weren't alone with your thoughts and misgivings last night. He was with you. And he told you what to do and what not to do."

"I told him I wasn't going to say anything," she said. She took her coat off the chair, put it on, picked up her handbag. "What I told you and Whitmore yesterday is the way I'm going to handle myself before that committee. Let them ask me anything. I don't know anything."

"Have it your way," I said, "but you're making a mistake." I reached to open the door for her. She caught my hand. "What are you going to tell the mouthpiece?"

"That you reacted significantly to some key questions—which means you haven't been entirely truthful."

"Well," she gave a little relieved laugh, "I guess that'll do it, won't it? Make it easier for me to shed him and get the guy Joey wants me to use, somebody who'll handle the case without asking so many personal questions."

"It's not the questions that are going to hurt you," I said. "It's the answers. If this lawyer you're talking about doesn't know that, he's no good. Joey will be paying him for nothing."

She only smiled. Whitmore, when he learned the results of the polygraph tests, and what Betsy Filler had said about him, withdrew from the case. He was as convinced as I was that, if only through her short-fused temper, Betsy was going to make a poor witness before the committee. She was bound to say too much and trip herself up. The outcome wasn't hard to predict. It happened just as we told each other it would that day in my office. Betsy was cited for perjury and sentenced to prison. That Christmas I received a card from her:

If it makes you any happier, you were right. I lied, and now I'm paying for it—but I still have my friends!

Love—Betsy

198

17
The $30,000 Kidnapping

Lee Tyler winced and thumbed the remote-control switch of the television set. The color picture rolled from a beer commercial featuring a bear to the freckled face of a sportscaster reading with high-pitched excitement a list of baseball scores. It was dusk. The only light in the long, luxurious room filtered through loose-woven curtains across glass sliding doors. Tyler's blowsy, red-haired wife, Babs, had been curled up asleep in a deeply cushioned chair. Now she stirred. An empty martini glass by her hand tipped over. She yawned, glared at the TV set, and reached to turn on a lamp. Outside, a big dog barked.

"What's wrong with Shep?" she said.

"He probably saw a squirrel," Tyler grunted. "Shut up."

"There's the doorbell." She got out of her chair, pushing at her hair. "Look at me. I'm a sight."

"Do I have to?" Tyler said.

"I can't face company, looking like this. I've got to fix up. Answer the door. Go on, Lee."

"I'm not expecting anybody," he grumbled, but he switched off the television set and moved down the room, a short, sturdy man of fifty. He walked up the few steps to the front entryway and opened the door grumpily, all set to blast the stupid salesman who'd chosen to break up his quiet evening at home. He squinted at the tall figure in the half-dark. He wasn't carrying any sample case. He was carrying a gun. It looked very big. Lee Tyler had a momentary sense of unreality. This sort of thing didn't happen in real life, only on TV. To actors. "What the hell!" he said.

"Shut up and get back inside." The tall man's voice was young and tense. He shoved the gun barrel into Tyler's belly. Tyler backed away, too frightened to speak. The man slammed the door, grabbed Tyler's shoulder, and turned him around. Now the gun barrel was in Tyler's back. "Move. We want your wife too. Where is she?"

"Bathroom," Tyler croaked.

"Call her. Nice and sweet. Tell her it's a friend."

"Look, what's this all about?" Tyler asked.

The gun barrel rapped the side of his head. Through the ringing in his ears he could hear the man's voice ordering, "Just do what I tell you. Call her."

"Babs?" Tyler heard his own voice, weak and shaky. The gun barrel tapped his head again. He swallowed in a dry throat and called loudly, "Babs? Come on out, sweetheart. Hurry. You won't believe who's here."

Shep barked. He was in the fenced backyard. The sound of his barking echoed off the water of the swimming pool. A door closed in the rear of the house. Babs appeared at the far end of the living room. She'd put on a fresh green denim pants suit over a yellow-green tank top that showed off her big breasts. She stopped. Her eyes grew round. Her mouth dropped open. The gun barrel was cold and hurtful poking into Tyler's ear. The tall man said:

"This is a gun, lady. If you don't want me to blast his head off, you'll come here, nice and quiet." Babs gulped. It looked to Lee as if her knees were going to give out. She clutched the door frame for a second. "Come on, move your ass!" the man shouted. There was hysteria in his voice and it scared Tyler.

"Come on, Babs," he pleaded.

She came. The tall man herded them out the front door. A shabby car was parked in the driveway. A bony blonde female sat in the rear seat. Tyler couldn't make out her age in the dying daylight. The tall man yanked open the back door and pushed Tyler roughly inside. He fell against the woman. She was young. She shoved him off her with a gun that looked to Tyler even bigger than the man's. Babs fell against him then, and the door slammed. The man got behind the wheel, started the car, jammed it into reverse and, with tires squealing, backed it careening into the street.

"Wait!" Tyler said. "The dog."

The man at the wheel didn't hear. He jammed the car into low and they tore along the street.

"You can't leave the dog!" Tyler shouted, trying to ignore the prod of the girl's gun barrel in his ribs. "If we don't let him in at night, he raises hell. He'll bark all night. And the neighbors don't like it. They come over."

The man jammed on the brakes. He made a U turn and they drove back the way they'd come. They jounced into the driveway. The man got out and tore open the door.

"All right. Get the dog. Then get back here. Don't try anything. You've got ninety seconds—then we shoot Babs. You got that?"

"What for?" Tyler stumbled out of the car. "What do you want with us?"

"Get the damn dog," the man said.

Tyler raced through the house, tore open the patio sliding doors, and called Shep to him. The big German shepherd wagged his tail happily and jumped up on Tyler to be petted. The dog was nearly as big as the man. "Get off me," Tyler said. "Come on. We're going in the car."

Shep raced ahead and out the open front door. Tyler passed the telephone. He put his hand on it. Outside, the man shouted for him. He ran outside. Shep was winding himself happily around the man's legs. For a split second, Tyler was disgusted with the dog. Then he thought it was a good thing Shep hadn't gone for the man's throat.

He'd have ended up dead, and so, probably would Babs. In answer to the man's curt, impatient gesture with the gun, Tyler climbed into the back seat again. The door slammed. Shep jumped into the front seat, his favorite spot for an automobile ride. Then they were off again. They ended up in some foothills Tyler didn't know, the springs of the car squeaking and wrenching under them. When they came to a halt and the engine was turned off, the silence was as wide and empty as the country night sky above them. Babs wept hysterically.

"Get out," the man said.

"Are you going to kill us?" Babs wailed.

"Shut up, lady. You, Tyler. Shut her up, will you?"

Tyler stroked Babs's plump shoulders. "Come on, Babs. This isn't helping. Quit whining. You're driving him nuts with that noise. You're driving me nuts."

"Oh, sure!" she said fiercely. "You take their side."

"Here's Shep," Tyler said. "Look, you're worrying him. You don't want to worry him." Trying to choke back her sobs, but with little, shaky hiccups still jerking out of her, Babs knelt and put her arms around the big dog. Tyler looked at the tall young man in the night blackness. "What the hell did you bring us out here for?"

"No phones, no unexpected visitors, no nosy neighbors. We'll wait here till morning."

A wild protesting cry from Babs. The blonde girl struck her hard across the face. Babs sprawled backward. Shep ran off a few feet and stood staring, tensed, ready to run again. Babs started to crawl toward him across the weedy ground, sobbing, calling out his name.

"If you don't shut up," the young man said, "I'll kill the dog, lady. I'll put a bullet right through his dumb head. Now, shut up, damn it!"

The blonde girl kicked Babs. Babs shut up, except for a low whimpering she couldn't help.

"All night," Tyler said. "And then what?"

"Then in the morning, you get me thirty thousand bucks."

"Thirty—!" Tyler laughed. "From where?"

"Your office. I heard from reliable sources you always keep that much cash on hand."

202

"Unreliable,'" Tyler said, shaking his head. "Someone was putting you on."

"Not in some safe," the kidnapper said. "You got it hidden. I want it."

"I haven't got it hidden," Tyler said. "I keep my money in banks like everybody else."

"Sit down." The young man shoved him suddenly, and Tyler was flat on his backside in the scrub. "Not like everybody else. Not like me. Not like most people in this lousy country. Most people haven't got money to put in banks. Where the hell would they get it? Working for you and your kind? You share the profits, do you? Don't make me laugh."

"I don't want an economics lecture," Tyler said. He tried to scramble to his feet and the man used a shoe planted in the middle of his chest to push him back down.

"You may not want it, but you need it," the young man said. "And I am going to give it to you. All night. So get ready. And keep awake, you exploiting son of a bitch, or I'll kill you and your fat wife and your dog too." He sat cross-legged a few feet from Tyler, facing him. "You know that dog eats better than most of the poor people in this country? Did that ever cross your mind? Did it ever penetrate your skull that those two cars of yours could keep a disadvantaged family in food and shelter and clothing for a couple of *years*, man? Ten families like that could live for twenty years on what you paid for that fancy house."

"You sound like a caring person," Tyler said. "You don't sound like a criminal. How is it going to do poor people any good to kidnap me?"

"It's going to teach you a lesson," the young man said. "Now, shut your rotten, capitalist mouth and listen to me."

Babs gasped out something in the dark. There were the sounds of blows. The blonde girl spoke. Shep whimpered. There was silence. The young man droned on. Tyler's head ached from the pistol-barrel blows. He didn't know what was happening to Babs. He strained his eyes to try to pick out her shape in the dark, the blonde girl's, Shep's. He couldn't. Then, suddenly, he was asleep. They'd shifted ground by then. His back was against the rough trunk

203

of a scrub oak. So was the young man's, his face a pale blur in the dark, but his voice grinding angrily on and on—half the vocabulary out of Marx and Engels, half of it obscenities. A kick in the stomach woke him. The man towered over him.

"Don't fall asleep on me again," he said, "you bloodsucking, thieving bastard, or I'll kill your wife and I'll kill the dog too. And I mean it, and you know I mean it."

Clutching his stomach, trying to suck in air, Tyler gasped out, "All right, all right. I know you mean it. I fell asleep. I couldn't help it."

The young man made a disgusted sound and turned away. He called into the dark, "Is she awake? I don't want her to sleep. I want her to hear this."

"She's awake," the blonde called. "I've got my gun aimed at Shep. If she falls alseep, I shoot him."

At dawn, Tyler and Babs were hustled back into the car. Babs's face was swollen almost shapeless. The girl had kept slapping her. Or maybe she'd used her fist—that was what it looked like. Tyler seethed. His own belly ached from the kick he'd received. His head was still sore. The car doors slammed. The engine snarled into life. They began jouncing down the rutted dirt road.

"Where are you taking us?" Tyler asked.

"If it's in the bank," the young man said, "then you are going to get it out of the bank and hand it to me. For that you need passbooks and junk. Those at your house?"

"They're at my house," Tyler mumbled.

No one was about in the neighborhood. He'd hoped to see someone who would look at the dented old car, recognize him and Babs, and be smart enough to realize that something was wrong. He wouldn't dare yell to them. The blonde would shoot Babs if he did, or the man would shoot Shep. Shep was the only one of the party who'd slept through the night. He had his head out the front window on the passenger side, enjoying the fresh morning air. He might bark if he saw a neighbor. That might draw attention and—but no one was about; not even a gardener. It was too early. The houses were spaced far apart on wide landscaped lots. There were trees that cut off the expensive places one from the other—assuring privacy. Only now privacy was what he didn't want. Once in the house, he tried drawing back the curtains, hoping somebody might look in and see the young man holding a gun on him. But the young man stopped him.

"Just get the fucking bankbooks and let's get out of here," he said. "Hear that? Your jerky wife is crying again. Come on, before she wakes up the neighborhood."

In the back seat of the car, the blonde was saying to Babs, between clenched teeth, "Shut up, shut up, shut up, you bitch." And with every *Shut up*, she punched Babs savagely in the ribs. When Tyler went into the back seat, it was with a shove from the young man. Again he struck against the blonde. She turned eyes on him that were blank and crazy. Tyler thought she must be on some drug or other. He clutched the bankbooks. He hoped to God there was enough in them to bring this nightmare to an end. And not in death—for Shep, for Babs, for any of them.

"The banks won't be open yet," the young man said as they started down the street away from the house again. "Anyway, we have to eat. You got money in that fat wallet of yours, Tyler?"

"Where are we going?" Tyler said. "Frascatti's?"

"Banks!" Babs said. "Are you going to give him money?"

"All of it," Tyler snarled at her. He spread the passbooks in his hands to show her. "Or did you want to spend another night like last night?"

"Oh, God, no!" Babs wailed.

The girl struck her in the mouth. "Shut up, bitch!"

"Lay off her," Tyler said. "She looks like a punching bag already. She can't help it."

The girl turned and struck him in the mouth with the gun barrel. He tasted blood. "Shut up!" she said.

The car went blocks in silence. It pulled into the empty parking lot of a franchise fast-food restaurant, brick and beams, planters and stained glass. Tyler expected the man to go inside and bring food out, but he was either crazier or more spaced-out on drugs than that. He ordered them all out of the car and they crossed the parking lot together. Behind them, Shep barked in the car. Tyler's mouth still bled. His teeth had cut it when the girl's gun barrel hit him. He ought to let the blood show so the waitress would see it and wonder. He dodged a glance at Babs. Her face was swollen and discolored.

One eye was almost closed. Her clothes were soiled and rumpled, her hair had twigs tangled in it. Surely the restaurant help would spot that. He wiped the blood off his mouth with his handkerchief. The man yanked open the restaurant door and ushered them inside. As they took a table, he said:

"Look natural. We're friends having an early breakfast before we hit the road together. Got that? I hope so. One false move, one word, and I'll shoot up this whole place and everybody in it. Believe it." Babs's mouth trembled but she didn't whimper. Tyler had seen the gun go into the pocket of the man's leather jacket. It was right next to him. Could he reach in and drag it out himself? He moved his arm slowly, but the booth was too crowded. He accepted the glossy menu the man handed him.

The waitress appeared. Tyler looked into her eyes. She didn't seem to notice anything wrong. She was a teenager. Tyler wished they'd gotten an older woman. The man told the waitress, "We'll all have coffee and the number eight breakfast, okay? Keep things simple." He smiled for the first time since he'd walked into the Tyler house last night. Tyler thought his smile was uglier than the scowl he normally wore. He held out his hand for the menus and put them in their slot.

Tyler thought this was like a dream. It was so crazy no one was going to believe it. Far off down the restaurant he saw three pay telephones in a row beside an opening in a stone wall with a discreet sign RESTROOMS. He thought of asking to go to the men's room, but the man with the gun would tag along anyway. The coffee came. It was delicious. He hadn't realized how he'd been craving it—and the food. He mopped up his plate. So did poor Babs. That was no surprise. She was an emotional eater. Upset her a little and she'd gobble food down like a pig in an apple orchard. At least it shut her up. Her eyes had that dreamy, faraway look of contentment they always got when she had an excuse to stuff herself. For the moment, there wasn't any danger she'd start the hysterical sobbing that could get them both killed right here. That was a relief. He half forgot the trouble they were in.

It seemed even more unreal when the man let them go wash up. But there was no escape. The man and the blonde were waiting when they came out. He told himself the man wouldn't shoot anybody—not at this distance. He should yell that he and Babs were being kidnapped and that somebody should call the police. He stopped. He looked at the black short-order cook behind the tall brick wall under the gleaming hoods. The man was busy at the grill. Half a dozen customers were on stools at the counter. A family with a little baby was in a booth. He looked at the tall man again and decided he would shoot, after all. Babs touched him. He gave her a sorry little smile and they went to join their captors.

"No funny business inside," the man said when they pulled into the bank's parking lot. "Just remember we've got Babs and Shep here. One sign of trouble, and we kill them both. Believe it."

Babs whimpered. The blonde slapped her. Tyler got out of the car and trudged up the shallow stone steps toward the plate-glass doors of the new, low-roofed bank. He was the first customer. He kept only savings here. That meant he didn't come in often. The teller didn't recognize him. She was an Oriental woman. She gave him a warm, mechanical smile. He slid the passbook out of its plastic case, opened it, and pushed it across the counter at her.

"I'll need ten thousand dollars in cash," he said. "In twenties and fifties, please,"

She looked surprised. She blinked at his face. She ran a finger down the entries in the passbook. She tilted her neat head, looking doubtful, and went away with the passbook to murmur something to a man in a gray suit and rimless glasses. The man looked toward him and Tyler felt himself break into a cold sweat. But nothing went wrong. The Oriental woman came back with bundles of currency. It took time to count it all out. He kept listening for the explosion of the man's gun in the car out in the parking lot, but it didn't happen. Finally the money was pushed into his hands. He was so nervous he almost forgot the passbook. Then he was out in the morning air again. He was at the car.

"What took you so long?" The man brushed back the cuff of his leather jacket with the hand that held the gun. "You were in there damn near twenty minutes. Get in." He started the engine. Tyler got in. The man turned. "Give me the money. How much did you get?"

"Ten thousand," Tyler said.

"What! I told you thirty." The man dumped the bundles of

currency on the seat beside Shep. He backed out of the parking slot and drove into the street. "How the hell many banks do you want to go to, for Christ's sake?"

"I don't know," Tyler stammered. "God, I don't know. If I ask for too much, they'll get suspicious."

The man laughed. "You trying to protect me. That's very funny? Get twenty thou at the next stop."

The teller this time was a young black man who looked startled and said he wasn't authorized to handle that kind of transaction. Tyler would have to see the head cashier. This was a woman nearing sixty. She eyed Tyler with undisguised curiosity. Her thickly made-up mouth formed a question but she didn't speak it. She gave him a strained smile and pointed him across the way to where glossy desks stood apart from each other on acres of wall-to-wall carpeting. The manager wasn't afraid to ask:

"Mr. Tyler, is there something wrong?"

His cool blue eyes surveyed Tyler's unshaven face, his clothes that were creased from long sitting in the car, from sitting on the ground out in that godforsaken field last night. He'd been able to wash his face and hands in the restaurant men's room, but he hadn't been able to do anything else about his appearance. He smelled of sweat, too—the sweat of fear.

"I was up all night at a business meeting," Tyler lied. "I realize I look dreadful. I'm sorry about that. But I need to close the deal and I need to close it before noon. And it has to be cash. It can't go through in time if the suppliers have to delay while checks are cashed."

"I understand." The manager excused himself and went off with the passbook. Tyler sat and fidgeted for a while. One minute turned to five. Five turned to ten. He didn't know what would happen if the delay got too long. He rose and went to the older woman again.

"Tell the manager I had to step outside for a moment," he said. "I'll be back." At the car he explained, "They're taking a lot of time counting it out. It's a lot of money. The bills are small, the way you wanted."

"What did you come out here for?" the man snapped. "You

208

trying to get us busted? Get back in there. Act normal, will you? You look scared to death.''

"I wonder why," Tyler said.

Half an hour later, the manager of the bank came toward him. A young employee followed, lugging a canvas sack. The manager had prepared the withdrawal receipt. Tyler signed it with a shaking hand. He picked up the bag from the desk. It was heavy. The manager touched him.

"You're quite sure everything is all right?''

Tyler forced a smile. "Now? Everything is fine.''

But of course it wasn't fine. Ten thousand dollars more wasn't enough. He dumped it on the seat beside the driver. The man with the gun said, "Okay, now on to the Savings and Loan, right?''

"No—that's all," Tyler said. "If I try this one more time, they'll suspect me. You can't get away with this. It's crazy to think so." The girl hit him across the bridge of his nose with her gun barrel. Blood gushed out. Babs screamed. The woman put a hand over Babs's mouth. The car careened with screaming tires out of the bank parking lot. The driver yelled:

"Okay. Now do you want to go to that Savings and Loan and get the rest of the thirty thousand, or do you want me to drive us out to the foothills again and shoot you full of holes and bury you there?''

Tyler mopped at his bloody nose with his handkerchief. "The Savings and Loan," he said. "All right, all right. Shut up, Babs. It's almost over." Half a second after he'd said that, he wished he hadn't. It had a deadly sound about it. "You get the rest of the money," he called to the man, "and then you let us go. That's what you said.''

"Ten thousand more," the man said.

"And you let us go," Tyler said.

"And we talk about it," the man said. "Look, you stinking capitalist slave driver, you think you can bargain with me? You're not in any position to bargain. If I want to let you go, I'll let you go. If I want to kill you, I'll kill you. And there's not a thing you can do either way. But I'll tell you this: If you don't get that ten thousand—there's no chance I'll let you go. No chance at all.''

Tyler didn't try a teller this time. Nor a cashier, either. He went straight for the manager's desk. A client of the bank was already sitting there talking to the manager. Tyler had to wait. He kept touching his nose gingerly. The bleeding had stopped but he was sure the bridge was broken. He thought grimly that if these two maniacs didn't get caught this time it wasn't for lack of messing things up. He must look like an accident going someplace to happen. He laughed a bitter laugh to himself. Maybe he was. Finally the little old lady who had been talking to the bank manager shook his hand and left. Tyler almost ran to get to him. He fumbled and dropped the passbook in his haste to hand it over. The manager bent quietly to retrieve it.

"You seem disturbed, Mr. . . . ah"— He read the name off the inside of the passbook—"Mr. Tyler. Are you sure you're all right."

"It's been a long night," Tyler smiled. "Business meeting. I must have fallen asleep at the wheel for a second driving here. Bumped my nose. Look, I've got to close this deal before noon. That's why I need the cash."

"I see," the manager said. "You understand, it will take some time to get this much cash ready." His eyes searched Tyler's. "Especially in such small denominations."

"I understand," Tyler nodded. "I'll wait. Sorry to put you to the trouble."

"Quite all right," the manager said mechanically. But he looked doubtful as he walked away. And Tyler froze when he saw the man pick up a telephone. *He'll be calling my office,* he thought. *He'll ask my son if everything is okay, and Billy will tell him absolutely not. And the manager will send for the cops. And that lunatic out there in the car will kill Shep and the blonde will kill Babs and*—But none of it happened. The money came in twenty minutes, this time in bulky brown envelopes.

"Don't you want to count it?" the manager asked.

"I trust you," Tyler said, and had to force himself not to run for the doors that glared with daylight. He dropped heavily onto the back seat of the car. He slammed the door, exhausted. He threw the heavy packages of money at the driver. He suddenly didn't give a damn what happened. He was tired out. He'd had it. Let it end. He couldn't take any more. He looked at Babs and almost burst out

210

crying himself. Both her eyes were swollen shut and the flesh around them was turning purple.

"Don't do anything like that again," the driver warned him, dumping the packages on the floor and gunning the car out of the parking lot.

"Oh, shut up," Tyler said. "You've got your money. Take us home."

But home wasn't where the driver headed. He floored the throttle. Luckily the car was old and in bad shape. It wouldn't do more than sixty miles an hour. But it did that steadily. He ran red lights. Three times they nearly collided with cars at cross streets. Rubber screamed. Horns blared. They cleared the business district. Not a cop had seen them. It figured, Tyler told himself sourly. Where the hell were they being taken now? He opened his mouth to ask. He shut his mouth again. Maybe he didn't want to know the answer. If they were going to be shot and buried, what difference did it make where it happened? They left the main road and followed a secondary road into the foothills again, hills beginning to turn brown after the rain-drenched green of winter. They left the secondary road for a bumpy dirt track. Was this where they'd come last night? Tyler didn't think so. The car rocked to a halt in a crooked barranca where a stream trickled over rocks sheltered by leaning, white-barked sycamores. In the silence, a blue jay squawked.

"Get out," the tall man said, opening Tyler's door. "You too, Babs."

"What now?" Tyler asked. "You've got your money."

"I want maybe one thing," the tall man said, "maybe another. I can't make up my mind. Do I want you dead or just scared? Too scared ever to tell anybody about this."

Babs started jabbering. "Oh, we won't tell. We won't say a word. Oh, please! Please don't kill us!"

"I give you my word," Tyler said. "We won't tell."

The tall man didn't answer. He studied Tyler. His hand was in his pocket, fingering the gun. *Is he going to execute us now?* Tyler wondered. The spot was perfect. Not a sign of human life in miles. Who would ever come here and what for? He thought of those stories in the papers of bodies uncovered in wilderness places years after burial. Babs moaned and clung to him. She was heavy. He felt sorry for her—she was so stupid. He felt sorry for himself—he was so smart.

"Will you shut up?" the blonde said and slapped Babs.

Tyler slapped the blonde. The tall man's hand came out of the jacket pocket with the gun. The gun swung in a wide arc, sunlight glaring off the metal. It struck Tyler's forehead and he was on his back on the ground. Blood streamed into his eyes. With a scream—horror, outrage, despair—Babs fell on him. The blonde started beating her with a fallen tree branch. The branch was rotten and kept breaking. Babs kept screaming. Tyler squinted through the blood at the figure of the man against the sun. The man had the gun pointed at him. Then he seemed to jerk awake. He pushed the gun into the jacket pocket, grabbed the blonde, and dragged her to the car. He shoved her inside, slammed her door, ran around to the driver's side and got in. Babs kept screaming. The motor thrashed into life.

"Get up," Tyler told Babs, and pushed at her soft, bulky weight. "Get off me. Get in the trees. They're going to run over us." He rolled from under her, staggered to his feet. He grabbed her under the arms, trying to get her up. "Come on, damn it, Babs— try, try!" He was crying. Then he stopped tugging at her. Because the car didn't come at them. Instead, it lurched around and, kicking up dust, it jolted, tilting, squeaking, back down the barranca the way it had come. Babs still screamed. Tyler shook her. "Stop it. Babs, stop it, now. They're gone. It's all over." He looked around. "Shep?" He whistled. The dog came out of the trees. "I'm going to find help," Tyler told Babs. She still lay crumpled, sobbing, on the ground. He stroked her shoulder. "Here's Shep. He'll stay with you. I'll be back as soon as I can . . . "

That afternoon my telephone rang. The caller was Jed Seeger, an attorney in the northern California town where Lee and Babs Tyler lived. "They claim they've been kidnapped, rousted around, beaten up, threatened. Even wilder than that—they say the kidnappers drove them around to Tyler's various banks and savings and loans and made him draw out thirty thousands bucks to buy them off." He gave me details. "It's too wild. I don't believe it."

"But they both tell the same story?" I asked.

"They say they won't go to the police with it. They claim they're scared the kidnappers will come back and kill them if they do."

"Which means to you," I said, "that they're lying."

"Can you fly up here and give them lie-detector tests? The whole thing is so crazy. I don't know what to think. I mean— kidnapping the dog, for heaven's sake?"

"I can't test the dog," I said.

"Come anyway," he said.

Babs Tyler's face was a lumpy mass of green, yellow, and purple bruises. Her mouth was swollen shapeless. Her eyes were nearly closed. Tyler's head was bandaged. There was tape and gauze across the bridge of his nose. His mouth, too, was shapeless. It didn't prevent his talking. He had a rasping voice. Babs whined. They were a treat to listen to together. Jed Seeger had typed up a complete report of their story. It read like a whodunit.

"Is this really true?" I asked Tyler.

"You're goddamn right it's true. Those sons of bitches damn near murdered us ten different times."

"You saw to that," Babs said. She turned her puffed face toward me. "He was completely out of control. He threw the money at that man."

"You were calm and collected at all times, though," Tyler sneered. "Sure you were."

"You were the one who almost got us killed," she said. "Slapping that girl."

"For slapping you," Tyler said, "because you wouldn't shut the hell up. Screaming, whining. You should have heard her. She nearly drove me nuts herself."

"Oh, sure!" she screeched. "It's all my fault."

I stood up. "Come on, Mr. Tyler. I want to talk to you alone for a while." I led him into a private room of Seeger's suite, where I'd set up my polygraph instrument and tape recorder on a table stacked with law books and blue-backed briefs. "Sit down," I told Tyler. "With your permission, I'll turn on the tape recorder and you tell me exactly what happened in your own words." He told me, just as I've told it in the preceding pages. He finished:

"I don't know who they are. They never once called each other by name. The car license was all splattered with dried mud so you couldn't read it. Look, check out the banks and savings places. They saw me. They gave me the money. Here." He dragged the passbooks in their clear plastic envelopes from a pocket and slapped them into my hands. "The withdrawals are recorded right there."

"That isn't evidence you were kidnapped," I said. "Jed Seeger said he explained that to you already." I handed back the books. "That's why I'm here. A polygraph examination can verify that what you've said happened."

"Let's get on with it," he said.

"I think you're in pain," I said. "You may still be in shock. The instrument won't work under those conditions."

"I'm all right." He reached for the hanging polygraph attachments. "Fasten these on me. Turn the gismo on. You'll see. I'm scared but that's all."

"That they'll come back and kill you?" I said.

"They could be parked outside right now," he said. "They came to my house and found us, didn't they? Why did they pick us? He claimed somebody told him things about money hidden in my offices. Mine. Not the guy next door."

"Only there wasn't any money," I said, "so that makes no sense. I think he picked you at random. You live in an expensive suburb."

"He knew our name" Tyler said.

"Most of the mailboxes out that way have the names on them. Mr. Tyler, I don't think those people are coming back. They got the money. They're long gone from here."

"He was a Communist nut," Tyler said, "a revolutionary, a terrorist. He defended those terrorists to me, you know that? Who can predict what that kind is going to do?"

"That was a cover," I said. "Stop getting excited. I want you calm for the test."

"Right. Put these things on. Let's go."

Surprisingly enough, agitated as he was, he made a good subject. I ran three tests. Every one indicated the same thing—that the kidnapping story was true. I told the attorney. Seeger said to Tyler:

"Good. Now we call the police. You've been robbed. You've

214

been brutalized. You've been threatened with death. It's a police matter."

"Oh, no!" Babs tugged at his sleeve. Tears leaked from her puffy eyes. "Please. They made us promise never to tell. They'll kill us for sure if we tell the police."

"She's right," Tyler said stubbornly. "No police."

"Those people have to be stopped," I said. "You claim they nearly killed you. Do you think you'll be the last? Kidnapping worked for them in your case. They'll try it again. And the next people they take they may really kill. Who do you think will be responsible for that? How will you feel knowing you could have stopped them and did nothing?"

Tyler sulked. Babs whimpered softly and wrung her hands. But in the end they saw my point and let me ring the police. Then a new farce began. The desk officer thought I was some drunk. He couldn't believe two people and a dog had been kidnapped, run around town to three different banks to collect the ransom money, and then let go. I handed the phone over to Jed Seeger. The desk officer still thought it was a joke. Angrily, Seeger gave his name and said he was listed as an attorney in the telephone directory; the officer could look him up and call him back. The officer did. He said he would send a patrol car to Seeger's office—but that it would be a few minutes. Ten minutes passed. The Tylers were snapping at each other. The tension was getting to the lawyer and me too. Seeger dialed the police station again.

"Yeah, yeah," the duty officer said. "I reported your call to the sergeant. He's trying to get a hold of a couple of detectives, only they're off duty and hard to find. Take it easy, counselor."

When Seeger told me this, I became annoyed. I rang the police, gave my name, and asked to talk to the lieutenant in charge. I gave him the story all over again. He listened without much comment. But he promised to get right on the matter and he was as good as his word. Not that it helped a lot. Within a few minutes, the lieutenant himself, with a uniformed officer and two detectives, piled through the door of Seeger's offices. Seeger introduced the Tylers, he introduced me, and he repeated the kidnapping story to the lieutenant. His name was Merill but it could have been Doubting Thomas, the way he listened. He had a square, blood-shot face, eyes like gun-metal and just that expressionless. Seeger finished. Merill grunted.

"I've run a polygraph test on Mr. Tyler," I told him. "He's telling the truth."

Merill jerked his head at the detectives. "Take Mr. Tyler inside and talk to him."

"I'd like to be present," I said.

"Forget it," Merill said. "We'll take over now."

"You don't have to put him through another examination," I said. "I talked to him for hours. He's been through a terrific ordeal. He's tired. I've got a complete tape of my interview. You're welcome to it."

"We'll make our own tape, thanks," Merill said.

I looked at Seeger. Perhaps he knew these men. I didn't. Whether he did or not, he gave his head a quick shake, signaling me to let the matter go. Merill took Mrs. Tyler away for questioning. Seeger and I cooled our heels. Seeger told me he felt the police in this small town weren't much good at interrogation, but since the Tylers had agreed to tell the truth, no harm was going to be done. Certainly, the police didn't take long. In a half hour they all came out together. Merill looked sour.

"Okay, counselor. So maybe it's true. What do you expect me to do about it?"

I couldn't believe this. "For openers," I told him, "check out those banks. Next, put out an all-points bulletin on a battered four-door Plymouth with a tall young man in a leather jacket and a skinny blonde."

One of the detectives said, "We know our job. We don't need sarcastic comments from some private eye."

"How about honest help from a former criminal investigations expert for the U.S. Mission in Europe?" I asked.

Seeger said, "Who is also in the L.A. Police reserves. And the L.A. County Sheriff reserves. And the U.S. Marine reserves assigned to criminal investigations."

"I'm only trying to speed up your investigation," I told Merill. "Use the radio in your patrol car. Get out that APB before those people can get any farther away."

"What did you say your name was?" Merill growled.

216

I told him. He quit scowling and reached for a smile. "No kidding? Why, hell, I've read your articles in the police journals." He stuck out his hand. "Say, it's a real honor to meet you. Sorry I didn't know. People are always trying to tell us how to do our work."

"Put out the bulletin," I said. "Get to those banks."

"Right," Merill said.

But nothing happened. He was only being polite. The police didn't solve the Tyler kidnapping. It solved itself. Six months later the skinny blonde girl turned herself in—not because she was tired of freedom but because she was sore at the tall dude in the leather jacket. They'd traveled the country after the Tyler kidnapping, spending the money like water, until there was only eight thousand of it left. Then one morning Blondie had wakened in an empty bed: Leather Jacket had driven off in the night, leaving her flat. Oh, yes, they'd taken the Tyler couple at gunpoint, she admitted. They'd done everything the Tylers had claimed. And if the cops really wanted to know, Leather Jacket could be found, if she knew him, and she did know him, in or around Lancaster. She was right. And she got her wish: He went to jail. So did she.

As for Tyler, he'd never had many friends. It wasn't only his voice that was raspy—something about his personality grated on people. Yet he craved attention, and the kidnapping, the great adventure of his life, got it for him. He told the story endlessly, everywhere he got the chance. And as his associates tried to avoid giving him the chance, he went right on telling it. He kept trying to add details to make it more exciting when he saw his hearers, after the second or third recounting, yawn and turn away. I wonder how the story sounds today. Would it still register as true on the polygraph chart?

18

Terry Moore and Howard Hughes' Baby

When Howard Robard Hughes died, a bony, bearded recluse, he left an estate worth billions, and all sorts of people lined up with claims on that estate. Terry Moore, a well-known film actress who claims she married Hughes in 1949 aboard a cruise ship off the California coast, says, "Howard only wrote one will, and it directed that all his money go to a medical institute he planned to set up. In fact, that's all he talked about on our wedding night."

Terry Moore told me this when I interviewed her before a polygraph examination she'd agreed to take to verify her story about having been married to Hughes. She was as lovely and vivacious as she'd appeared in her films of the forties and fifties. She was now in her late forties, had been three times married and divorced, and lived with her two children in Hollywood. Chuck Ashman had sent her to me. Miss Moore's agent while she was busy with her career, he now did a late-night television news program for a Los Angeles station and wanted to break the story about Terry Moore's marriage to Howard Hughes, but he needed some verification of her claim.

That Hughes and Miss Moore had lived together for years was no secret, but no one seemed to believe they'd been married at the time. I searched my own files and combed newspaper morgues, but no record of any marriage between the two showed up. When Terry breezed into my office, she was accompanied by her mother and Chuck Ashman. I asked them to wait outside the examining room until I'd finished with the pre-test interview and had completed however many tests proved necessary. I'd asked Ashman to make a list of the questions he wanted answers to, and he handed me an envelope before he sat down to wait.

"Tell me about your marriage to Howard Hughes," I said, once Miss Moore was comfortable. "Do you know the exact date?"

"No. I'm not even sure of the exact year but I think it was 1949. Mother and I went aboard the *Helga*. It's a yacht—how long? Sixty-five, eighty-five feet?" She gave a little smiling shrug. "I do remember the captain's name. He was a personal employee of Howard's. Naturally, there were a number of Howard's aides on board. One was a witness to the marriage."

"He's still around," I said. "Has he come forward and admitted being present at the ceremony?"

"He hasn't made any public announcement, as far as I know," she answered. "But he told me over the telephone that Howard had the captain destroy the log showing that we were married. I have that conversation on tape."

"Can anyone else verify the marriage?"

"Howard's cook, the ship steward. But I don't know where he is now. I don't know if he's even still alive. And mother, of course. She was there."

"How did you meet Mr. Hughes?" I asked.

"I was sixteen or seventeen when I first met him. I liked him from the beginning. He was fascinating and loveable. We courted for about a year before he asked me to marry him. He wanted to let everyone know we were married, but I insisted it be kept a secret. Because of my film career."

"How long were you married to him?"

"About eight years."

I slit open the envelope Chuck Ashman had given me and read over his list of questions. One of them concerned a baby born to Terry Moore when she was in West Germany in 1951. This startled me. None of what I'd read about Miss Moore after Ashman had first called me had mentioned any child being born to the couple. I looked up.

"Is this right? You had a child by Howard Hughes?"

"Yes. A baby girl. Lisa Marie. She was premature. She came into the world in October 1951. I was in Munich making a film. She died the next day of blood poisoning. I was heartbroken. I really wanted that child."

"Did Mr. Hughes get to Germany at the time?"

"He wanted to come over but I told him I was all right, and he shouldn't bother. He did send over his personal physician because he was concerned about my health." Terry Moore bit her lip and fought back tears. It was obvious that she was still emotional about that moment of her life.

"Did you and Howard Hughes have other children?"

"No. He didn't even want that child. He didn't want children because he was afraid they'd have a claim on his estate. No, he made sure I would never again have any children. I thought he was being selfish. His argument was that unless you were around children constantly, to create and mold them, they would damage your image and blacken your name. He really meant it. And I suppose he was being honest with himself. He hadn't time to raise children. He was always working—too hard to suit me."

"Did you live together," I asked, "as man and wife, after the marriage?"

"In Beverly Hills," she said. "For eight years."

"At the Beverly Hills Hotel, wasn't it?"

She nodded. "For a long time."

I took a deep breath. "Do you have any proof that you were married to Howard Hughes?"

"I have a tape recording of his voice when he called me from his office and told me he couldn't come home, one evening. I was upset and he bawled me out for not understanding that he was a busy man

220

and had to keep on top of things so his stockholders would be happy."

"Nothing else?" I asked unhappily.

She gave a little regretful smile. "I'm afraid not now. Not that I can think of. I'm trying to locate others who were on the S.S. *Helga* when we got married. I'm sure then I'll have all the proof I need."

"Do you plan to make a claim on his estate?"

"No, I don't want a dime. I only want to make sure that his wishes are carried out, that the money goes to the medical institute, as he wanted it to. No, I don't want anything for myself. That's why I haven't filed a claim."

I was studying Ashman's list again. "You say you were never divorced by Hughes. In other words, when you two decided to call it quits, and you married again, you were committing bigamy, is that correct?"

Her smile was wry. "Believe me, it kept me up nights worrying about going to jail as a bigamist. It worried me through all my other marriages. Now you know why I kept quiet about my marriage to Howard all these years."

I studied her. "He married again too. Right?"

She said, "I've tried to run down that marriage license. I can't locate it." Her wry little smile was back. "I can't even find out where they filed for divorce. Well, that's water over the dam right now. I just want the world to know I was married to Howard Hughes on the *Helga* and that I had his child in 1951. I don't want his money—but I want to make sure it goes where he meant for it to go."

"Did his body have scars, marks, tattoos?"

"Oh, sure. Three scars on his chest from that plane crash that almost killed him. Everyone knows about the scar on his face near his eye. But not everyone knows where it came from. I put it there once when I was furious with him and hit him with something. It was stitched by a doctor one Easter Sunday while we were living at the Beverly Hills Hotel. The little finger on his right hand—that was permanently bent from the airplane crash. Another actress hit him when they were going together. That left a pretty good scar near one eyebrow. Colitis always bothered him. It was really a bad case. And

221

he was also deaf—did you know that? But he wouldn't wear a hearing aid. He did have an amplifier on his telephone, though. I—I guess that's all. I can't think of anything else right now."

"Tell me your feelings about him," I said.

"I really loved him," she said. "It was a shame things didn't work out for us. He was always so busy and so conscientious in everything he did. I wanted him around all the time, but his business came first. Howard was the greatest lover I ever had. He was the best."

It was easy to see that Terry's first love was really her only true love. Whether they'd been married or not, if they had been able to remain together, Hughes might have had a much happier life and not have died as he did—half-starved, neglected, almost alone. I went over the questions I intended to use during the polygraph examination with Terry. She didn't object to any of them. As I fastened the blood-pressure cuff, the respiration tube, the electrodes, I asked her if she'd ever been polygraphed before.

"No. I'm fascinated."

Here are the questions I asked and her responses.

"Were you ever married to Howard Hughes?"

"Yes."

"Were you ever made pregnant by Howard Hughes?"

"Yes."

"To your knowledge, was your marriage to Howard Robard Hughes ever annulled or ended by divorce?"

"No."

"Did one of his associates tell you that Howard Robard Hughes destroyed the evidence of your marriage to Hughes?"

"Yes."

When the examination was completed and I knew I had a set of charts that left no doubts as to their meaning, I undid the polygraph attachments and showed Terry the lines on the graph paper that indicated to me that she'd been telling the truth when she claimed she'd been married to Hughes and had borne him a child in Germany. She smiled.

"I really didn't have any doubts that I'd check out all right." She rose. "Thank you for listening to my life."

222

"Thanks for your cooperation." I opened the door of the examining room. In the outer office, Chuck Ashman and Terry Moore's mother looked up anxiously. I told Terry, "If you don't mind waiting a few minutes, I'd better have a word with Mr. Ashman."

Almost before the door had closed behind him, the television newsman was asking, "Well, what's the verdict?"

"No problem," I said. "She's telling the truth about her marriage and the baby."

"Great. I was sure she was. I just needed some outside verification. Thanks." He shook my hand. "I'll put the story on the air tonight. And I'll have Terry with me. Can you write up a report for me on your tests so I can read it for the cameras?"

I readied the report as quickly as I could, while Ashman brought in a still photographer to take shots of Terry in my office. I had a secretary type up the report. While we waited for it, Terry introduced me to her mother, a charming and lovely woman.

"Oh, yes," she said, "I was there on the yacht. I witnessed the marriage. I'm so happy you've confirmed that. You know, Terry's writing a book about Howard. It's going to be fascinating. There'll be things in it that have never been told before. It's not going to be sensational, scandalous, anything like that. It's going to be an honest appraisal of a very unique human being who was misunderstood by almost everyone."

"I'll look forward to reading it," I said.

"You know—I loved that man, almost as much as Terry did. He was very good to me. He often took me to lunch and dinner. He bought me many presents. I know he loved Terry deeply. It was just that his whole life was his work, his companies. It was a terrible shame the way he died and how he avoided people in his later years."

"All that money didn't bring him much happiness," I said. "I don't know that I've ever found a millionaire who got much joy out of life."

"Well," Terry's mother said, "I think people will see Howard Hughes in a better light when Terry's book comes out."

"I'm sure of it," I said. The secretary handed me the typed report on the Moore examination, and I passed it to Chuck Ashman.

"Thanks for your patience," I told him. I took Mrs. Moore's hand. "And yours. Sorry to have kept you waiting." I helped Terry Moore on with her coat. "I'm happy it worked out so well."

"So am I," she said. "Thank you."

Later on, Jack Anderson, the syndicated columnist, had Terry Moore appear with him on his television show, where she told a nationwide audience the same story she'd told me in the soundproof privacy of my examining room—of her shipboard marriage to Howard Hughes in 1949 and the pitiful death of their only child in faraway Munich. She still has entered no legal claim against Howard Hughes's estate. But she is a close and concerned observer of the ongoing turmoil over his fortune. Her only interest is to do everything she can to see to it that his wishes for a medical institute are carried out. She is quite a little scrapper, and if she feels for one minute that justice is not going to be done, she'll fight until it is. That's Terry Moore, who, though many years have passed, is still in love with her first husband.

19

The Murder of Dr. Martin Luther King, Jr.

On April 4, 1968, a single rifle bullet struck and killed Dr. Martin Luther King, Jr., as he stood with aides on a balcony of the Lorraine Motel in Memphis, Tennessee. King was not yet forty years old, yet he had become the most powerful black leader of this century. Twelve years earlier he had launched, against fierce opposition, a year-long boycott of the public transportation system of Montgomery, Alabama, which led to a U.S. Supreme Court decision banning segregation on buses. This in turn effectively ended segregation in other areas. In the years that followed, King was at the forefront of vast protest marches by American blacks demanding civil rights denied them for a century. An advocate of nonviolence, awarded the Nobel Peace Prize in 1964, King, like his model, Gandhi, died by violence. And in the wake of his murder, in a fury of grief and despair, blacks rioted and cities burned.

Within minutes of the shooting, Memphis police had cordoned off the district and begun a house-to-house search for the killer. He escaped. But beside a dingy rooming house opposite the motel, they found a rifle with a telescopic sight, a pair of binoculars, and a portable radio, all bundled hastily into a blanket. They decided the shot had been fired from the window of a washroom in the house by the man records showed to be the owner of the rifle: James Earl Ray, an escaped felon from the Missouri State Penitentiary. Ray had also owned a two-year-old white Mustang automobile. An all-points bulletin was broadcast for the car and its driver to all law-enforcement agencies in the surrounding states. But Ray slipped past them—first into Canada, then all the way to London.

The FBI joined in the search, bringing in its own investigators. Dr. King's lieutenants, shocked and grieved, accused the Memphis police of deliberately having pulled off security teams supposedly assigned to protect their leader. The police claimed that King and his staff had not wanted protection and had insisted the police back off. The federal agencies upset the local forces, who felt that they had done a thorough job on the case and resented Washington's interference. And while they all bickered, James Earl Ray made his way out of the country and the continent.

When he was finally caught in England and returned to Memphis for trial, Ray was represented by topflight attorneys, until he pleaded guilty and was sentenced to prison for ninety-nine years. A few days later, he went back on his confession, claiming he'd been coerced into it by threats that his father and brother were about to be arrested as his accomplices. The court refused to order a new hearing or a new trial, but Ray wasn't ready to give up. He began a long fight to gain the right to let a jury decide his guilt or innocence. Finally he got a new attorney, Mark Lane, well known for his research into and books on the Kennedy assassination.

It was Jack Anderson, the nationally syndicated columnist, who called me in to polygraph James Earl Ray. He wanted to present the results of my examination on a new television series he was developing with producer Ralph Andrews in California. Ray had been polygraphed earlier—by Douglas Wicklander of the John Reid firm in Chicago. Wicklander had determined that Ray was lying when he denied killing King, and that he was lying about a number of other aspects of the case. Mark Lane had not been Ray's lawyer at the time of this test and felt it might not have been conducted under proper conditions. Lane was also disturbed by the tone of an extensive interview with Ray published in *Playboy* magazine. He thought the questions had been slanted and that the piece showed Ray in an unfavorable light. For these reasons he welcomed my entry into the case.

I spent every moment I could find in the next days reading anything and everything on the tragedy of April 4, 1968, and on James Earl Ray. The Hollywood Library, not far from my offices, had bulging files of clippings. I boarded a flight for Tennessee on a cold night in late December 1977. A taxi took me to a Memphis hotel, where I met Mark Lane and members of Ralph Andrews' television production staff. I liked Lane at once. I'd read about his probing of the Kennedy assassination and found him a thorough, competent, intelligent lawyer, and a first-rate interrogator. His keen, inquisitive mind showed up at once in our talk, and I knew that if Ray were ever given the chance at a new trial, Lane would present an outstanding defense.

"Ray has been used as a political football," Lane said. "That's why there's got to be a new trial. His side of the story never even got told. The case wasn't decided on the evidence. It was decided in the papers."

I met James Earl Ray in a small room in the Brushy Mountain Tennessee State Prison. He wore drab prison garb, he was thin, and his face was rather sallow. Though plainly tired, his eyes were clear. I closed the door and told him to sit down. I had a tape recorder with me, but I thought it best not to use it until I was sure Ray had accepted me as objective and disinterested. I set it on the floor and didn't move to take off the lid.

"We don't have to use this yet," I said.

He looked relieved. He was edgy and unsure of me. "I didn't like my last brush with a lie detector," he said. "I was in lousy physical shape."

"How do you feel now?" I said. "I don't want to examine you if you feel ill."

"I'm all right," he said.

He didn't give his words any tone. He kept a barrier between us.

He'd been conned by this authority and that. So Mark Lane had told me. So I'd read. It wasn't much of a surprise, then, that he distrusted me. But he wasn't the only nervous man in that room. If he was tense, my own blood pressure was high and my pulse rate was faster than the normal seventy-two beats a minute. I was sweating and he noticed it. I had to break through his reserve.

"Look," I said, "I don't have any preconceived ideas about you or what you did or did not do that got you here. I'm not concerned about the escape attempt you made. I know what the police are saying but I'm an old hand and I don't let anything anybody says influence me. A polygraph examination is going to clear up any questions I have. And all that examination is going to be about is the Martin Luther King matter. You want to tell me about it.

Ray made a false start, stopped, cleared his throat, started again. With a lot of hesitations, he told me what he'd done after his escape from the Missouri prison, and before the death of King. He'd traveled to Canada, then to Mexico. He'd moved around the U.S. under a variety of assumed names.

"How did you make a living?" I asked.

"Smuggling. From the States into Canada."

"Smuggling what?" I asked.

"I don't know." He shrugged his shoulders. "I didn't look in the packages. Maybe drugs, narcotics. I don't know."

"You didn't do anything else?" I asked. "In the States?"

He didn't answer.

"The FBI claims you committed armed robberies to support yourself," I said. "Are they right?"

Again he didn't answer. I let the matter go for the time being and took another tack. I didn't want to get tangled up in details of his past, but I needed control questions to use in his tests, questions that would prompt lies I could identify as lies. He stopped me.

"I know what you're doing," he said. "I read up on the polygraph after that last fellow from Reid's gave me my test. He called me a liar, and I wanted to make sure I knew something about the polygraph before I took your test."

That surprised me. "Well," I told him, "I don't know what you've read, or how much you learned from your research, but I have to tell you, I have my own technique that I've used for many years. Don't worry about how the instrument works. Don't try to use it. Just cooperate with me and what we'll come out with is an objective examination. If you are telling the truth, I'll know it, and so will the whole world."

Again he didn't use words. He looked at me with his small, piercing eyes, and nodded. It was a quick nod. Just as quickly, he looked away. He waited for my next question.

"A little bit of knowledge," I warned him, "could just create certain physiological problems that could distort the examination. You know that, don't you?"

"Yes. Sorry. I'll cooperate in every way, Mr. Gugas."

"Right," I said. "Now, let's go back to Canada, where you met this man, Raoul. You said he told you to leave Canada and go to Birmingham, Alabama, and buy a rifle. What was his purpose in asking you to get the rifle?"

"It was him I'd been doing the smuggling for—drugs or whatever. He paid me well. I had no reason to question him. He asked me to get the rifle because he wanted to check it out and see if it was the kind he could sell on a quantity basis to—interested persons."

"What was Raoul's last name?"

"I've already told everybody I don't know that. I never asked him. I doubt very much that even Raoul was his real name. In our business, you're always using other names to protect yourself from the law. Asking questions is out of line. Asking for his last name or asking to see identification or any of that would be the last thing I'd do."

"Describe him for me," I said.

Ray only repeated the description of Raoul he'd many times given his attorneys and the press. I'd just read the printed accounts—over and over again—and it was as if he'd memorized them. I kept looking him straight in the eyes. When I touched a subject he didn't like, he turned his eyes away from mine.

"Just when was it Raoul asked you to buy the rifle?"

"Well, we'd gone to Atlanta. He asked me to buy a big-bore rifle, a deer rifle, with a telescopic sight, so he could show it to some people who were interested in buying rifles, new and used ones. I had identification showing that I was from Alabama, so I drove over to Birmingham. Raoul met me there and we found out that the Aeromarine Supply Company had a lot of guns for sale. Raoul gave me about seven hundred and fifty dollars and told me to get a deer rifle.''

"Did you get it?" I asked.

''Not the one he wanted. When I got back to the motel, he didn't like the rifle. He said for me to take it back and get the one he'd picked out of a catalogue. He was taking off for Memphis. I was supposed to meet him at the Rebel Motel there on April third and bring the rifle with me. I said I would exchange the rifle and get the one he wanted and then drive to Memphis.''

"Why was the first rifle you picked the wrong kind?" I asked. "Did Raoul explain that to you?"

''I didn't ask. He just told me it wasn't the right one and I didn't press for why. He'd said he had this buyer who wanted a whole bunch of guns, and I didn't figure it was any of my business to ask him what it was all about. When you operate outside the law, you keep your mouth shut and your eyes open.''

"What happened when you arrived in Memphis?"

''I got to the Rebel Motel sometime in the early evening on April third. Raoul was there and I gave him the rifle. He was satisfied with it. Then he sent me to get a pair of infrared binoculars. The store wasn't far off. I think it was called the York Arms. I couldn't get the infrared type there. They didn't have them. So I got another pair.''

"Did you take them to him?"

''No, I took them to a room I'd rented at 422½ South Main Street. He'd told me he'd meet me there around four in the afternoon. This was April fourth, now.''

"When did you rent the room?"

''Earlier that day. Under the name George Willard. I was in and out of that room at least a dozen times. Raoul had me going to the drugstore, the gun shop, a couple of bars, and a gas station to get air for my tires. I didn't spend a lot of time in the room, really, because of all the running around I did.''

"Did he meet you at four as he said he would?"

"Yeah. I gave him the binoculars.''

"Where were you when Dr. King was shot?"

"To be perfectly honest with you, I don't really remember. I think I'd just left the gas station and I was heading back toward the rooming house on Main when I heard sirens all over the place and I saw the police had blocked off the whole area. They were everyplace. I didn't know what had happened, but I knew I had to get out of there right away, because I was a fugitive and I didn't want to get caught by the cops."

"Where did you decide to go?" I asked.

"I was really shaken up. I thought about going to New Orleans, because I knew I could meet up with Raoul there after all this King confusion. I heard King had been shot at a place called the Lorraine Hotel. It turned out to be right near my rooming house. I swear I didn't even know that, didn't know where the place was. The news came over my car radio about seven o'clock. It was evening by now, right? And the news said that the suspect was driving a white Mustang. That didn't make me feel any better. With my record and being in that rooming house, if I got caught they'd be sure to blame King's death on me. I wondered if Raoul had set me up. Maybe Raoul and his friends were trying to get rid of me. I was really in a tight mess."

"Do you think Raoul killed Dr. King?"

"It would only be conjecture on my part. I don't know, but I suspect he had something to do with it."

"What about the stuff found in the blanket beside the rooming house—the rifle, the binoculars, the radio? How did it get left behind? It was your stuff. All of it was identifiable as yours."

Ray shifted on his chair and looked away from me. I asked the same question again. He said impatiently:

"All I can tell you is that either Raoul left it there or someone who was with him in my room. How do I know who dumped it there? I wasn't anywhere near that rooming house when King was shot. I suspect Raoul could fill in that puzzle but I can't."

"Was there a conspiracy to kill Dr. King?"

"I can't be sure, but if it was Raoul who set the whole thing up to kill King, then I was an unsuspecting accomplice, that's all. I don't know if Raoul was mixed up in the killing. But I guess if he

231

did it, then I was an unwitting part of the deal. I know I didn't kill King, and I know I didn't have any prior knowledge that he was going to be killed."

My own nerves were well under control by now, but Ray had begun to sweat. I didn't want him upset. I changed the subject. "Where did you get the money to travel around the country after you left Canada?"

He turned away again. I repeated the question.

"Raoul had paid me plenty of money for the smuggling. I had enough to get around."

"You didn't commit those robberies the FBI says you did to get travel money?"

"I'm not going to talk about those bank robberies," Ray said. "I don't want to get in any more trouble than I'm in right now."

I switched subjects right away. I knew I'd turned up the kind of control question I'd been looking for. He'd be almost sure to have a strong reaction about the bank robberies when I gave him his polygraph test.

"We can skip the bank stuff," I said, "because it doesn't have anything to do with what I'm here to examine you about—Dr. King's murder. Anyway, the statute of limitations has run out. They couldn't prosecute you now."

Later, I was to wonder why Ray had become so shaken up about those bank robberies. James Earl Ray is no dummy. He's been around and knows the laws and the statutes of limitations. Why, then, did the color leave his face and his eyes shun mine? I don't suppose I'll ever know the answer, and at the time I wasn't really concerned with it. I needed more answers, and I began a new approach.

"What about the allegation that your brother Jerry was involved with you in a conspiracy to kill Dr. King?"

"That's a lot of baloney. My brother and I had nothing to do with King's killing. Jerry was in Chicago, working, when King was shot. That's been proved."

"Your father's also been mentioned," I said.

"That's all phony," he answered. "The government was pushing to have him and Jerry arrested, and that was why I decided to plead guilty—to protect my family. No, I wasn't guilty, but they weren't guilty either. And Percy Foreman said they'd be out of trouble if I just pleaded guilty. He said all I'd get would be a prison term. That was better than being barbecued, he said. He gave me every reason you could think of why I should plead guilty to King's murder. So I finally agreed. But it was against my better judgment."

"He was your defense attorney," I said.

"He'd told me to start with that my case would be easy to win. Now he was telling me I didn't have a chance because the press was against me, public opinion was against me. All that stuff about the good defense he was going to put up for me? He never even contacted witnesses who could prove that the State's big witness against me was dead drunk in bed. He could never have identified the person running away from the bathroom where they said the shot was fired from."

I was deeply disturbed by all I'd read and gathered from other sources about the trial. I could sympathize with Ray when he asked me how he could trust anyone again.

"I know investigation techniques," I said. "And Mark Lane has done an outstanding job for you."

"Yes. He's been a true friend and an honest attorney. I only wish I'd met up with him sooner. I probably wouldn't be in this mess now. I sure hope he can get me a trial. He says, 'There is the truth, and there is the legal truth.' And he's right. The evidence they have against me won't stand up in any objective court. I sure hope he makes out for me."

"He's doing all he can," I said.

Ray seemed a little less edgy. I wondered if we could start testing. The prison hospital ward was just down the hall. I sent for a medical technician to check Ray's blood pressure. I'd been mistaken. He was still uptight. The meter read one-thirty over a hundred. His pulse was racing, a hundred and twenty-five beats per minute. He was in no shape to face a polygraph test. Not yet.

"You need to relax," I said. "Have some lunch and lie down for half an hour." He had a sandwich, washed down with two little cartons of milk. He ate and drank quickly. He lay down in the hospital ward for twenty-five minutes. But he didn't wind down. His blood pressure still checked out above normal. So did his pulse.

I wondered if anxiety about getting started on the tests was keeping him stressed. Maybe he'd settle down once the polygraph attachments were made and the test was underway.

"Sit here," I said. "Let's give the instrument a try." He took the chair and I fastened on the tube, cuff, and electrodes. "Try to relax. You're still keyed up."

"I want to get the tests done," he said, "so Mark will know I've been telling him the truth."

"Your blood pressure's too high," I said, and unfastened the cuff. "It's important that you feel well, that you feel up to the test."

"I'm all right. Put that thing back on. Don't you understand? I flunked the last test, the one the Reid guy gave me. I have to take this. I have to pass it. Look, I know I'm a little nervous, but the book on lie detectors I read says that's normal.

"That's true," I said. "But you're overanxious. Don't be in a hurry. There are several things we have to do before I can begin the actual examination. If you read the book right, you know we have to review all the questions in detail, so you'll know and understand each question I ask and there won't be any chance of error."

"Okay." He nodded, but he didn't relax and he wasn't about to. I took a deep breath and began reviewing the questions with him. This was the first series. I'm giving here the answers he later gave when the polygraph was activated and the graph paper moving.

"Is your name James Earl Ray?"

"Yes."

"Did you have breakfast this morning?"

"Yes."

"Do you know who shot Dr. Martin Luther King, Jr.?"

"No."

"Did you have any soft drink today?"

"Yes."

"Did you shoot Dr. Martin Luther King, Jr.?"

"No."

Now here came the first control question: "Between the ages of eighteen and thirty-five, did you ever think about causing any physical harm to any person?"

"No."

"Were you born in Alton, Illinois?"

"Yes."

"Between 1960 and April fourth, 1968, do you recall telling any person in the United States that you were going to shoot or harm Dr. Martin Luther King, Jr.?"

During the preliminary run-through of the questions, Ray stopped me here. He wanted this question reworded so that it included the United States only, and not Canada.

"I might have said something negative about King when I was in Canada."

I changed the wording. His answer on the test was "No."

"Did you fire any rifle at any person in Memphis in April 1968?"

"No."

Now came the second control question: "Were there others involved in planning your escape from Brushy Mountain Penitentiary?"

"No."

There were four questions about the assassination of Dr. Martin Luther King, Jr., and Ray's possible association with it, in that first series. As I've said before in this book, that's about the limit for a successful polygraph examination. But there were more questions to be asked, and they formed a second series. Again, I'm listing them here with Ray's responses given during the actual running of the test.

"Do you wear glasses?"

"Yes."

"Were you involved with any other person or persons in a conspiracy to shoot Dr. Martin Luther King, Jr.?"

"No."

"Do you have three brothers?"

"Yes."

"Did you know Dr. Martin Luther King, Jr., was going to be shot?"

"No."

Next came the third control question: "Did you ever think about harming Dr. Martin Luther King, Jr.?"

Ray answered "No."

I asked, "Were you ever legally married?"

235

"No," Ray said.

"Did you ever have any rifle or pistol with you in the rooming house at 422½ South Main Street on April fourth, 1968?"

"No."

"Did you point any weapon toward Dr. Martin Luther King, Jr., on April fourth, 1968?"

"No."

I wound up the second set of questions in the same way as the first, with a control question: "Between the ages of eighteen and forty, did you ever lie to any government official?"

"No," Ray said.

I ran several charts on both series of questions, watching Ray closely all the time. He kept applying pressure to his left arm, the one that held the blood-pressure cuff. When this happens, it causes a pen deflection on the chart, a deflection easy to notice. As the tests were repeated, I saw that Ray applied this pressure only at certain questions. His purpose fascinated me. He meant the chart to show an increase in blood pressure that would tell the examiner on evaluating the charts that at these points the subject was lying. And the questions he picked out were the control questions—the ones I'd used with some certainty that the physiological responses would contradict the spoken ones. Ray's forced overresponses were so dramatic on these control questions, I thought he was attempting to beat the polygraph. I removed the attachments and had his blood pressure checked again. It was higher than ever, one forty-five over a hundred now. His heartbeat had dropped to a hundred per minute before the test; now it was back to a hundred twenty-four. When the technician had left, Ray asked me:

"Well, how did it come out?"

"James," I said, "did any of the questions I asked you disturb you in any way?"

He tried to look puzzled. "No, not a bit."

"Well, in a couple of areas, there were definite responses after your answers."

"I can't understand that," he said. "I didn't feel anything different."

I looked straight into his eyes and he turned away. He mumbled, "I was tired, I was nervous."

236

I gave my head a regretful shake. "I'm sorry," I said. "I'm sorry your charts aren't as clear as they should be. But you do show the same significant reactions on most of the critical questions, chart after chart. If none of the questions troubled you, why did this happen? Why did you show disturbance on the same ones time after time?"

"I don't know," he said. "Nerves, I guess."

"Did you understand all of the questions?"

"Oh, sure." He muttered it. He didn't look at me.

"Do you think I was objective and thorough in our pre-test interviews?"

"Yes." He still didn't look at me.

I didn't tell him that I'd noticed him forcing some of his responses. He was too intelligent ever to admit it. I told him I would review his charts carefully and make a final determination about the tests as soon as I could. He nodded, still keeping his face and eyes turned away. It didn't cheer me up. I was convinced he'd not been truthful during his tests and that he'd tried to manipulate the process so that I couldn't make any determination from the charts. I was disappointed for Mark Lane, who'd been patiently waiting, hour after hour, downstairs, hoping for good news from me. I told him I needed time to recheck carefully all of the charts. I'd give him an answer that evening at the motel.

Ray was interviewed by Jack Anderson about an hour after my examination, with cameras and microphones. He told Anderson he had not shot Dr. King and that he knew nothing about the assassination. Anderson asked me for my opinion, based on the polygraph tests I'd given Ray. I told him I thought Ray had lied about not shooting Dr. King, but had told the truth when he said there was no conspiracy. I said this meant to me that Ray had acted on his own. The broadcast would not take place for a while. If the intensive study I wanted to give Ray's charts left any doubts, my own part in the Anderson show could be filmed again. But as I examined the charts closely throughout the rest of the afternoon in my motel room, it simply became more and more apparent that Ray had lied on the vital questions.

Heavyhearted, I picked up the telephone. Mark Lane came to my motel unit and I gave him the bad news. Pain was written in his face, but he said nothing. I told him I meant to have other qualified examiners review my findings and offer a final opinion but that I doubted the outcome would be any different. He thanked me and left. I needn't have felt sorry for him. He wasn't going to let one setback stop his effort to get James Earl Ray a new trial.

The next day I went with him to Memphis, where he had located a taxi driver named James McCraw who could be very important to Ray's defense. McCraw insisted that the State's one and only witness, Charles Q. Stephens, had been inaccurate in claiming to have seen Ray leave the washroom at 422½ South Main Street just after the bullet had been fired from there that killed Dr. King. He told Mark Lane and me:

"I saw Charlie Stephens lying on his bed stone drunk about five forty-five P.M. on April fourth, 1968. I'd received a call from the dispatcher to pick up a fare at the Main Street place. Stephens was living there with Grace, his common-law wife. She was there. When I saw what condition Charlie was in, I wasn't about to take him in my cab."

"You call him Charlie," I said.

"I've known him for more than twenty years," McCraw answered. "He was dead drunk."

"This man is a polygraph expert," Mark Lane told McCraw. "A lie-detector man. Would you be willing to let him test you to see if you're telling the truth?"

"I'm telling the truth," McCraw said. "Why not?"

McCraw passed my tests without a hitch. Lane asked me if I would give polygraph examinations to Charles Q. Stephens' common-law wife. It turned out that she'd been committed to a state hospital for alcoholism, but she had previously told Lane that McCraw's account of Stephens' condition at the time he claimed to have seen James Earl Ray leave the rooming house washroom was correct—that Stephens had been drunk and unconscious at the time of the shooting.

"She won't make a satisfactory subject," I said. "I'm sorry. Treatment, confinement, medication—all those things can work against a successful polygraph examination."

"I'm going to get her out of there," Lane said.

"If you can," I said, "and if she recovers from the experience, just let me know, and I'll be happy to test her for you."

Grace Stephens is now in a California rehabilitation center. She is getting along well in her new surroundings. Maybe, in time, Mark Lane will send for me again in the James Earl Ray case. For if it can be established that Grace is telling the truth about Charles Stephens' condition, she can be a most important witness should a new trial be arranged for Ray.

The charts from those tests I gave him at Brushy Mountain Penitentiary make me absolutely certain that James Earl Ray fired the shot that killed Martin Luther King, Jr., and that he acted not as part of any conspiracy but solely on his own. The John Reid polygraph experts in Chicago agree with me. And I'm certain of another thing: Should James Earl Ray not receive a new trial, he will attempt another prison escape. It's his pattern. He's even been known to make it sometimes. But whether he does or does not, one thing is sure. Controversy will continue to swirl about his name for many years to come.

20

Vesco and the 224 Million Dollars

It was southern California's rainiest winter in decades. The runways at Los Angeles International Airport gleamed like gray and desolate mirrors. The huge tires hissed as the wide-bodied jet lumbered toward the ocean. The engines whined, the bulky craft shuddered and gained speed. The yellow runway marker lights became wet streaks beyond the windows. The engines screamed. The jet was airborne. It curved out over the dull gunmetal color of the Pacific, climbed through layers of wooly gray cloud into layers of ragged black, and at last broke into sunlight and unblemished blue sky. Above my head the seat belt and No Smoking signs winked off. The plane swung southward. I was on my way to Costa Rica.

In the seats around me sat Ralph Andrews; his producer, Stan Berk; and his right-hand assistant, Nancy Willock. Andrews, a tall, nervous man with a gleaming shaven head, was preparing a pilot film for a syndicated television series, "The Truth With Jack Anderson." The national newspaper columnist, famous for his investigative reporting, was not with us. He would come to Costa Rica after the television team had made everything ready for filming. It didn't look to me as if this was going to be the easy part: I'd traveled in happier company. Andrews, Berk, and Willock were anxious. The venture was costing a bundle. Adding up transport costs, the wages of technicians, and the leasing fees on video and audio equipment, the investment came out at something like fifty thousand dollars. Then there was the uncertainty factor—the man on whom all this expense and anxiety were focused: Robert Lee Vesco.

Vesco, a rugged, two-fisted type who'd grown up on the tough streets of Detroit and never even finished high school, had cut a spectacular swath through the world of high finance—buying troubled companies, propping them up, reselling them, rounding up investors from all over the world, building an international business empire, piling up a personal fortune of untold millions. To some, he was a genius; to others, a slick manipulator at best, at worst a swindler. Finally, the U.S. Securities and Exchange Commission got on his case. They alleged he'd deprived shareholders in Investor's Overseas Service of $224 million!

Vesco shifted his headquarters to the Central American republic of Costa Rica, out of reach of those trying to get at him. Watergate followed. Vesco was charged with having contributed an illegal fifty thousand dollars to enable Richard Nixon to aid the men accused of, and jailed for, the break-in at Democratic National Headquarters: the incident that was to put an end to Nixon's presidency. Other accusations were flung at Vesco: that Mafia money financed his operations, that he was involved in drug trafficking, that he was running guns into a Miami warehouse. Robert Lee Vesco was a hot subject.

He'd agreed to let Jack Anderson interview him in front of cameras so that he could tell his side of the confusing and contentious story to the American television public. He'd gone even further. He'd agreed to let himself be polygraphed, convinced that in this way he could prove that the charges against him were lies. But in the minds of Ralph Andrews and his staff, so much hung on the success of this segment of his projected pilot that Vesco's very

241

name had them shaky with nerves. Nothing must go wrong. Naturally, they were convinced that their own part in putting the segment together would be flawless. That left only one person to worry about: Chris Gugas.

When I'd been approached by an intermediary to talk with Ralph Andrews about taking part in the Jack Anderson project, I'd refused. Andrews had made use of the polygraph on an earlier series that had not been a hit. I had disliked the way he'd presented the polygraph, and I'd predicted to him that it would not take hold. There is no way the polygraph can be seriously used among a crowd of cameramen and floor directors and in front of an audience in a television studio. It isn't a show-biz gimmick. I felt Andrews' whole concept was a poor one and would confuse the public about the value of the polygraph and harm the future of something I deeply believed in. I was relieved when my prediction proved correct and the show went off the air after only a few weeks.

"This time," Andrews assured me, "things are going to be different. The idea is to polygraph well-known personalities who feel they've been wronged and who want to be polygraphed to prove they're telling the truth."

I started shaking my head. He held up a hand.

"Wait, just listen for a minute. Everything will be kept on a high, professional level. I know how you feel about the polygraph. This time we're not going to do a thing that will offend your ethics—not in any way whatever. That's a promise. Look, work with us, please."

"I've got a full schedule," I said. "More than I can handle. Get hold of John Reid in Chicago. He's one of the most experienced examiners in the world, and he's got a raft of associates. I've got only three examiners working for me. I can't afford to be away from my office, flying all over the world."

Nancy Willock sat nearby taking notes. She looked up. "We've already contacted Mr. Reid. He can't come aboard."

Andrews said, "He offered one of his staff members but I want a name. I want a polygraph man with experience and a reputation. Besides, I'm not in Chicago, I'm here and you're here. I want you, Chris."

"I appreciate your confidence," I said. "But there's really no way I can do it. I'm overworked as it is."

But Andrews wasn't taking no for an answer. He insisted that his program would be beneficial to the polygraph field. It would open a new understanding of the value of using the instrument in business and in the courts. I had to agree with that, and I couldn't have wanted anything more. But facts were facts. I'd told him the truth—I was simply too busy. What resulted was a compromise. I sighed.

"All right, I'll work on the pilot with you. I won't promise anything beyond that. And we have to have an understanding: There'll be no gimmicks. Everything has to be professional and in good taste—right?"

"Right. Now, your first test will be in Costa Rica. We plan to leave in a couple of weeks, as soon as we can get our technical equipment together and ship it down there. Can you be ready?"

"Costa Rica?" I said. "Is it Vesco?"

"You've got it," Andrews said.

"I'll need background material," I said. "Can Jack Anderson's office supply that?"

Nancy Willock said, "I'm afraid he hasn't anything available himself yet."

I was on my own for research. First I contacted a friend at the Los Angeles *Times* and read through heaps of yellowed newspaper clippings. Robert Lee Vesco had made a lot of headlines in his time. He was still headline material. Books had been written about him too. I did what any researcher does. I went to my local public library—the Hollywood Branch. A man who'd piloted Vesco around the world in pursuit of his debatable business projects on his own 747 had some pretty unpleasant things to say about him. The pilot's name was Captain A. L. Eisenhower (nickname Ike, of course) and his book was titled *The Flying Carpetbagger*. Another book less than charitable to its subject was *Vesco: the Infernal Money Making Machine,* by Michael Dornan. I wasn't getting an unbiased view. I would have to furnish that myself, but such a task was nothing new for me. It's part of a polygraph examiner's equipment. He can't do a good job unless he goes in with an open mind.

243

The Costa Rican trek was postponed once, when Vesco came down with a virus. When the new date came, and I met Andrews and Willock at the rainy airport for this flight, I knew my subject. I'd had thirty years of experience at my job: I was as ready to do my part as the TV people were to do theirs. But Andrews, once on the plane, seemed to forget all the faith in me and my reputation he'd talked about on the ground. Now they were actually turning me loose to talk face to face with this notably troublesome tough guy with millions of powerful dollars behind him. I was going to ask him questions—about very touchy subjects, subjects that made him angry.

"Be careful," Andrews said. "Take it easy. Don't do anything to annoy him."

"He could cancel the interview," Nancy Willock said.

"And there goes fifty thousand bucks down the tube," Ralph Andrews said.

It became a litany. I thought the plane trip would never end. But nothing got better when it did. At the Hotel Irazu in San José, I had to listen to it all through dinner that evening. And at breakfast the next morning. And at lunch. The rest of the time, I avoided Andrews and Berk, holing up in my room reading over yet again all the Xerox copies of material on Vesco I'd brought along. But while we were in the same hotel together, there was no real way I could dodge the constant reminders:

"Chris, for God's sake, keep the man happy till Jack Anderson gets here and we film the interview. Keep the man happy." I appreciated their concern, but I was getting more nervous each day.

A glossy brochure on the hotel reception desk outlined a train trip through Costa Rica. We had a couple of days, yet, so I decided to take the tour. I can stand being shut up in a hotel room for only so long. I wasn't concerned about testing Vesco, but the television people were going to make me that way unless I got away from them. As it turned out, I didn't—they took the train trip with me. But the subject of Vesco was forgotten in the loveliness of the landscape. I have seen some beautiful countries, but I'd have to rank Costa Rica close to the top. Its lush vegetation, pure clean air, and many winding rivers and streams reminded me of South Pacific islands I'd visited before World War II. There were wide stretches

244

of banana plantations, the long, leathery leaves shiny in the sun, the stalks of harvested fruit piled up, awaiting transport to the far corners of the world. Coffee bushes, with their lovely red berries, were everywhere. Cocoa beans lay drying on racks along the railroad. The harvest workers lived and raised their families in little shacks, but food was everywhere. In the eight hours of that trip, during which the train made some seventy stops, I didn't see one barren acre of land. All was lush and green and fruitful between San José and the port town of Limón.

We took a plane back to San José and on Monday morning, November 18, 1977, I met with Jack Anderson, who had reached Costa Rica on Saturday evening. I told him I felt it was important that I polygraph Vesco before he did his interview.

"That's fine with me," he said. "Here's the list of questions I've prepared." He handed me typewritten sheets. I ran my eye down them, flipping the pages over. There were something like fifty questions in all. I looked at Anderson. "Something wrong?" he said.

"The limit on any one polygraph test," I said, "is five key questions. It hasn't anything to do with you or me—it's simply the way things are. Any polygraph expert would tell you the same thing." I handed back the sheets.

"Can't you give him more than one test?"

"Depending on what kind of subject he makes," I said. "But with the tight schedule you're working on, I'd say the limit would be three."

"Good. Then let's pick out fifteen questions," Anderson said. "You can ask him five on each test."

As I was driven in a Vesco limousine through the sunny San José streets, I hoped Robert Vesco would agree. After all, he was at least as busy as Jack Anderson. The car stopped at a white building roofed in red tile and I was shown upstairs to the office of Alberto Abru, Vesco's Costa Rican chief of staff. Abru had been with Vesco for years. He struck me as forthright, and we got along well from the start. It was plain that he was expertly protective of his employer, but he shared with me a lot of information about the Vesco financial empire and promised me that when the polygraph tests were finished, he would supply me with documents to back up

Vesco's answers. Books stood on shelves behind Abru's desk, among them biographies of Vesco, including those by Captain Eisenhower and Michael Dornan. Abru saw me eyeing the books.

"You have read them all, I suppose?" he asked.

"Only three," I said, "but I promise you, I've kept an open mind. I don't always believe what I read. I want to hear the other side of the story. That's why I'm here."

Abru smiled. "I'm glad to hear you say that, Chris. Bob has been lied to by so many of his so-called friends, he doesn't know whom to trust anymore. I can assure you, he will answer every question you ask him truthfully."

"That will make a good impression," I said.

"Of course," Abru added hastily, "there are certain details he can't give you. But I'm sure you understand that there are reasons for that. He is still under indictment in the States, and he doesn't want to have any more hassles with the government. Not if he can help it."

"The questions are simple and to the point," I said.

Abru glanced over his shoulder at the bookshelves. "Those writers," he said contemptuously. "They will say anything, Chris, anything. Vesco is a thief. Vesco is a swindler, a gunrunner, a drug dealer, part of the Mafia. It is disgusting."

Vesco was late. I wasn't surprised. He'd wanted to give Abru time to brief me and, I supposed, to put me at ease. We chatted about Chicago, where Abru had once lived, and where he'd met and married his American wife. He told me he was going to open his home here in San José to Ralph Andrews and his television staff. It would be there that the Jack Anderson interview with Vesco would take place in front of the cameras.

"That's generous of you," I said.

Abru's smile was wry. "Mr. Anderson suggested Bob's house, but that's out of the question. You understand. He has so often been threatened. He will tell you about a particular incident that will shock you. You will see why to photograph his house, inside or out, would be dangerous. Who can tell who may be watching this television program? He has his family's safety to consider."

I was aware of someone behind me and turned. Robert Vesco

246

himself stood in the doorway of Abru's office. He came forward as I rose, and shook my hand. His grip was firm and his smile was genuine. He took a seat next to Abru, facing me. Before I sat down again, I took off my jacket. Under a jacket or in a jacket pocket a tape recorder can be concealed. Attaché cases are not always what they seem to be, and I made a point of opening mine on Abru's desk. It held only papers. Vesco might be recording what went on in his room for his own protection against misquotation or misrepresentation later on, but I wanted him and Abru to know that as far as I was concerned, what was said in this interview was strictly between us. I took from the attaché case Anderson's long list of questions.

"Hold it," Vesco laughed. "I've got my own." He showed me a list almost as long as Anderson's. "My lawyer drew it up—Edward Bennett Williams, Washington, D.C. You know him?"

"I've heard of him," I said. "He's a high-powered attorney, but he apparently doesn't know there's a strict limit on how many questions can be asked in a polygraph examination." I explained the situation. "We'll have to try to find fifteen questions in all, taken from your list and Jack Anderson's, that will do the job."

"Let's get going," Vesco said.

But it wasn't a quick task, or an easy one. We sweated and haggled on that tropical morning. Vesco had a lot of grievances against a lot of individuals and government agencies and he wanted to answer every charge ever made against him. I had to keep corralling him, reminding him we could cover only a very few core areas and that every key question we decided to use had to hinge directly on those matters. It took hours, but finally I had what I felt was a workable set of questions.

"Is this going to cover it?" Vesco asked warily. "Is this going to show the American people I'm only a businessman? That I'm not a crook, a swindler, a gangster? Look—if I stole two hundred and twenty-four million bucks, why haven't they charged me? The only thing I've been charged with is an illegal contribution of fifty thousand dollars to Nixon—nothing else. And what does that add up to? Maurice Stans and John Mitchell were tried for accepting that money and acquitted."

247

"So why not go back to the States," I asked, "go into court against the charges the government's threatening to bring, and get it over with?"

Vesco's smile was grim. "Chris, you don't understand how the government works. I'm supposed to be rich, right? They've got so much money and so much manpower, they could turn me into a poor man by the time I got through protesting my innocence. 'A man is innocent until he's proven guilty'? Bullshit. When the government indicts you, you're guilty. That's the real truth."

"What about your family, your friends?" I said. "Don't you owe it to them to get it on record once and for all that you didn't steal millions from Investors Overseas Services—that you're not a swindler?"

"Do you know what it would cost me," Vesco answered, "to defend myself today? No? Well, I don't have that much money, not without tying myself up for the next ten years. Howard Hughes was right when he worried about going to court. You can get murdered there, innocent or not. No thanks." He glanced out the window at the sunny blue sky. "I like it here. I'm going to become a Costa Rican citizen as soon as possible. My wife's already a citizen. My wife and family are exactly the ones I'm thinking of. I'm not subjecting them to an endless court battle in the States. No way. Anyway, there's no guarantee I'd live that long if I went back there."

"What are you talking about?" I asked.

"Something not many people know," he said. He leaned forward. "Uncle Sam hired an ex-convict to kidnap me. Or my family. To force me back to the States to stand trial." He sat back in his chair. "I wouldn't put anything past the government." He glanced at Abru. "We've got documentation, haven't we?"

Abru nodded. I stared. It sounded too fantastic to believe. I hoped Vesco wasn't paranoid. I was here to give him a polygraph examination; that won't work with the mentally unstable. Evidently Vesco saw the incredulity on my face. He jerked his head in a silent command to Abru. The man moved to a file cabinet and rolled open a drawer. From it he tugged a thick folder. The drawer rolled shut. Abru glanced at Vesco. Vesco nodded. Abru put the binder into my hands. There were forty-five pages. I flipped them over. There were documents, affidavits, statements.

"Read that when you've got time," Vesco said. "I know it sounds incredible, but every goddamn word is true. You'll see the convict's signature in there."

"Did he actually say the government had hired him?"

"A deputy U.S. Attorney in New York and an SEC attorney. They told him to kidnap me and bring me to the States. If they couldn't get me, he was supposed to kidnap anybody he could from my family—as a hostage. And if he couldn't do either one," Vesco finished, "he was supposed to kill me."

I weighed the Xerox copies of the documents in my hand. "I'll read about it before we do the examination," I said.

"Right. Because I want you to ask me about that," Vesco said. He checked the question lists in front of him. "Oh, and don't leave out the Nixon contribution business. About Murray Chotiner asking me for money."

"He was supposed to have met with you in Nassau," I said. "After the Watergate break-in. He was Nixon's big fund-raiser. What was he trying to get from you? The million dollars Nixon said it wouldn't be any trouble to raise? You met more than once. Was fifty thousand all you gave him?"

"Yes—at the Paradise Club in Nassau," Vesco said. "Let's not worry about the details. I'll tell it to Anderson in the interview." He did, though not how much he'd given Chotiner to pass on to Nixon. Anderson's staff later dug out the truth: The cash contributions Vesco had turned over amounted not to fifty thousand dollars, but to five times that much—close to a quarter of a million.

"What about these Mafia charges?" I asked.

"Everybody with money and an Italian name hears those," Vesco said. He laughed ironically. "If I had any connections to the Mafia, it wouldn't be me working for them—it would be them working for me."

"I don't want to keep you." I got out of my chair, placed the binder of documents in my attaché case, and closed it. I put on my jacket. "We've got our fifteen questions. We'll finalize them to-morrow morning—right?"

249

"Early," Vesco said, and shook my hand.

Abru escorted me out to the street, where a car was waiting for me. "What about those gunrunning charges?" I asked him. "You rented a warehouse in Miami."

"I did," Abru said. "But not for guns."

Ralph Andrews, Stan Berk, and Nancy Willock were waiting for me in the hotel lobby, tense and anxious. They jumped out of their chairs as I came through the door. They crowded around me, asking excitedly:

"How did it go? Is everything still okay?"

"You can rest easily," I told them. "Vesco was cooperative. We matched Jack Anderson's questions with the ones his own lawyer wants on the tests, and he's willing to answer them all."

"Great." Andrews clapped me on the shoulder. "Come on, let's have a drink." We followed him to the hotel bar. For the first time, Andrews and his staff were relaxed. We spent an enjoyable hour. I didn't know then, and it was just as well, that I'd been slightly inaccurate. Vesco was not going to be quite as cooperative as I'd hoped.

We met alone at the beautiful, sprawling Spanish-style home of Alberto Abru early the next morning. Through rear doors, past a patio, I could see workmen putting the finishing touches on a big tile swimming pool. Vesco was more relaxed than at yesterday's meeting. He removed his jacket, loosened his tie, and rolled up his shirt sleeves. He looked interestedly at the polygraph instrument and tape recorder I'd brought along.

"Let's get going," he said. "Did we cover the ground completely yesterday? Is there any more stuff you need?"

"I'd like to ask you about the two-hundred-twenty-four-million-dollar accusation," I said.

His face hardened. "I told you I didn't steal that money. I don't care what the government says. I don't care what the newspapers say."

"It's not going to shut them up," I said, "if you stop at that point, if you say only that you didn't steal that specific amount. The question—and your answer—have to be more general."

"Oh, no." Vesco shook his head. "Two hundred and twenty-four million is what they're charging me with. Two hundred and twenty-four million is all I should be asked about."

"But don't you see," I argued, "if I ask you only about that amount, they're going to turn around and say, all right, it wasn't two hundred and twenty-four million, it could have been two hundred and twenty-three million, or a hundred and ninety-five million, or some other amount—any amount. You won't have given them an answer at all."

"We could sit here all day," Vesco said, "naming off sums, and it wouldn't get us anywhere. Look, Chris, I can pass your test on any amount you want to name, but that's not the issue. They claim I stole two hundred and twenty-four million and that's all that needs to be answered. My lawyer says so, and I say so. Now let's stop wasting time and get to the other questions."

He was making a mistake, but I didn't want him upset. It would only make the test process harder. "Have you been using your money and influence in Costa Rican politics? It's been charged that you contributed money to the presidential campaigns down here."

"Why would I?" Vesco wondered.

"One of the candidates said he would kick you out of the country if he got elected. It was on the news reports."

"No campaign contributions," Vesco said. "They claim I've got so much money invested in Costa Rica that I control the economy. That's not true, either. Be sure you get those questions in. I want to put a stop to those lies."

"Good," I said. "Now—what about this business of your talking to Richard Nixon, trying to persuade him to get the SEC off your back?"

"I didn't talk to him," Vesco said. "I sent someone."

"Who was that?" I asked.

"Someone close to the President," Vesco said. "I don't want to involve them in this."

The tests went smoothly. There were three, each one containing five critical questions. Altogether, with simulation tests to assure myself that Vesco was responding properly once the polygraph units had been attached, and with additional control questions to give me an indication of his physical reactions when he told an untruth, the whole process took a little under two hours. The room in Alberto Abru's handsome home in which we conducted the tests was pleasant, cool, and quiet. Here are the key questions and Vesco's answers.

"Did you steal two hundred and twenty-four million from investors of the I.O.S. Limited, or its funds?"

"No."

"Did you ever use organized-crime money to gain control of any U.S. or foreign companies?"

"No."

"Did you willfully, knowingly, or intentionally violate U.S. criminal laws during your involvement with I.O.S., Limited?"

"No."

"Did you obtain and consider reputable U.S. legal advice during your involvement with I.O.S., Limited?"

"Yes."

"Have you ever knowingly financed or participated in trafficking of heroin or other illegal drugs or narcotics?"

"No," Vesco answered.

After a break, we ran more key questions.

"Did you ever communicate with President Nixon about the alleged contribution to his campaign or your SEC controversy?"

"Yes."

"Were you aware that your alleged cash contribution to the Nixon campaign was to be used for the Watergate break-in?"

"No," Vesco said.

"Did Murray Chotiner visit you about the time of President Nixon's taped conversation in which he said that 'there would be no problem obtaining hush money' for the Watergate participants?"

"Yes."

We took another brief breather, then finished the job with four final questions.

"Did you give money to ex-President Figueres to permit you originally to come to Costa Rica?"

"No," Vesco said.

"Do you have investments in Costa Rica of such importance that they could affect the economy of the country?"

"No."

"Have you personally contributed money to the leading Costa Rican presidential candidates, Monge or Carazo?"

"No," Vesco said.

"Are you a member of the Mafia, or any organized crime syndicate?"

"No," Vesco answered.

He was understandably eager to learn how he'd come out on the tests. A glance at his charts showed me nothing to indicate he'd been less than truthful, but I told him I'd need to study them thoroughly before I could make a report. I detached him from the polygraph.

"You were a good subject," I said. "Thank you."

"Get me your report as soon as you can," he said. "I have to have it translated into Spanish for my people here." He stood up and stretched. He looked at the polygraph instrument as I began packing it away. "I told the truth. I hope that machine will prove it. I wish it could be used in court for my defense."

"I'll go over the charts right away," I promised. "And when I get back to the States I'll have a couple of other examiners check them out to be sure my conclusions are right."

While I'd been polygraphing Vesco, Ralph Andrews, Stan Berk, and the technicians had been setting up cameras and lights, microphones and recording equipment in the large, beautifully furnished living room of the Abru home. I'd had an unsettling brush with Berk earlier. He'd wanted to film the tests. This was the gimmicky, sensationalized approach Andrews had promised I wouldn't be subjected to. I didn't have to argue against it for long when it became clear that not only could it ruin the test results and give the TV viewing public a false idea of the polygraph, but it could very well also make Vesco change his mind. Instead, Andrews arranged for Berk to photograph Vesco attached to the polygraph after the tests were completed. Once these shots were taken, Jack Anderson took me aside.

"How did the tests go?" he wondered.

"He told the truth on all the questions," I said.

"Did you really get deep into the two-hundred-and-twenty-four-million-dollar thing?"

"He wouldn't go deep," I said.

253

"But people watching the show are going to see through that," Anderson protested. "It could have been less. It could have been more."

"Ralph Andrews kept after me not to get Vesco angry," I said. "I told him what you've told me. That's how it's going to look—as if he's dodging. But he wouldn't budge."

"I'll try to open him up in the interview," Anderson said. "Come on, you look tired." In an adjoining sunlit room, the television crew were helping themselves at an elegant buffet, with dozens of tempting dishes, and flowers on the table. As I walked in with Anderson, he said, "Ah, there's also a bar. A drink will pick you up."

I had a crisply cold beer. But I found I couldn't enjoy the laughing company around me. And I wasn't hungry. I wandered out into the tropical garden for a while to be by myself. I hadn't realized how tense I'd been about the Vesco examination. Now that it was over, instead of feeling pleasantly relaxed, I felt exhausted. The beer did me some good, and the brief part I had to play in the television filming that followed went off without a hitch.

In his interview with Vesco, Jack Anderson's questions could range wider and probe deeper than mine. The two men were well matched: Anderson smooth, thoughtful, relentless; Vesco wryly amused, shrewd, fast on his feet. Their meeting made fascinating listening. But in the end, the truth about the I.O.S. millions remained as much a mystery as ever. Did Robert Lee Vesco loot the investors in his international mutual fund—of some amount? Maybe the world will learn the answer when Vesco stands trial in the U.S. But that could be a long time off. It could be never.